a practical guide to
VISUAL MERCHANDISING

**The Wiley Retail Fashion Merchandising
and Management Series**

Under the consulting editorship of Joseph C. Hecht
Montclair State College

a practical guide to
VISUAL MERCHANDISING

Linda Cahan
CAHAN COMPANY, CONSULTING

Joseph Robinson
UNIVERSITY OF WYOMING, LARAMIE

John Wiley & Sons
New York • Chichester • Brisbane • Toronto • Singapore

To James Gaughan, Thank You!

Cover photo by Chet Seymour/THE PICTURE CUBE

Library of Congress Cataloging in Publication Data

Cahan, Linda.
  A practical guide to visual merchandising.

  Includes index.
    1. Display of merchandise—Handbooks, manuals, etc.
2. Merchandising—Handbooks, manual, etc.   I. Robinson,
Joseph.   II. Title.   III. Title: Visual merchandising.
HF5845.C28 1984   659.1'57   83-16745
ISBN 0-471-86441-2

Printed in the United States of America

10 9 8 7 6 5

Foreword

How many times in my career has someone said to me, "Gee, you're in display; that sounds like a fun job." I would like to set the record straight. First, I am in visual merchandising, not display. Second, if you think of it as a fun job, get yourself invited to spend a couple of hours in any major department store's visual merchandising department. Get a front row seat and keep your eyes and ears open because it will surely change your mind!

Visual merchandising is a business like any other business and is run for the most part by professionals who have worked hard to gain their reputations.

I started in visual merchandising 15 years ago working for Tom Nichol while he was at Joseph Magnin. That was the beginning of a career that has been very satisfying. It wasn't easy, and often during those years I asked myself if I wasn't a little crazy and perhaps I should go into something else. But, once you get retailing and visual merchandising in your blood, you're hooked and there's no getting it out!

Here is a book compiled from years of experience in the visual merchandising field. It takes a no-nonsense approach to helping you develop an understanding of the language, ideas, and points of view of the professional. It will aid you greatly in your study of visual merchandising and throughout your career.

Good luck, for you're about to undertake a mind-opening experience.

William Watson
Visual Merchandising Consultant

v

Preface

This book is based on many years of experience in the visual merchandising field. Since theories and styles change yearly in both retailing and visual merchandising, an effort was made to give the reader an educated appreciation of many different styles as well as the understanding that there is no "one right way" to design something in this business. Visual merchandising is one small part of the retail community, yet its impact can potentially make or break a store. Visual merchandising and image are synonymous in the retail world. Customers buy for price and image. If one doesn't work with the other, sales go down.

The community of visual merchandisers is small and close. Everyone comes up through the ranks because there is no substitute for experience. This shared experience gives visual merchandisers an appreciation of each other's work and problems. Although a spirit of competitiveness exists between VMs, it serves to strengthen the individual presentations. Visual excitement is heightened in this combination of art, design, and merchandising.

Reading this book is good preparation for beginning a retailing career. Keep it for reference if continuing in the visual merchandising field. Although the book is no substitute for experience, a lot of knowledge gained through trial and error is given here.

Over the years, many individuals shared their knowledge and experience: department managers, store and operations managers, maintenance and operations staff, carpenters, printers, and advertising and promotional people. Specific persons to whom I am grateful are: Don Wolfe, Syracuse, N.Y.; Colin Birch, New York, N.Y.; William Watson, New York, N.Y.; and Frank Keller, Atlanta, Ga. Special recognition goes to those who reviewed the manuscript: Sylvia Smith (Brookdale Community College, New Jersey); Arthur A. Birkland (Newberry Community College, Massachusetts); Lea Johnstone (District 916 Area Vocational Technical Institute, Minnesota); Carolyn Fix Blount (Shoreline Community College, Washington); and Marion H. Jernigan (North Texas State University, Texas). Thank you all.

Linda Cahan

Acknowledgments

Very special thanks to Leonard Kruk, Joseph Hecht and Pat Fitzgerald, whose help, knowledge, and support have been invaluable.

Thanks to Donald Schneider for his constant support. Jeanne P. Waller, Director, Westhampton Free Library, N.Y., for all her advice   William John Cahan, architect, Anshen & Allen, San Francisco, CA   Nancy Cahan, Laurence Treatment Center, Laurence, MA   William Watson, VM Consultant, New York, N.Y.   Charles Balas, Owner, Anchor Street Inn, Nantucket, R.I.   Bea Borrower, Bergdorf Goodman, New York, N.Y.   Edward Korn, R. H. Macy, Co., New Haven, Conn.   Colin Birch, Bloomingdales, New York, N.Y.   Terry Dobris, Toshi Inc.   Toshi, Freelancer   Marc Block, R. H. Macy Co.   Ilene Rosenthal, HBSA, New York, N.Y.   Tom and Pat Kochie, Freelancers, Southampton, N.Y.   Dr. Melvin Sorcher, Richardson-Vicks   Joe Yandoli, Edron Fixture Co.   Cliff Baumgardner, Comptroller, Trumbull, Conn.   Glen Terrace Nurseries, Hamden, Conn.   John DeStefano, DeStefano Studio   Nellie Fink, Adel Rootstein   Ken Knaeblein, Carlisles, Erie, Penn.   John Rossio, Bonwit Teller, New York, N.Y.   Jim Crilley, Jr., David Orgill, Beverly Hills, Cal.   Paul Cogswell, D.M. Read Co., Trumbull, Conn.   Jerry Melmed, SUNY, Staten Island, N.Y.   William O'Brien, Oriel Corp.   Eileen Freidenreich, New York, N.Y.   Johanna Bohoy, Charrette, Woburn, Mass.   Daniel O'Conner, manufacturers representative, New York, N.Y.   Henry Brimmer, designer, San Francisco, Cal.   Fran Oestricher—D.G. Williams, New York, N.Y.   Ernest Hindrichen, R. H. Macy, Co.   Vickie Vartanian, Bloomingdales,

New York, N.Y.   Jonathan Hurwitz, Functional Display   Bob Koenigsberg, Display Presentations   Robert Currie, Gloworm, New York, N.Y.   Greg Turpan, Turpan & Sanders, New York, N.Y.   Angela Weir and Family

Thank you to the reviewers who helped me learn: Art Birkland, Newberry Jr. College, Mass.   Lea Johnstone, White Bear Lake, Minn.   Carolyn Blount, Shoreline Community College, Washington   Marian Jernigan, North Texas State University, Texas   Sylvia Smith, Brookdale Community College, N.J.

Contents

1. VISUAL MERCHANDISING—A PROFILE   1

What is visual merchandising and why is it needed? Visual merchandising as a career: the department structure, and how to get into the field. The visual merchandising manager: how to prioritize, management styles, and how to budget.

2. DESIGN   30

Design as it relates to merchandise and presentation in terms of image, market, customer, concept, location, and objectives. Design's basic elements and principles as they relate to visual merchandising: space, lighting, color, rhythm, theme, props, signing, proportion, and balance.

3. TOOLS AND MATERIALS OF THE TRADE   74

How to plan for on-the-job tool use. How to do basic visual merchandising and display jobs. Explanations of tools that cut, join, attach, are used daily, and basic materials.

12. WHAT'S NEW—WHAT'S NOT: A LOOK INTO THE FUTURE   319

Trends of the past and their impact on present and future visual merchandising. How to use and improve on old trends to create new ones.

CHAPTER 1

Visual Merchandising — A Profile

LEARNING OBJECTIVES

At the completion of this chapter, you will be able to:

1. Explain the relationship of the VMM and the atmosphere, image, and environment of a store.

2. List the basic skills necessary for entry level employment as a visual merchandiser.

3. Outline the history of visual merchandising.

4. Discriminate between *display* and *visual merchandising.*

5. Construct a chart showing the chain of command for a major department store.

6. List the qualifications needed by a person applying for an entry level staff position as a visual merchant.

7. Compare the responsibilities of a VM in a small store to a VM in a large store.

8. Compare the responsibilities of a VM in a union store to a VM in a nonunion store.

9. Describe the advantages of working as a VM freelancer.

10. Identify the basic principles of prioritization.

11. Describe the hiring procedures that should be followed by a VMM.

1

12. List the management philosophies necessary to create incentive and employee motivation.

13. Explain the importance of having a visual merchandising budget.

14. Describe the development of visual merchandising from the pre-1970s through the 1980s.

15. Discuss the information needed by VMMs before they can effectively prepare the display budget.

16. Set up a VM budget book.

17. Describe the accrual process as it relates to visual merchandising.

Visual merchandising can be challenging and enjoyable. It also can be extremely frustrating, depending on the current project and the quality of support given by management. For the beginning visual merchant (VM) there may be days of stapling fabric to pads for caseline color. Interspersed with the pad covering can easily be a major fashion show setup or boutique opening. A promotion in 1971 at Sibleys, Syracuse, N.Y., convinced the author that a career in retail visual merchandising offered a challenge to both her creativity and her physical endurance. Her first three days in display at Sibleys were spent in the shop. After covering what seemed like 2,000 pads for a seasonal change in the cosmetics department (an easily learned task as pads are covered like artists' canvases and the author was a fine arts major with interest in fashion at Syracuse University), her help was required on the third floor for a Wedgwood china promotion. The promotion involved balancing a brand new MG Midget on four teacups. The purpose was to illustrate the strength of the fragile-looking Wedgwood china. The author directed the car onto the freight elevator that went to the third floor and helped clear the aisles for the car to be driven through the stockroom and onto the selling floor. A lot of excitement was generated when the car rolled into the fine china department and revved its engine for a finale. Six men were on hand to lift the car onto the cups while the author's job was to place the teacups under the wheels. The author discovered (after two broken teacups) that a piece of wood would have to be placed over the top of each cup to distribute the weight over the rims evenly. This worked beautifully and the promotion was a success. The next day, when the author had to staple more pads, it didn't seem quite as boring.

A job in visual merchandising varies daily. The responsibilities are unchanging but the situations around them are in constant flux. The mannequins, shops, signing, decor, wall displays, fixture treatment, windows, plants, and cases are often the responsibility of the VM department, yet what is needed to complete these duties often changes. The constant changes and keeping on top of them is what makes visual merchandising an exciting and challenging field.

A VERY SHORT HISTORY

The term *visual merchandising* was originally used in 1944 by Albert Bliss, a display manufacturer. Before this term existed, *display* was used to describe the job of the "trimmers." The history of the display trimmer/visual merchandiser in the United States really begins in the early 1900s. At that time the display man (there are no records of women working in the field in the early 1900s) had little authority and received less respect. He was considered a temperamental artist, not a businessman. An organization was formed in 1914 in Chicago out of the already existing display trade group. Named the International Association of Display Men (IADM), this organization hoped to develop the display field into a profession instead of a job. The "trimmer" became "a display man" and the organization held yearly conventions to keep the trade aware of new trends and ideas. During the late 1940s the IADM disbanded due to internal regional arguments and in 1942 the National Association of Display Industries (NADI) formed. This was composed of display manufacturers on the east coast. In the 1960s the west coast saw the formation of the Western Association of Visual Merchandisers (WAVM). This is also composed of manufacturers of display materials. The IADM was the only organization made up of actual display professionals. There is no organization currently for visual merchandisers who work in the field. Both NADI and WAVM provide a job posting service to the field and *Visual Merchandising and Store Planning* magazine acts as a monthly newspaper. Visual merchandising today is a profession that is constantly gaining focus and importance. Retailers now realize that good visual merchandising is essential if they wish to get ahead of the competition.

Visual merchandising and *visual merchandiser* are the popular and accepted terms for the display function. Display alone denotes the importance of the visual/artistic aspect of the merchandise presentation. Visual merchandising encompasses the entire merchandising concept. It includes both the artistic and the marketing functions of the retail environment. Display is one aspect of visual merchandising. The visual merchandiser must also be responsible for and aware of total merchandise presentation, image, store design, and management interaction.

THE VISUAL MERCHANDISER AS AN EMPLOYEE

The visual merchandiser's role in the retail hierarchy varies with each store and situation. Visual merchandising jobs are available in large or small department stores, large or small specialty stores, union or nonunion shops, and on a free-lance basis for all stores.

Large Department and Specialty Stores

If a large department store chain has a main store plus several branches, the visual merchandising staff most often has its central/corporate office in the main store. The VM staff is usually set up as shown in Figure 1–1.

In a large store the senior VP of visual merchandising reports either to the

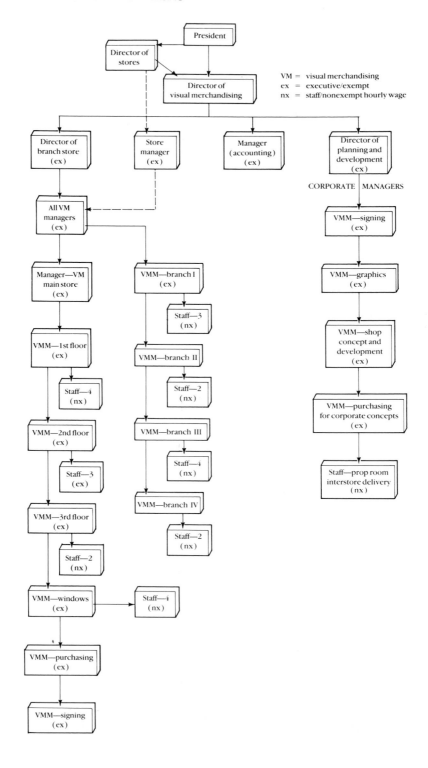

VM = visual merchandising
ex = executive/exempt
nx = staff/nonexempt hourly wage

president or chief executive officer of the chain of stores. If the VM director is a vice president (not senior) or an executive, he or she will report to the vice president of branch stores and the president of the company. Store planning is usually a parallel group (with a smaller staff) that reports to the VP of operations and the CEO (chief executive officer). Recently, there has been more interaction between the visual merchandising and store planning departments in many forward-looking stores to better coordinate the image and ambiance of the stores.

Store planning is generally responsible for the site, plans, construction, and interior/exterior design (including fixtures) of each new store and most of the renovations of older stores.

In many department store chains, visual merchandising is now becoming involved in these decisions. The visual merchandising staff reports directly to their store's VM manager, who then reports to both the store manager and the corporate VM branch store manager. The VMM (visual merchandising manager) is at the same level, in many cases, as the merchandising executives in the store. In most stores the VM staff is on a different pay scale than the sales personnel. Although they are all paid by the hour and "punch a clock," the VM staff usually starts at a higher base salary. Smaller branches of major specialty stores may only have one person in visual merchandising to take care of the entire store. This person may be an executive, a salaried employee, or a freelancer depending on the store's needs.

Apprentices in visual merchandising will gain all of their rudimentary knowledge from their first jobs. Ideally, the first "boss" will also be an excellent teacher. Larger stores attract experienced visual merchandisers and also hire newcomers to the field in entry level staff positions. Larger department and specialty stores look for certain qualities during an interview for an entry level staff position (Figure 1–2). These qualities are as follows:

1. **Enthusiasm.** Genuine, not feigned, excitement about learning the retail business is desired for this position.

2. **Intelligence.** The ability to learn quickly is necessary in this field because mistakes can be very costly.

3. **Experience in art, graphics, design carpentry, or fashion.** Any or all of these fields are good beginning experience for a career in visual merchandising.

4. **Ability to listen and understand/communication skills.** It is necessary to be able to *hear* and understand other people. The ability to make oneself understood to others is equally important.

Figure 1–1
Organization of a department store visual merchandising staff. Each branch has an individual budget allocated by the main VM office. It is broken down by month and season. The expenditures go to the individual branches' operations managers who record and then send the bills/expenses to the main store accounting VM. (Naturally, there are many different levels of management/executives.)

DISPLAY

Visual Merchandisers
....with Flairability

Can your talents and experience in hard goods retail display stop traffic in high volume, up-to-the-minute home furnishings departments?

OR do you have a unique flair for designing dramatic table arrangements that are trend setters?

Now you can put these talents where they will be appreciated and rewarded. Both openings are available at our fast-growing retail department stores in the metropolitan New York/New Jersey area. And we'll reward your creativity with excellent compensation and full company paid benefits. Send resume in confidence to: MANAGER, EXECUTIVE RECRUITMENT.

F4752 TIMES 10108

An equal opportunity employer

DISPLAY

Visual Presentation
-Assistants-

Prominent 5th Avenue flagship store, specializing in women's apparel only has excellent positions available for those experienced in Prop Production, Window and Interior Presentation. We offer an unusually attractive benefits package. Call for appointment.

LANE BRYANT
465 FIFTH AVE (40th St)
NEW YORK, NEW YORK 10017

(212) 532-0200
an equal opportunity employer

DISPLAY TRAINEE
Wanted, a creative person for showcase & seasonal display to work in a retail chain enviornment. Exp is helpful, will accept a recent art graduate. Strong growth pot'l for the right candidate. Salary commens w/exper. Please call 201-489-6031

DISPLAY DESIGNER
Qualified candidate must be skilled in color renderings, have ability to develop a concept and translate that into detailed drawings. Exp in thermoforming, injection molding. Plastic fabrication techniques essential. Vacation, holidays, benefits. Sal comm w/exp. 212-723-2486

DISPLAY   Join Our Staff!!!
WANTED: VISUAL DISPLAY PERSON
Must be exp'd in home furnishings. Windows & in-store merchandise displays. Full time. Call Mon-Sun; 288-9264 11AM-8:30PM Only.

DISPLAY
Creative V.M. co. seeks 5 yrs exp in design & construction. P/T, F/T. Include sal read UH297 TIMES 10108

DISPLAY TRIMMER
Exp draping fabrics and working with foamcore-avail immed for temporary position. 691-1286

Figure 1–2

A job advertisement for a beginner in the visual merchandising field.

5. Physical appearance. A job interview is not the time or place to have a "what you see is what you get" attitude unless what is seen looks professional and fashionable. Dressing as if you don't care generally will impress the interviewer that you really do not care about the job or yourself. Good health is also a necessity for a job in visual merchandising. As the job is very physical and demanding, strength, a strong back, and endurance are important for the applicant. (Good walking shoes are needed when starting a job because nine-tenths of the day will be spent either standing or walking.)

Small Department and Specialty Stores

The VMM in a smaller store has far more varied responsibilities than in a large store. The VMM in the small store is generally responsible for all windows, interior displays, seasonal changes, signs, plants, and fixturing. There will occasionally be a small staff to assist the VMM, but most often the VMM works alone. The planning, organizing, buying, and implementing of each job must be done by one person. This type of situation is excellent for learning visual merchandising skills. Several years of experience at the staff level is helpful to properly handle this job. The VMM of a small store reports to the store manager or president. This may or may not be considered an executive position. Each store handles the status of the visual merchandising job differently.

Requirements of this job are essentially the same as those needed in an entry level position. Experience is the only difference and must be considered first.

Experience for the VM position in a smaller store usually includes knowledge of budgets, purchasing, promotion, windows, interior merchandising, and display techniques. A rudimentary knowledge of these skills will be gained after working for a large store for several years. Advanced skills will be learned on the job at the smaller store.

The other important qualification is enthusiasm. The VMM in a small store must be highly self-motivated. The store manager runs the store with little help and doesn't have the time to lead the VMM step by step. Therefore, the job requires a self-starter.

Working in a Union Store

A store that is unionized or a union shop requires a different emphasis on certain of the VM's skills. When the employees are unionized, the VM's duties are more sharply defined. A VM cannot use a hammer on anything other than a display as only carpenters are allowed to do any carpentry or construction. Any electrical work must be done only by electricians. Although the visual merchandisers are limited in their physical activities, their communication and organization skills must be sharp.

The VM must be able to discuss and plan displays with the various tradespeople. Everything must be clear and planned ahead of time to ensure timely and accurate installation of shops and displays. Of course, there are many things the VM can do, such as work with mannequins, clothing, or windows, other than carpentry, painting displays, electrical work, and so on. The union membership gets upset when nonunion people do their jobs. A job steward or the union representative will protest any violations of the work codes to management. Each store negotiates a different code with every union. Therefore, restrictions on the VM staff vary from store to store. Strikes have been called over major violations of the contracts. Naturally, everyone wants to avoid strikes, so that staying within the work codes is an important consideration. The major issue usually brought up by the unions is job security. If the VMs try to take over their responsibilities, they feel their jobs may be in jeopardy.

Apprenticeship in a union store can give less of a full, rounded education in the visual merchandising field because the union prevents the VM from doing some of the actual work needed for a well-rounded education. To work knowledgeably with the unions, the VM must pursue a familiarity with every skill and have an understanding of all related jobs.

Working in a Nonunion Store

Most of this book is geared toward working in a nonunion environment. All visual merchandising skills should be understood, even if they aren't always physically practiced (by union store VMs).

In a nonunion store the visual merchandiser carries and climbs ladders, paints, cuts and nails wood, and changes bulbs and light fixtures. Although these activities are not usual in a union store, the VM must understand how to do all these jobs to plan for the various complications that may arise. It is also necessary to understand how long each job may take in order to plan projects with some accuracy.

In small stores the visual merchandiser will often be called on to "chip in" with help that may not be part of the original job description. The author has, during a 12-year career, cleaned bathrooms, dusted china departments, carried and planted heavy, live Christmas trees (thereby getting poison ivy in November), planned and did the commentary for fashion shows, organized a fund raising party for 500 guests and decorated two floors of a store to accommodate the party, mopped floors, designed promotional materials and had them printed, ironed huge table-cloths and draperies, watered 350 poinsettias three times a week for seven weeks, and moved 57 cartons of men's shirts in order to wheel Christmas trim from the stockroom to the selling floor. Sound like fun? Sometimes it was, and then there were the bathrooms and the cartons. In a nonunion store many things can become the responsibility of visual merchandising. The VM's relationship with the store manager will determine how involved each will become in the other's job. Chipping in with needed help in times of crisis is a welcome and appreciated attribute for a VM to have. Knowing when to say no is equally necessary. It's important to understand self-limitations and not take on more than is physically or mentally possible. It doesn't hurt to push one's strength and mental agility to their limits to understand where those limits are, but also know when to stop!

Freelancing

A visual merchandising freelancer is a person who works for several stores and/or companies simultaneously. Freelancers work for both the store and for themselves. The stores or companies that hire freelancers range from large department stores to small specialty shops. The freelancer usually reports to whomever hired him or her for the job. In a small store a freelancer usually works twice a month changing windows and/or interior displays. When working for a large store, the freelancer either works every day for a stated period of time, e.g., six weeks before Thanksgiving to help put up Christmas trim, or works on a particular job as needed, e.g., special mannequin makeup or wigs. The freelancer's role in the visual merchandising team for a large store is as a temporary employee with few, if any, benefits, except possibly a temporary discount. When working for a small shop, the freelancer may receive a sizable discount but, as with the larger store, no medical benefits or profit sharing. Working for companies other than retail stores, the freelancer will often report to the head of promotions, marketing, or advertising. These jobs often pay better than traditional retail jobs but require professional experience. All the freelancing jobs require a firm understanding of visual merchandising techniques. Very few people have successfully started freelancing careers without previous store experience. One example of this exception-to-the-rule success story is Toshi, a Japanese-born free-lance visual merchandiser who came to New York City several years ago as an artist and designer of props. After being asked to install his props at several locations by other freelancers, Toshi decided to try freelancing on his own. He now has as accounts many stores on Madison and Fifth Avenues.

Freelancing is a challenging and often lucrative way to approach a career in visual merchandising.

THE VISUAL MERCHANDISING MANAGER (VMM)

After learning how to be a visual merchandising assistant from other, more experienced teachers/VMs, the opportunities exist to progress to the next step: visual merchandising manager for a retail store. The VMM has responsibilities that are far beyond those of the assistants (Figure 1–3). As was discussed in the beginning of

VISUAL MERCHANDISING MANAGER

A management opportunity exists for an experienced, creative individual who understands the connection between visual merchandising and dynamic sales growth.

The ideal candidate will have the proven ability to create ambiance and visual excitement, shops, and merchandising statements. Management, purchasing and control of budgets is involved. A fashion approach to merchandise is a must.

If you possess these qualifications and are seeking to further your visual merchandising career in a dynamic organization, we are interested in talking with you.

PLEASE CALL FOR APPOINTMENT
PERSONNEL MANAGER

Figure 1–3
An advertisement for a visual merchandising manager for the branch store of a large, well known retailer.

this chapter, the VMM is responsible to management for the total look of the store at all times. Prioritization (first things first), employee relations, and budgeting are three very important learned skills needed to effectively handle the complexities of the job.

Prioritizing

Prioritization, or selecting priorities, means deciding what jobs take precedence over others. Prioritizing is another word for organization. Being organized is essential for success in visual merchandising or any business career.

The basic principles of prioritization are to break down all projects as follows:

A projects. Jobs that *only* you can do

B projects. Jobs that others can do if you get them started in the right direction

C projects. Jobs that others can do without your help

To become organized, keep a calendar that has the days broken down by time of day. List all events and their setup dates. List all meetings as they are posted. All requests made by fellow employees should be listed separately on small sheets of paper and placed in an appropriate section on the calendar. All promises to others should also be written down and put into appropriate spots on the calendar (Figure 1–4).

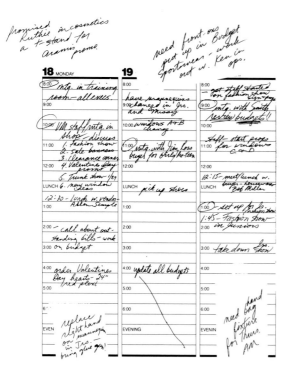

Figure 1–4

A typical calendar for a VMM's week.

Judging correctly what project has priority over another is one skill that must be learned on the job. This skill separates the good from the bad VMMs. A VMM can be very creative or talented, but if he or she is disorganized and cannot meet deadlines the creativity is wasted. The retail business (like many others) works on deadlines. The deadlines are usually coordinated with advertising schedules, special events, and holidays. If a special promotion is advertised as "beginning September 20 in our new Jungle Shop," there had better be a Jungle Shop installed before the morning of that date!

To organize a day's activities, separate jobs into A, B, and C categories. Then organize them by time.

1. Which job needs to be done first?

2. What project must be completed so that another related job can be started?

3. What are the deadlines for each job?

4. What projects can be worked on in the same area to save time?

5. How many projects can be done in one day?

6. How many people are needed for each job?

Get everyone started on the C projects. These jobs can be done without any effort on your part and may consist of mannequin changes, case-boutiquing changes, removal or installation of promotional posters and signs, pad covering, prop cutting and painting, shop cleaning, and many other routine assignments.

Next order of priority is to help all the B projects to get started. Feedback from the VMM will be needed on many varied jobs. Some of these may be a mannequin presentation, an end panel "shop statement," window changes, signing, fabric selection for any projects, merchandising fixture moves, and so on.

Finally, you can begin the A projects. While the VM staff works on the on-floor or behind-the-scenes jobs that make a store look exciting, the VMM now has time to either plan or pay for all that excitement. Planning and budgets/bills are two responsibilities that are often handled solely by the VMM. In a very large store or chain of stores, the VMM will usually have an accountant or someone responsible for budgeting and bill payment only. Planning in a very large store may also be handled by an assistant. But primary responsibility rests with the VMM. The VMM in a moderate-sized store often has both of these responsibilities with little help. Having the full support and cooperation of the VM staff can make the job of the VMM much more easy and pleasant.

Employee Relations

Every visual merchandising staff works best as a team. Establishing this team and inspiring good work should be a goal of every VMM.

Employee relations in traditional terms consists of the entire personnel function. The VMM must employ good employee relations in order to develop the work habits, creativity, and potential of the team. The VMM often hires people but usually the personnel department will take care of the initial screening, interviewing, and firing.

There are so many laws governing hiring and firing practices today to protect the employee that only people trained in these skills should do the jobs. Personnel will most often interview an applicant before sending him or her to visual merchandising for another in-depth interview.

References should be checked *before* the person is hired. Often the references are not contacted until long after a person has begun working, and as a result many problems occur. Lying on an application in any way is just cause for immediate dismissal. The VM applying for a job should only use people as references who were good to work for and with, and be honest during the interview process. Lies are usually uncovered further into a career and can come back to haunt the employee.

When hiring or firing: age, physical disabilities, sex, health, religion, race, marital status, or nationality are not to be mentioned. Never fire someone by saying, "You're too old/sick/weak/pregnant to do the job." It would be cause for a law suit by the fired employee. If in doubt, go through all procedures with the personnel department. The best question to ask when interviewing a prospective employee is, "What are the things you liked the most and the least about your last two jobs?" The answer to this will give a good idea of what is important to that person and what his or her work habits are.

There are many different management styles. Managers of workers (such as VMMs) all have different approaches to dealing with people. These differences are known as styles, i.e., management style. Some managers rule like monarchs and don't allow any feedback from their employees while others ask for openness and ideas from their staff. One management style is to rule with fear by creating a situation where the employee is always afraid for the job. Another style consists of positive reinforcement. This is when the manager compliments good work and discusses (not screams at) bad work. Which management style sounds most promising to create a good working team? Ideally, a positive reinforcement style combined with an open exchange of ideas will create an excellent work atmosphere.

The fear of losing creative control rules many VMMs. Remember, the VMM is directly responsible for everything that is done in the store by the employees of the VM department. Therefore, the "monarchs" and "fear rulers" often act that way to protect themselves against the possible mistakes of their staff. Much personal growth comes as a result of mistakes made in the learning process. If a person lives in fear of making a mistake, he or she may well be afraid to make a decision. Human robots as employees may work hard but they rarely learn or improve their skills. A frequently heard phrase on the part of employees working for this type of manager is, "I'm not paid to think."

There is no one right way to paint or sculpt a work of art. In visual merchandising there are also many right ways to develop a theme and create a display. The old saying "two heads are better than one" makes a lot of sense in the visual merchandising field. Of course, not everything has to be designed by a committee, but listening to others' ideas can be very helpful and a good learning experience for the VMM.

The visual merchandising manager sets the example of employee standards. The VMM who is lazy, deceitful, chronically late, unresponsive, and uncreative can expect the same behavior from the VM staff. As the VMM is in the position of teacher/boss, the responsibility for the employees' futures rest in the VMM's capabilities as a creative and positive manager.

How to create incentive and encourage employees to perform better?

1. Listen to their needs and wants.

2. Try to be responsive to these needs and wants without hurting the work progress and without creating an unrealistic precedent.

3. Listen to other people's ideas and use them on occasion, giving credit where and when credit is due.

4. Compliment good work when it is done. Don't wait several weeks or until reviews are due.

5. Discuss bad performance and work habits as they arise. Don't yell or scream at poorly completed jobs. Instead, try to talk about the good work that the person has done and then question the problems that created the bad. Naturally, insist that the bad work be redone, but do so with understanding and compassion.

6. Reward work well done with fun projects. Treating someone to lunch is also a nice way of saying thank you for a good job.

7. Planning and idea meetings help a staff understand the direction the visual merchandising department and the store are heading in the future. Interaction between the staff members and the VMMs is often an excellent learning experience. During meetings an exchange of creative ideas, helpful hints, and tips on vendors help all the VM individuals in their understanding of the job.

Budgets and Budgeting

Working within a budget can be the most frustrating and challenging problem that a visual merchant encounters on a daily basis. The display budget generally fluctuates with the profits of the store. If the profits are low, the budget is usually lowered proportionately. The reverse is true when the profits are high. When the budget is exceeded, the extra expense cuts directly into the profits. In the early years of "window trimming," elaborate displays were concocted in the windows to show off the merchandise as well as the props. Vast sums of money were spent in turning entire stores into Christmas wonderlands, Easter festivals, or, occasionally, entire other countries. This style of opulance faded during the early 1970s when profits were down as a result of a slight depression in the economy. Display took on a more modern, clean look which lasted until the early 1980s. More attention was paid to the merchandise and to found objects for props in order to stay within tight budgets. Visual merchandising then became an important concept as budgets dictated that more attention be paid to the merchandise than the display goods.

Around 1980 a new attitude toward display developed throughout the United States. The power of effective visual merchandising was felt from San Francisco to New York. The R. H. Macy Company, who were always very effective merchants, decided to become exciting visual merchandisers as well. This didn't develop overnight but evolved from upper management's financial decision to put some of the profits into making the stores more theatrical—a more exciting environment to shop in. Other stores in the country were discovering the profits from exciting visual presentation at the same time and a new wave of old style display was reborn. Large chains of stores started to tie the buyers in with the visual people in huge "foreign" promotions. Bloomingdales became Indian, then Chinese. The Bon in Seattle went Chinese and then Jordan Marsh of Boston did the same with Orient Express. Indian and Chinese artisans were imported to exhibit their skills and wares and to add authenticity to the merchandise and the feeling of shopping in another country. Many stores are having Italian Weeks, French Weeks, and the like, to promote merchandise and to add excitement. Christmas has become more traditional and "redder." The decision has been made to give money to display— but with the money comes tremendous responsibility. Every penny must be accounted for.

Effective budgeting is fairly easy. Sticking to it is the difficult part. Generally, a store owner or manager will decide how much will be spent for display according to the profit picture at the time. Then the display manager will be asked for feedback on the amount. Is it enough or too little to accomplish what is wanted and needed by management? Questions that the display manager should ask of management at the planning stage are:

1. What shops are being planned for installation during the season now being budgeted?

2. What renovations are being discussed for this budget period that would affect display in terms of signing, mannequins, platforms, props, and paint? Are the actual renovations going to be charged to the display account, or is there a special budget allocated for construction/renovation?

3. What direction does the management want to take in terms of the overall look of the store? Is management looking for the most amount of color and coverage but no quality props, or smaller exciting areas but no storewide display theme? Possibly management is looking for both. The theme should be discussed at that time, as should the extent of the use within the store.

4. What promotions are being planned that will affect the display budget?

5. Which major tools will need replacement or refurbishing for the upcoming season?

6. How many mannequins are needed? How many need to be reconditioned? Are cubes needed for housewares areas?

7. Are new fixtures being planned for any areas? Will the expense of these fixtures fall on display? Are sign holders needed?

8. The sign program often comes under the display budget. Will extra signing be required for the upcoming season?

9. Is the staff sufficient to handle the work load? Also, how much must be planned into the budget to take care of raises?

10. The fall season traditionally has a larger budget than spring. There are two main reasons: Christmas and back-to-school. More money is made during the fall season and therefore more money should be in the budget. Consider Christmas trim and the yearly replacement of lights, ornaments, poinsettias, and so on.

Based on the questions asked of management, plan the budget by considering the following problems:

1. Within each requested shop there are built-in expenses. These are as follows:

   a. Materials needed to build the shop, e.g., platforms, wood for walls, fabric, paint.

   b. The shop name signage, e.g., "The Classic Corner."

   c. Props to further identify the shop.

   d. If the shop is to be a permanent addition, perhaps store directories will need to be amended to include the new shop.

2. When renovations are made to a store, they come out of either the display budget, the director of stores corporate budget, or the corporation capital expense account. (Capital expense allows the company to write off the expenses of a renovation over a period of time while depreciating the renovation at the same time, thereby lowering the taxes on the profits.) Generally, only small renovations are charged to the display budget, but check in advance what building and fixtures are planned and what may be charged to the VM account. At the end of this chapter are basic costs of simple renovations. Add a 10 percent cost increase per year past 1982.

3. If a total coverage look is requested, what props will best suit the image of the store and be reasonable in price? What can be made by display personnel in-house to avoid extra production costs from vendors? What theme can

be interpreted in similar ways for different areas without getting too repetitive and expensive?

4. Promotions that will affect the display budget are:

   a. Fashion shows: runways, runway covers, tablecloths for refreshments, plants, extra lighting, and the like.

   b. Vendor demonstrations: signing, special setups within the department for the demonstrator, tablecloths, flowers if required.

   c. Father's Day, Mother's Day, Valentine's Day, Fourth of July, swimwear supersale, Bridal Week, and trunk shows.

   Mother's Day usually requires fragrance outposts (an outpost is merchandise set up in an area separate from its regular home, e.g., a duplicate fragrance bar in the lingerie department). Often flowers are given away, which falls under the promotions budget, but the special signing comes within the display area.

   Father's Day also makes a lot of use of outposts. Outposts need to be signed and merchandised. Their construction usually falls within the display budget.

   Valentine's Day can cost a lot; the more outposts, the better. Everyone is involved in this day, so sales are usually varied and strong across the store. The traditional outposts are perfumes, lingerie, valentine-boxed underwear for men, anything red, candy, cards, and shirt/tie combinations.

   Trunk shows are given by vendors within the store. A buyer will only buy a portion of a "line" (total designs or items in a collection). The vendor will bring the entire line to the store for a trunk show, whether it's dresses or jewelry. This creates excitement for both store and customer. Signing and a special area should be set up for this.

   Bridal Week combines ready-to-wear (clothes) with hard lines (gifts, china, domestics, etc.) in a sales pitch to brides-to-be. Often signing, special tables, gift areas, and bridal boutiques are set up by display to prepare for this week.

   Swimwear Sales are big business in July. There are many stores that hang expensive banners and set up a large quantity of signs advertising the sale.

5. Add in the cost of basic supplies and the refurbishing of existing ones. Basic supplies include staple guns, staples, glue guns, hot glue, masking tape, double-stick tape, epoxy glue, nails, pins, chrome hangers, felt-tip pens, paint, brushes, and the like. These may sound like small expenses, but if you add them up they amount to a respectable figure. A staple gun is about $18

and a box of staples around $5. Double-stick tape is around $14 a roll while boxes of hot glue are $6 and the glue guns $11. Chrome hangers for hanging signs, etc., are about $0.25–$1.00 each. If you're working under a tight budget, an extra cost of $350 could ruin the best laid plans.

6. No one expects a customer or display person to knock over a mannequin, but unfortunately, it happens on a regular basis. In order to recondition a mannequin, money has to be planned and budgeted ahead of time in anticipation of accidents. Another anticipated cost is for makeup updates for mannequins as the styles change. Reconditioning can cost anywhere from $80 to $125 per mannequin. Also plan for several wigs and hands to be stolen per season (more for downtown stores); these are very popular items.

7. Plexiglas for visual merchandising is very popular and very fragile. It won't break easily, but it scratches and cracks with abuse. Sign holders are often stashed in odd places so that department managers will have them when needed. These holders can get very scratched in their hiding places and as a result look shoddy on the selling floor. Provisions should be made to add to the sign holder supply every season to compensate for the damaged holders.

8. If new major promotions are planned, new signs will have to be printed. These are generally one or two colors. For impact and attractiveness, they may be printed on glossy paper. These new signs are expensive and should be considered when planning.

9. Add to the cost of all props ordered the cost for delivery and the tax. Both will be charged to display by the control department.

There are many methods of setting up your budget book so that staying within the budget becomes a matter of entering all expenses as they come up. A book should be created listing your purchase orders and all information pertaining to them. An example would be:

DATE	PURCHASE ORDER #	AMOUNT VENDOR	DATE ITEM	AMOUNT	PAID	PAID

This is very simple and columns should be added with:

MONTH-TO-DATE EXPENDITURES	SEASON-TO-DATE EXPENDITURES

The most important point to remember is to enter your purchase orders as they are placed—and fill them in at the same time so that you don't forget what you ordered and any questions about the amount can be checked out in the beginning (Figure 1–5). You will be required in most cases to have your purchase orders approved by your store manager or director of stores before they become valid. This is a formal check and balance on expenses.

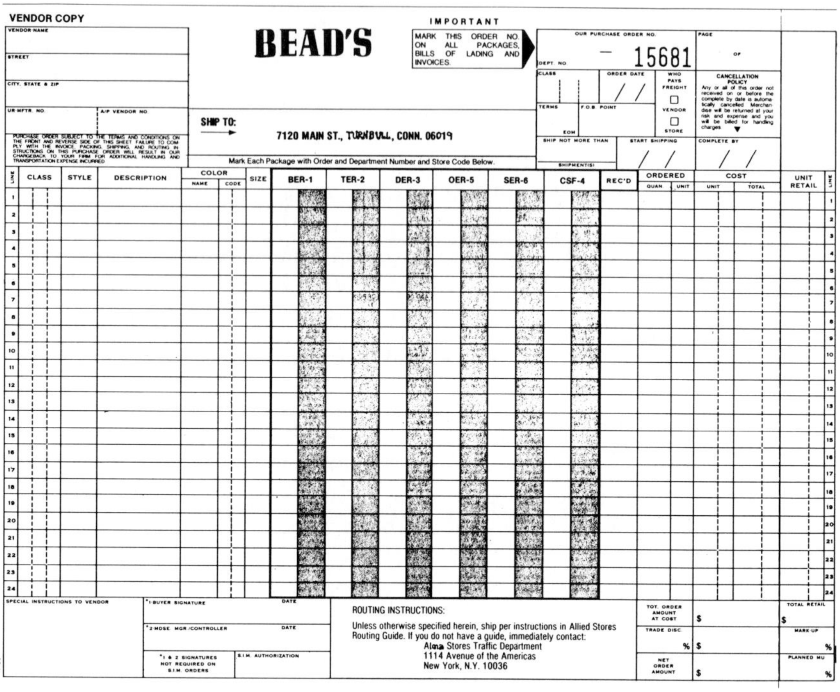

VENDOR COPY

VENDOR NAME

STREET

CITY, STATE & ZIP

UR MFTR. NO. | A/P VENDOR NO.

PURCHASE ORDER SUBJECT TO THE TERMS AND CONDITIONS ON THE FRONT AND REVERSE SIDE OF THIS SHEET. FAILURE TO COMPLY WITH THE INVOICE, PACKING, SHIPPING, AND ROUTING INSTRUCTIONS ON THIS PURCHASE ORDER WILL RESULT IN OUR CHARGEBACK TO YOUR FIRM FOR ADDITIONAL HANDLING AND TRANSPORTATION EXPENSE INCURRED.

BEAD'S

IMPORTANT

MARK THIS ORDER NO. ON ALL PACKAGES, BILLS OF LADING AND INVOICES.

SHIP TO: 7120 MAIN ST., TURNBULL, CONN. 06019

Mark Each Package with Order and Department Number and Store Code Below.

OUR PURCHASE ORDER NO. | PAGE

DEPT. NO. — 15681 OF

CLASS | ORDER DATE / / | WHO PAYS FREIGHT VENDOR STORE

TERMS | F.O.B. POINT | EOM

SHIP NOT MORE THAN | START SHIPPING / / | COMPLETE BY / /

SHIPMENTS

CANCELLATION POLICY: Any or all of this order not received on or before the complete by date is automatically cancelled. Merchandise will be returned at your risk and expense and you will be billed for handling charges.

LINE	CLASS	STYLE	DESCRIPTION	COLOR NAME	COLOR CODE	SIZE	BER-1	TER-2	DER-3	OER-5	SER-6	CSF-4	REC'D	ORDERED QUAN.	ORDERED UNIT	COST UNIT	COST TOTAL	UNIT RETAIL	LINE
1																			1
2																			2
3																			3
4																			4
5																			5
6																			6
7																			7
8																			8
9																			9
10																			10
11																			11
12																			12
13																			13
14																			14
15																			15
16																			16
17																			17
18																			18
19																			19
20																			20
21																			21
22																			22
23																			23
24																			24

SPECIAL INSTRUCTIONS TO VENDOR

*1 BUYER SIGNATURE | DATE

*2 MDSE. MGR./CONTROLLER | DATE

*1 & 2 SIGNATURES NOT REQUIRED ON S.I.M. ORDERS | S.I.M. AUTHORIZATION

ROUTING INSTRUCTIONS:

Unless otherwise specified herein, ship per instructions in Allied Stores Routing Guide. If you do not have a guide, immediately contact:
Alma Stores Traffic Department
1114 Avenue of the Americas
New York, N.Y. 10036

TOT. ORDER AMOUNT AT COST $ | TOTAL RETAIL $

TRADE DISC % $ | MARK-UP %

NET ORDER AMOUNT $ | PLANNED MU %

1-80

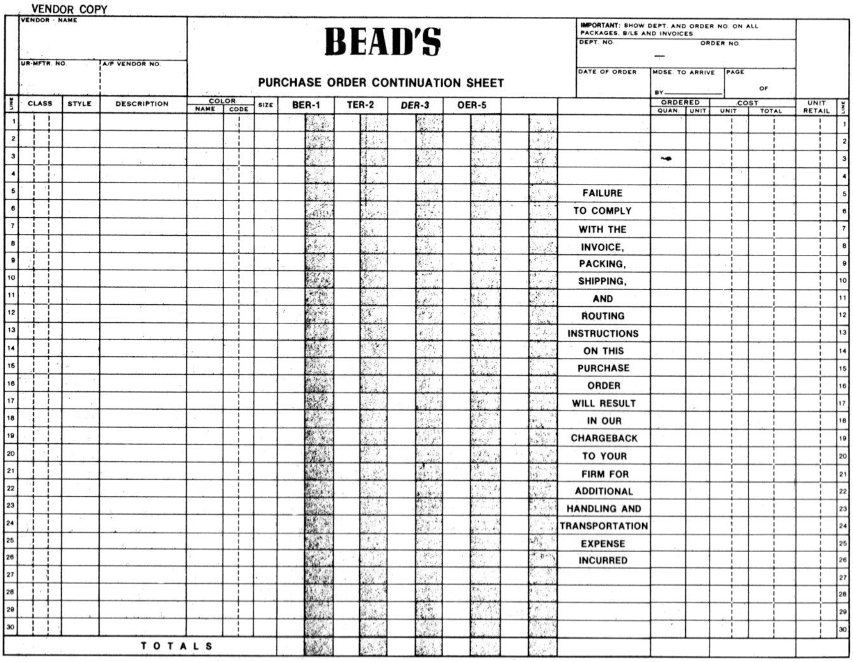

VENDOR COPY

VENDOR - NAME

UR-MFTR. NO. | A/P VENDOR NO.

BEAD'S

PURCHASE ORDER CONTINUATION SHEET

IMPORTANT: SHOW DEPT. AND ORDER NO. ON ALL PACKAGES, B/LS AND INVOICES

DEPT. NO. | ORDER NO.

DATE OF ORDER | MDSE. TO ARRIVE BY | PAGE OF

LINE	CLASS	STYLE	DESCRIPTION	COLOR NAME	COLOR CODE	SIZE	BER-1	TER-2	DER-3	OER-5				ORDERED QUAN.	ORDERED UNIT	COST UNIT	COST TOTAL	UNIT RETAIL	LINE
1																			1
2																			2
3																			3
4																			4
5													FAILURE						5
6													TO COMPLY						6
7													WITH THE						7
8													INVOICE,						8
9													PACKING,						9
10													SHIPPING,						10
11													AND						11
12													ROUTING						12
13													INSTRUCTIONS						13
14													ON THIS						14
15													PURCHASE						15
16													ORDER						16
17													WILL RESULT						17
18													IN OUR						18
19													CHARGEBACK						19
20													TO YOUR						20
21													FIRM FOR						21
22													ADDITIONAL						22
23													HANDLING AND						23
24													TRANSPORTATION						24
25													EXPENSE						25
26													INCURRED						26
27																			27
28																			28
29																			29
30																			30
TOTALS																			

Figure 1–5

A sample purchase order and order continuation form.

Accruals will become part of your budgeting experience. If you are planned for $10,000 for one month and you place $9,000 worth of orders and only $5,000 are delivered, $4,000 can be accrued to the month it was spent in, even though it wasn't delivered. This will prevent overages in other months. For example:

Spent: $9,000 on purchase orders for February

Arrived: $5,000 worth of merchandise ordered

Outstanding: $4,000 worth of merchandise and bills

Accrued: $4,000 for the month of February

Transferred from other departments: $1,000 for the month of March

1. Plan them correctly by asking questions and researching expenses, leaving an allowance for inflation.

2. Set up bookkeeping and stick to the system.

3. Always write down and enter your purchases as they are made—don't wait even one hour—it is very easy to forget exact items and amounts when busy.

BASIC CONSTRUCTION COSTS

BASIC WALLS

CONSTRUCTION		COST/PER LIN. FOOT 1982
WALLS	8' high framed in 2″ x 4′ pine and covered in sheet rock, sanded, taped and painted	
	1. One sided—Finished	6.50
	2. One sided—with key strip. With double hanging Jet Rail or 4–14″ glass shelves	28.50
	3. One sided—with light valance—Key strip with double hanging Jet Rail or 4–14″ glass shelves	44.50
T-WALLS	8' high framed in 2″ x 4″ pine and covered in sheet rock, sanded, taped and painted	
	1. Finished	13.50
	2. With Key strip, with double hanging Jet Rail or 4–14″ Glass Shelves	52.00
	3. With Key Strip, with double hanging Jet Rail or 4–14″ Glass Shelves and light balance	83.00
ADDITIONS	To walls finished (no key strip) (for recessed Key Strip add 12.00 per ft.)	
	1. Jet Rail and Bars	25.00

CONSTRUCTION	COST/PER LIN. FOOT 1982
2. Cross Bars and Waterfalls	5.50
3. Cross Bars and sock/tie hooks	21.50
4. Glass Shelves 4–14″	25.00
5. Slot bd. 8′ high gum finish (varnished or painted)	23.00
6. Slot bd. (varnished or painted)	28.00
7. Slot board (varnished or painted) with hooks for Ties/Belts or socks	41.00
8. Slot board Bra Wall	38.00
9. Slot Board Shoe Wall	39.00
10. Paint walls (12′high—two coates)	1.50
11. Wall covering (suede cloth)	4.00
12. Light Valance	16.25
13. Slanted wood shelf with 3″ lip for Table top Placemats—three shelves high	26.00
14. Slanted Glass Shelves with plastic lip (stationary) 4-shelves high	32.00
15. Glass Shelves with dividers for Underwear or Knits—six shelves high	79.00
16. Shirt Glass Bin Units with plastic clips	25.00
17. Blanket Bins	50.00

FIXTURES		1982 EACH
GLASS CUBE UNITS ON FORMICA	1. Shirt, Towel—4 box high, 4 box wide	500
	2. Knit Unit 4 Box high, 5—wide	550
Cibe Bases	3. Gift Units (4x4 as per GRT)	350
	4. Gift Cubes with risers	150
	5. R-100 Bath Rug	550
	6. B-I00 Bedspread/Blanket	550
	7. DP-50 Dec. Pillows	500
	8. C-100 Comforter Fixture	500
CUBES (formica with glass risers for above)	1. 18″high 24″ wide 24″ wide	80
	2. 24 high 24 wide 24 wide	100
	3. 30 high 24 wide 24 wide	120
	4. 24 high 48 wide 48 wide	250
	5. Parson tables	200
	6. Round Table	30
	7. Round Table with cloth	57
	8. Mannequin cube 24″ × 24″ × 8″	75
	9. Mannequin cube 48″ x 48 ″ x 24″	250
	10. Wrap stand 1	250
	11. Cas. China Cube set-up	350
	12. Luggage cube	150

FIXTURES		1982 EACH
	13. Lamp large cube—set-up	250
DRAPERIES	1. T-Wall 8'high 8'long, light with valance	250
	2. with beds	400
ASST.		
	1. ½" case of 12 pc—4' x 8'	334.80
	2. Track and Lamps every 2"	20.50/lin. ft
	3. Plain fits on 1" bar	8.20
	4. with parts arm	18.90
	5. Cutlery unit with 4" bunker	100
	6. Cut. Unit with 4" Bunker	300
	7. Sign Holders 5 x 7	6.50
	7 x 11	7.50
	22 x 28	60.00
	8. 3-lay mirror	285.00

STORE FIXTURE BREAK-DOWN SHOWING UNIT PRICES

J/2	Garment Racks & M/P Units—See Attachment	
	Painting	1982
	Taping & Spackling	.30 Sq. Ft.
	Wall painting—one prime coat & one finish coat	.28 Sq. Ft.
	Column Painting—one prime coat & one finish coat	.33 Sq. Ft.
	Furnish & install vinyl wallcovering	1.55 Sq. Ft.
	Furnish & install vinyl wallcovering (for cornices)	1.80 Sq. Ft.
	Stucco finish—walls	.85 Sq. Ft.
	Stucco finish—cornices	1.10 Sq. Ft.

VISUAL MERCHANDISING AS A CAREER

The visual merchandising field is becoming more viable as a career every year. Gene Moore of Tiffany's (a master in the visual merchandising field) was one of the first "display people" to become a vice president of his firm. Many more have followed as visual merchandising gains acceptance and importance in the business world.

The visual merchandising field can be compared with a pyramid (Figure 1–6). There is much room at the bottom and very little on top. The VMs who make it to the top have a combination of talent, dedication, hard work, assertiveness, strength and charm of character, plus a dose of luck. Not every retail store in the world employs visual merchandisers but each exhibits some form of visual merchandising in their store. The opportunities for the enthusiastic and persistent VM are

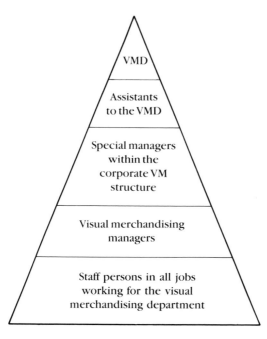

Figure 1–6
The visual merchandising hierarchy.

limitless. Although most opportunities exist in the large department chain stores, smaller stores also employ visual merchandisers or freelancers.

Ways to enter the visual merchandising field are touched on throughout this chapter. A summary of the different points follows. What stores look for in an applicant for an entry level VM position are:

1. Enthusiasm.

2. Intelligence.

3. Experience direct or in a related field of study.

4. Communication skills.

5. Physical appearance (important in an interview).

6. Health and stamina.

What stores look for in a VMM applicant are:

1. Experience. The length and duration of service (is the applicant a job hopper?) as well as the type of stores worked in are both important. The type of store worked for will indicate the style to which the VMM is accustomed.

2. An excellent portfolio.

3. Communication skills.

4. Enthusiasm.

5. Professional attitude and grasp of job responsibilities.

6. Overall intelligence.

7. Professional appearance.

The best way to get a job in the VM field is to talk to visual merchandisers who are currently working in the field. Find someone who is willing to spend some time with you and ask him or her about his or her job, the store, its visual merchandising policies, and who would be the best person to contact in the personnel department. He or she will be able to tell you if there are any current openings and if he or she knows of anyone planning to leave the store in the near future. Often, VMs know of openings in other stores "through the grapevine." The VM staff person will usually not know who on the staff may be laid off or fired. Therefore, the applicant should apply to personnel even if the VM employee says there are no current openings. One never knows!

Don't get discouraged. An enthusiastic nature combined with perseverence will work well together to help you get a job. If nothing is available at the store with the best visual merchandising in town, set your sights a little lower to get into the field and gain some experience. But keep in touch with the best store to further your educational experience and to get their name on your resume.

Visual merchandising will continue to develop as a viable profession in the future. The economy continues to force retailers to compete on many levels. Price breaks, special sales, unique merchandise, and major renovations are all designed to separate the aggressive merchants from those less flexible. Visual merchandising will always be a major factor in aggressive/flexible retailing. The image and individuality of a store is created, reinforced, and maintained by the VM department.

As business becomes more competitive the role of visual merchandising will be expanded to include additional input and control over the merchandising and design of retail stores. Visual merchandising is an exciting career challenge that demands intellectual, creative, and physical agility.

SUMMARY CHECKLIST

Key Concepts

1. Visual merchandising is a term that encompasses a large realm of responsibilities and skills.
2. Visual merchandising is making a store and its merchandise look so appealing that the customer enjoys the shopping experience and will want to return.
3. Visual merchandising skills are gained through years of experience working in the field.
4. A job in visual merchandising requires a person who can adapt to change.
5. The term *visual merchandising* encompasses the entire merchandising concept.

6. Visual merchandising jobs are available in large or small department stores, large or small speciality stores, union or nonunion stores, and on a free-lance basis.
7. The VMM in a smaller store has more varied responsibilities than in a large store.
8. In a store where the employees are unionized, the VM duties are more sharply defined.
9. Visual merchandising freelancing jobs require a good understanding of visual merchandising techniques.
10. Prioritizing is another word for organization—a skill necessary for a quality VMM or VM.
11. It is critical that the VMM utilize good employee relations with the staff.
12. A VMM who utilizes a positive reinforcement management style combined with an open exchange of ideas will create an excellent work atmosphere.
13. The visual merchandising field is becoming more viable as a career every year.
14. Competition will cause the role of the VMM to be expanded to include additional input and control over the merchandising and design of retail stores.
15. Display budgets generally fluctuate with the profits of the store.
16. Management usually decides how much money will be available in the display budget. The display manager may have some input as to the size of the budget.
17. All activities planned by management should be accounted for in the yearly budget.
18. Promotions will affect the display budgets.
19. All display managers should utilize a budget book.
20. Store policies control the acceptance of gifts by buyers.
21. The visual merchant must always consider security when planning displays.
22. All merchandise should be signed out using proper procedures.

KEY TERMS

1. Caseline color
2. NADI
3. Display budget
4. Found objects
5. Capital expense account
6. WAVM
7. Freelancer
8. Trunk shows
9. Accruals

DISCUSSION QUESTIONS

1. Discuss the importance of visual merchandising and its relationship to the total store.
2. What are the basic skills required of a person who would like an entry level position in visual merchandising?
3. Discuss the history of visual merchandising from 1900 to the present.

4. How do the responsibilities of a VM in a nonunion store differ from those of union store VM?
5. What are the advantages of working as a VM freelancer?
6. What is meant by prioritization? Give an example.
7. Why is it important that the visual merchandising staff work as a team?
8. What are two types of management styles that could be utilized by a VMM?
9. List the management philosophies that a VMM could utilize to create incentive and employee motivation.
10. List the pros and cons of a career in visual merchandising.
11. What is the relationship between profit and the display budget?
12. List at least five of the issues that should be discussed with management prior to preparing the visual merchandising budget.
13. Within each display shop there are built-in expenses. What are these expenses?
14. Why does a manager prefer that the cost of store renovations be taken from the capital expense account?
15. What are the major column headings you should include in a budget book?
16. What are the three most important items to remember when dealing with budgets?

STUDENT EXERCISES

Number 1

Interview the personnel manager at two department stores located in your community. The purpose of your interview will be to discuss the personnel structure (chain of command) that presently exists. Include the following discussion points when summarizing your interviews.

1. Is there a policy or flow chart in writing?
2. Who does the VMM report to?
3. Would you change the structure in any way as it relates to the VMM? (explain your answer)

Number 2

Assume the role of a VMM in a large department store. You have a staff of seven employees who are under your direct supervision. The store manager has given you the responsibility of hiring your own staff.

Develop a personnel policy that you will utilize when hiring your visual merchandising staff. Develop the policy using a step-by-step procedure.

Number 3

It is March 1 of the present year. As assistant VM manager, it is your responsibility to take care of all bookkeeping functions for the VM unit. The VM manager has asked you to prepare a financial summary of all purchases and orders received for January and February. Your financial headings should include the following headings: amount spent, orders arrived, amount outstanding, amount accrued, amount transferred. Your yearly budget is $60,000. A summary of activities is indicated below:

ITEM	AMOUNT	DATE ORDERED	DATE RECEIVED	KEREC #	P.O. #
1	$5,000.00	1/17	1/24	06438	436
2	4,000.00	1/22	2/14	06487	437
3	6,000.00	1/26	1/28	06451	438
4	1,000.00	1/31	Not Received		439
5	2,000.00	2/2	2/7	06472	440
6	3,000.00	2/14	2/23	06480	441
7	2,000.00	2/27	Not Received		442

Number 4

Visit three community businesses with which you are familiar and obtain a copy of the security procedures that must be followed by all employees.

1. Do any of the policies relate directly to visual merchandising activities?
2. Is there a signout procedure when merchandise is taken from a department?
3. Who is responsible for lost merchandise?
4. Are buyers allowed to accept gifts from manufacturers or distributors?

CASE PROBLEM 1

The New Employee

The Lansen Brothers Department Store is a well-established firm that is operating in a city of over 350,000 located in the heart of a major industrial area in the Southeast. Store sales volume has been decreasing steadily for the past six months. The total volume of customer traffic seems to be about the same but the customers are not purchasing merchandise in the normal quantities for this time of year.

During the first half of the year, the sales volume was $21 million and decreased to $17 million during the second half of the year, which includes the major buying period. At the annual board meeting in January, the store manager proposed that the visual merchandising department budget be increased by 70 percent to allow for the purchase of new materials and the hiring of three additional VM assistants. After considerable discussion the board approved the plan and Alice Goldbuff, the VMM, was informed of the decision and given total responsibility for the hiring.

Throughout the month of February, Alice interviewed fourteen persons for the position and selected the top three applicants who began work March 1. April through June proved to be beneficial to the overall look of the store. The additional monies allocated had allowed Alice to purchase additional visual merchandising materials, and with the help of the extra staff support the store was taking on a new look. Sales had begun to increase. After their first six months, all three new employees received above average to excellent evaluations from Alice.

On July 15, the store manager, Tracy Felton, called Alice into her office. She had just received a call from a friend in another store who had seen Lou, one of the new VM assistants working at Lansen Brothers. He informed Tracy that he had fired Lou for stealing during December of last year. After analyzing the situation, Alice and Tracy listed the following facts:

1. Lou had received an excellent evaluation from Alice during his six-month review and is doing an outstanding job for Lansen Brothers.

2. Alice had not checked past employment records or references before hiring Lou.

3. Lou had lied on his employment application.

Questions To Discuss

1. What decision should Tracy and Alice make regarding Lou?
2. How could this situation have been prevented?
3. Should Alice have been given the hiring authority? (defend your answer)

CASE PROBLEM 2

The Union Shop

The Corner Store is a medium-sized department store located in a community of 320,000. Last year was a very successful sales year. The gross sales for the store were $14 million. The Corner Store has been a family-owned corporation for the past 14 years, but due to internal family problems, the business was purchased by Kinglo Corporation. Kinglo is a major conglomerate with diverse investments.

Lowell Anderson was immediately brought in as store manager and was instructed to make several changes. One major change was to allow the employees to decide if they would like to operate under a union shop. During the past 14 years under the previous management, the employees were never given this option, nor did they feel they needed it.

During a meeting with the employees, Mr. Anderson outlined the following facts relevant to the employees if they decided to join the union.

1. On the average, each employee would receive a 7 percent salary increase.

2. Union dues would be taken out of their pay checks automatically.

3. Duties for each employee would be specifically outlined.

4. If the majority of employees voted for the union, all would be required to join.

5. All department heads and managers would become "management" and would not be part of the union.

Mr. Anderson gave the employees a week to discuss the issue before the vote was taken. Two days after the initial meeting, Kari McIntosh, the VMM, called her staff together to discuss the issues.

Questions To Discuss

1. What are the advantages for the VM assistants if they join the union?

2. What are the disadvantages for the VM assistants if they join the union?

3. How would you vote if you were a VM assistant? (defend your answer)

4. How would you vote if you were the VMM? (defend your answer)

CASE PROBLEM 3

The New Department

"What a year it has been," remarked Sue Dennis, the VM manager for Albertons Apparel. Albertons is a clothing store that caters mainly to the middle-class customer. The merchandise is reasonably priced and of substantial quality. Albertons is located in an industrial community of approximately 425,000 people. Albertons recently opened a second store and Sue is visual merchandising manager for both stores.

Christmas is over, inventory is complete, and the months of January and February actually give Sue some time to do the planning, budgeting, and catch-up work that has been neglected for the past months. Sue was checking her budgets when the phone rang. It was Mr. Lakert, the store manager. He told Sue to report to his office immediately. The head carpenter was also summoned to Mr. Lakert's office.

A new men's/women's shoe department was going to be built in the original store. Sue was asked to prepare a detailed budget and present it to Mr. Lakert. She was given the following information:

1. Cost sheets
2. Size of department:
   a. Length, 20'
   b. Width, 16'
   c. Ceiling, 12'
3. Floor: carpeting over concrete
4. Walls: a vinyl material over ½" sheet rock
5. Ceiling: suspended grid system
6. One entrance into the stock room which has already been built

Sue's budget should reflect all items necessary to open the department excluding labor and sales merchandise. The budget summary sheet should include the following information: item, number needed, size, cost per item, and total cost.

Activities To Be Completed

1. Prepare the budget summary sheet that will be presented to the owner. Utilize cost estimates from vendors in your community.
2. Prepare a rough sketch of the department.

CHAPTER 2

Design

LEARNING OBJECTIVES

At the completion of this chapter, you will be able to:

1. Explain the value of design as an essential element in display.

2. Explain the primary points to consider when designing a display.

3. Cite the importance of image and design as it relates to customer attraction.

4. Describe the difference between displaying merchandise and merchandising a display.

5. List the questions that should be asked before designing a display.

6. Describe the basic display locations available in a retail store.

7. List and explain the elements that should be considered when beginning to design a display.

8. Discuss the six major principles necessary when developing a quality display.

Entire books have been dedicated to the concept of design and its relationship to art and life. Design by definition is a plan, outline, or sketch. In this chapter, design is treated as an essential ingredient in the creation of a display. Good design makes a visual presentation work. When a presentation or display works, this means the design attracts attention in a way that strengthens the image of the store as well as appropriately introducing the concept of the merchandise to the customer. The customer for this merchandise must be identified and the display planned to attract that particular person. A window or display usually has only three to eight seconds to attract attention, create desire, and sell a product. Confusion can arise when the visual merchandiser fails to think out all the aspects of design. An untraditional design for untraditional merchandise will naturally attract the right customer and direct attention to that merchandise. A traditional display for trendy merchandise will make that merchandise look like everything else and the customer who is attracted to the most current trends (usually in style for only one year) will not see or will ignore the traditional display. A trendy, innovative design for classic blazers may alienate the traditional customer but attract the style-conscious customer, who may then think that the traditional blazers are trendy. If this seems confusing, try to imagine classic bust forms and plants with vinyl jumpsuits and plastic visors. Confusion of style and images rarely works.

The primary points to remember when designing a display are:

1. What is the image of your store?

2. Who is the customer you are trying to attract?

3. What is the concept of the merchandise to be used in the display?

4. Where is the display being set up and how will the location determine the design?

5. Why is this merchandise rather than any other being put on display? How does this reason determine the visual presentation and design?

IMAGE AND DESIGN

There is a vast difference between the design images of Saks Fifth Avenue, Neiman-Marcus, Bonwit Teller, and other extremely elegant, high-priced stores and mass merchandisers such as Sears, Penney's, and Woolworth's. Between these two ends of the merchandising design spectrum lie Bloomingdale's, Macy's, Marshall Field, Jordan Marsh, and all other full-line department stores that cater to both ends of the customer spectrum ranging from better to moderately lower priced merchandise. All of these stores as well as smaller stores around the country have one thing in common: the desire to attract a customer to their establishment in order to sell merchandise. Each store selects an image to present to the world as uniquely its own. The customer then comes to identify a certain look with a store and expect this look to be echoed throughout the store, be it pizazz, excitement, elegance, or a total lack of all three. Mixing images within one store rarely works because it confuses the customer. An example would be the use of a plastic leaf garland at Saks Fifth Avenue. Plastic garlands (see Glossary) could work in a Penney's or Sears, but would look terribly out of place in Saks. But if an elegant oriental vase with a massive piece of gilded bamboo were placed with a very simple better dress display in a lower priced store, it would attract attention and give a feeling of luxury and richness to a department. This same display could also scare away customers who feel that the merchandise is too rich and therefore too expensive an item to even look at. Therefore, it is vital to know your customer and store well before designing a display.

The image of a store can be badly hurt by a sloppy or poorly designed display using improper elements. This applies to stores that run the spectrum of merchandise content from high priced to low.

Snobbery is out of place in a design image which relies on the quality of the goods sold. The pride a visual merchandiser feels should be in the quality of the visual merchandising design presentation, how well that display sells merchandise, and the successful correspondence to the store's image.

1. Visual merchandising designs must relate to the store's image.

2. Poorly designed displays work against a carefully cultivated image.

3. Merchandise quality, design, and image must all relate.

CUSTOMERS AND DESIGN

In the opening paragraph an example was made of trendy presentation for traditional merchandise and vice versa. This example applies directly to the store's customers. A large department store may have many types of shoppers. If the customers are properly educated by the store, they will come to expect a certain level of visual presentation whenever they enter the establishment. If a display design is tasteless and not in keeping with the expected image, the customer may become discouraged with the store's viewpoint and feel uncomfortable shopping there. An example of this is an actual incident in a town in the Hamptons, a sophisticated resort area on Long Island in New York. A high-priced, trendy shoe store had a window display of a male flasher with his raincoat open and nothing underneath, looking at two shocked female mannequins wearing skimpy clothing and the store's shoes. The entire community was annoyed by this unnecessarily tasteless display. Had the male mannequin been fully dressed and dangling a huge, hairy spider in front of the female mannequins, it would still have been funny but the shock and outrage considerably less. The flasher is a standard media joke, but dressing female mannequins in skimpy clothing raised the issue of women "asking for it" and the feminist viewpoint of the woman as a victim. Business went badly for the rest of the summer and the store was not reopened the following season. Know not only your customer but your community and its standards. Assuming too much sophistication or ennui and trying to shock people into buying can lead instead to a boycott.

Surrealism has been used in display since the early 1930s. It has taken both humorous and bizarre forms. In the mid to late 1970s, strange and shocking situations were commonplace in Bloomingdale's, New York City. An innovative visual merchandiser, Candy Pratts, developed shocking windows with violence and sex as themes. Rather than alienate customers, the windows were taken in most cases to be a comment on society and the apparent slide or decline of civilization. Female mannequins, seemingly murdered, were sometimes found lying on the floor in the windows with cool, detached, well-dressed mannequins nearby holding possible murder weapons.

In this case, the community of New York City could appreciate the commentary and relate it to the growth of white collar crime in the city.

1. Educate your customer.

2. Know your customer and community.

MERCHANDISE CONCEPT AND DESIGN

An excellent example of taking a concept and building a fantastic business from it is the Izod shirt phenomenon. The concept of Izod sport shirts for men revolved around their vast range of fashionable colors, their appropriateness for most occasions, and their wearability for sports (for which they were originally intended). An intelligent and inventive marketing person at Izod decided to develop the fashion concept and push the large choice of colors as opposed to the snob appeal. The snob appeal came through the price, but it was eventually usurped by Ralph Lauren and other brands as Izod became over promoted and worn by many people. (Snobbery relies on a select group wearing a particular item.) Business hasn't suffered from this overpromotion, but the snob appeal has lessened. The colors form a great display wall presentation and remain a joy for visual merchants to work with. By creating a spectrum of color across a wall with Izod shirts, several things are accomplished: great color impact and excitement, a strong Izod statement, and a major emphasis on the sportswear department.

Before designing a display always look at the merchandise first, and if you're unfamiliar with it, ask the buyer about the concept and meaning of it in a retail sense. Keep in mind that you are displaying merchandise, not merchandising a pretty display. If items are used in an inappropriate manner—such as Health-Tex (moderate-priced children's clothes) displayed in an elegant fashion as opposed to looking cute and fun as the merchandise is advertised—the customer will become confused and sales are lost.

A new ice cream making machine came onto the market in 1980 called Il Gelataio. It was costly and appealed to a small segment of the buying public. It was promoted heavily by demonstrators within the housewares areas of department and specialty stores and had good sales. When the concept of this machine was handled properly by the store's management and display team, it sold very well. When it was massed out (large quantities put on the selling floor) and sold like a popcorn popper—it failed. It was necessary to market Il Gelataio in its own area and treat it as a new concept in home entertainment and gourmet eating enjoyment. Ice cream parlors were set up around it to give the feeling of old fashioned ice cream taste. Sales were down when Il Gelataio was stacked on the shelves next to the lower priced models so that it blended in and lost its snob appeal.

Following are some questions to ask yourself before designing a display for a specific product:

1. What is the product?

2. Where does it belong (housewares, ready-to-wear, cosmetics, men's)?

3. What is its price point, or how much does it cost?

4. Is this price point higher or lower than the average cost for a similar product?

5. What is the concept behind the price factor of this product? Is it priced lower to be promotional (sale oriented) or is it priced higher because of its quality and potential for snob appeal?

6. To whom are you trying to appeal with this product? Who are your customers? Put yourself in their place and try to see the product through their eyes. What do they see, how will they use it, where and when will it be used?

All of these thoughts will give you ideas on how to display the product.

LOCATION AND DESIGN

Once you have determined the image of your store, your customer, the concept behind the merchandise, and several possible ways to market (display) the product, you're ready to start the hard part. Now you're faced with reality—a terrible location for the best product you've ever seen, or a terrific locale for garbage. Naturally, this doesn't happen all the time, but it can feel that way when your fantastic ideas for a design don't correspond to the reality of the space allotted for the display. The location often determines your setup and display, and it's up to you to make it work.

There are several basic types of locations to deal with in a retail environment.

A. The window (Figures 2–1 through 2–7):

1. Windows created on either side of a mall store entrance.

2. One large window or several windows in a straight line along the front of the building, also known as a "bank" of windows.

3. A large window broken into several sections by mullions (strips of 2" × 2" steel that hold large pieces of glass together).

Figure 2–1

The window that is gaining in importance throughout the country is the mall window. This is an area created on either side of a store entrance. Usually the window area behind the props is left open so that the customer can see into the store.

4. A very small window—the classic jewelry window.

5. The window that looks into the store.

6. The bay window with a platform and lights, and merchandise beyond it.

7. Two windows facing each other and the street—leading back to a door in the center—known as lobby windows. These windows have only a small frontal view from the street and the most visual area is in the walkway leading to the door. As the walkway is usually narrow, there is little stepping back and viewing room, so that the displays have to tell individual merchandising stories as the customer walks through the aisle to enter the store.

Figure 2—2
A bank of windows.

Figure 2—3
A large window expanse broken up by mullions.

Figure 2—4
A small window that is part of a store's exterior architecture. These are usually built for jewelry stores.

Figure 2—5
A window is often designed to allow the customer to see past the display into the merchandise area.

Figure 2—6

The bay window may be raised above street level and a small, stagelike area created for a display presentation. The background is usually left fairly open so that the customer can see through into the store.

Figure 2—7

Lobby windows are two sets of windows that are separated by a path into the main entrance of the store.

B. The walls (Figures 2–8 through 2–14):

1. A flat wall with standards for hanging merchandise.

2. A flat wall with shelves for sitting or folded merchandise.

3. A wing wall or T-wall.

4. A blank wall for display use only along an aisle or escalator.

5. A corner made by two intersecting walls.

6. A flat wall with a valance that has lighting attached behind it.

7. One half-wall with a ledge on top of it.

Figure 2–8
A basic wall with hang bar and waterfalled frontons. Notice the standards that are attached on the face of the wall to hold up the hang bars.

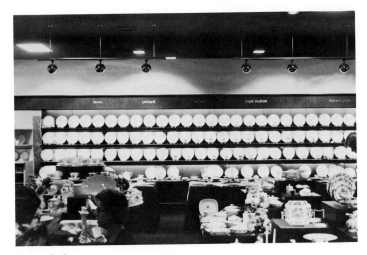

Figure 2–9
A shelved wall that holds sitting (hard goods) or folded (soft goods) merchandise. In this case, dish sets are arranged in a clean, geometric lineup.

Figure 2–10
A wing wall is an addition to the end of a freestanding wall.

Figure 2–11
Often the walls that are created by escalators are used for display or small shop areas.

Figure 2–12
A corner made by two intersecting walls is an excellent display area and is an architectural standby in store design.

Figure 2–13
An example of a classic valance with fluorescent lighting attached to its back or wall side.

Figure 2–14
A half-wall is seen in older stores, usually on the main floor. Softening props, such as floral arrangements or mannequins, are often used to highlight the short wall.

C. Cases (Figures 2–15 through 2–17):

1. Boutiquing (arranging a small selection of related items) the top shelf of a case.

2. A glass front case with no shelves.

3. A case with a display window behind it in the central core; also known as a shadow box.

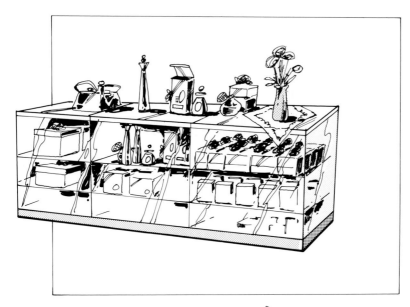

Figure 2–15
Boutiquing the top shelf of a case involves displaying related merchandise in an attractive manner closest to eye level.

Figure 2–16
A glass front case with no shelves can be used as a vignette or striking display area.

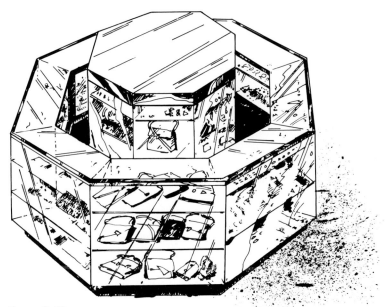

Figure 2–17
A window that is built into a core unit is often used to display the merchandise stocked in the cases in front of the core unit.

    D. Shops (Figures 2–18 through 2–19):

        1. Designed for a specific area with "permanent" construction.

        2. Designed as a temporary shop area for a limited amount of time.

Figure 2–18
A shoe area is often permanent construction. Slotwall is used in many shoe departments to get the most flexible use out of the wall space. The areas that are created on this wall perform two functions. One is to add visual stimulation by breaking up the flat wall and the other is to create separate areas for different shoe classifications.

Figure 2–19
*A temporary shop that was created
to house specific merchandise for
a limited period of time. In this case,
leg warmers are on display.*

E. Ledges (Figure 2–20): On top of core units, usually on the main floor of a store, on top of valance structures, or on escalator walls.

Figure 2–20
Ledge displays are usually on top of core units on the main floor of a store. They are either total impact displays, i.e., identical floral arrangements, or they display the merchandise stocked below as with this Etienne Aigner handbag display.

F. Islands (Figures 2–21 through 2–22):

1. An area set aside for display only. Can be raised or lowered depending on the surrounding architecture. If the area is lowered, there must be protection to keep customers from falling into the display area.

2. Can be made by cubes or buildups covered with either wood, formica, paint, or carpet.

3. Any area created by freestanding platforms to define a space and create a specific display presentation.

Figure 2–21

An area set aside specifically for display purposes. It may be changed architecturally by redoing the floor platforms.

Figure 2–22

A platform set up in a department store can become an instant display presentation. Lighting should always be focused on the display.

OBJECTIVES AND DESIGN

Why is this merchandise being put on display? Is it on sale? If so, are there enough pieces of the merchandise on and off the selling floor to warrant a display? If there are only a few items and one is on display, the merchandise will be sold out before the display item is removed and customers who react to the displayed item will be disappointed and annoyed when told that the goods are unavailable. Usually heard from irate customers is, "Why is it on display if you have none to sell?" A valid question! If the merchandise is not on sale but is a promotion—bought by the buyer at a special price (lower than usual)—usually there must be sufficient quantity to justify a mannequin or special presentation. Sale or promotional merchandise should be up front in the department for short major sales or promotions, and relegated to the rear of the department when the sale or promo lasts for several weeks or months. In the case of clearance merchandise (marked down/reduced in price more than once), the goods should be in a far corner of the department. It is amazing how customers will find the clearance area no matter where it is. There is no reason to take up valuable front promotional and image space for old, marked down merchandise.

Brand new, exciting, and innovative merchandise needs a display to introduce it to the customer and give it an identity. If the store has invested heavily in this product and related articles, then a shop to segregate these items may be called for. A well thought out shop will attract the customer most likely to buy this type of merchandise (Figure 2–23).

Figure 2–23

This display is a play on both the merchandise concept and the props. The flannel nightshirts are considered "as warm as toast." The presentation is more fun than a simple sign saying "flannel nightshirts." Although these garments are not innovative, the financial investment by the buyer warranted prime display space. As the winter was predicted to be unusually cold, the sales potential of this merchandise was considered to be very high.

Credit: Ilene Rosenthal..

Is the merchandise elegant? Expensive? Unique? Treat it accordingly with a display that segregates and identifies it as being special. A spacious feeling, unusual props, and signing can create an elegant atmosphere.

For lower priced but unusual or "fun" merchandise, "massing it out" (putting large quantities on appropriate fixtures) in the department with a special display area next to it will identify it to the customer. An outpost is another way to create a special merchandise feel. An outpost is an area developed outside the normal department for merchandise intending to reach customers who may not shop in the regular parent department. Customers will notice this unusual merchandise in their usual shopping haunts, e.g., gift items for women in an outpost within the men's department or men's fragrances in women's lingerie. Men rarely travel outside their department, so that bringing the impulse items to them will create more sales. An outpost may be the best solution when trying to decide where to display and merchandise a special item. Outposts work when there is a tremendous amount of merchandise to be sold; two locations will sell more goods than one. When items are special, to create more sales they need to be in areas that will draw the attention of shoppers not accustomed to looking in their usual shopping departments. This way they may find impulse items such as those offered in the outpost on their regular shopping paths. Rarely do outposts carry expensive merchandise that has to be tried on, requiring a dressing room, or heavy goods that need a delivery service. Outposts are for quick purchases or impulse items, and can usually create large sales when they are stocked with enough of the right merchandise and staffed by people who know their goods and can sell quickly (Figure 2–24).

Figure 2–24
A Christmas shop that is also an outpost. It consists of a wide assortment of stocking stuffers, ornaments, and other tree decorations. The overall visual impression is of red and green.

Special situations arise continually that require visual merchandisers to stretch their minds and creativity to find a viable reason for merchandise to be put on display—and an identity to make it work (sell) when it is displayed.

APPLIED DESIGN

Once you've identified your location and product-marketing strategy, you then have to work with the elements and principles of design to make the location work for your display. There is no one way to tell someone how to be good at design. In some cases it comes naturally, in others it is learned, but either way it is possible to develop a sense of good design through study, evaluation, trial and error, and observation. Taste is arbitrary, and you may develop what you consider to be excellent taste in design, yet another person with different ideas will consider your taste fussy, too stark, folksy, or just plain bad. Basically, in the business world, the taste level is determined by the person who directs the company. This person will usually hire a visual merchant who will best reflect the image and taste the merchandiser wants to project. This doesn't mean that it's the best or only way; it is what is wanted by that particular person for that particular store. A strong VM will probably have differences of opinion regarding taste level with both management and with the display staff. Remember that there is no one way to do anything in display art. There are many solutions to any problem and your way may be excellent, but there is also room for greatness in other ideas. An understanding of the basic elements of design will help you to develop a good sense and innate taste as well as make it easier to design a display from merchandise.

When you start to consider all the elements, look again at the merchandise you want to display. What are its physical properties and what will enhance them? Each element will act in a different way to work for or against the product. Ideally, they should all work together to create the desired effect. Design elements and principles that will be covered in this chapter other than the merchandise are positive and negative space, light, color, flow, proportion, balance, and how they relate to visual merchandising.

To summarize the discussion of objectives and design, the merchandise should create the message. Understand the concept behind the merchandise before attempting to display it because it fits into a preconceived design. Before starting a display ask these questions:

1. Why is the merchandise being displayed?

2. Is it on sale?

3. Are there enough pieces in stock to warrant a display?

4. What is the use of the merchandise?

5. What is the image or style of the item?

6. To whom are you trying to sell this?

7. How long will it remain on display?

8. What kind of area will it be located in and is there a need for security fixturing?

POSITIVE AND NEGATIVE SPACE

Positive and negative space are exactly what they sound like. The letters on this page are positive figures and the white space around the letters is negative space. If a large black box is placed in an empty room, the box is positive and the rest of the space is negative. In any design, using the negative space to your advantage will enhance the positive figures. If there is a large amount of negative space in an enclosed area, such as a case, shadow box, or window, the object placed in that stark environment will stand out strongly. The negative space can echo the positive figures to enhance it in another way. Using the negative space in the same basic shape of the positive figure will highlight the basic outline of the merchandise (Figure 2–25). Using exactly the same amount of positive and negative space will give a static somewhat boring look (Figure 2–26). You can make the negative space important and balance it by allowing a lot of negative space to counteract a strong positive element. In some cases the physical properties of the merchandise are so strong that they overwhelm weak negative space unless that space is made interest-

Figure 2–25
Mannequins placed behind a wall of fabric create exciting negative space by echoing the positive mannequins in the foreground.
Credit: Toshi, 1982. Giorgio Armani, N.Y.C.

Figure 2–26
The use of positive and negative space should be planned so that an exciting vibration is set up between the two. In this illustration the positive and negative areas are equal and are.therefore not very interesting.

ing by the placement of the object, the color of the space, the lighting, and texture. If the negative space is made exciting by its own physical properties other than with merchandising or props, the entire design takes on a more vital and eye-appealing quality (Plate 10).

On a mannequin platform, the use of negative space creates room for implied movement in the mannequins. Referring forward to Chapter 4 on safety, when a mannequin is on a platform in the middle of the selling floor, the negative space should be taken up by something visible to the customer so that the end of the platform is defined and the shopper doesn't trip over it. This should be planned into the display design so that the negative space falls within the platform as opposed to on the ends (Figure 2–27). If the mannequin or display is planned into an area that is set apart from the traffic flow, the negative space can be used more creatively. When the customer isn't in danger of tripping over platforms, an unbalanced design scheme can be employed to create interest.

LIGHTING

Although light is neither a traditional principle or an element of display design, it is the substance by which persons recognize all the basic visual elements. The visual elements are line, color, shape, direction, texture, scale (proportion), dimension, and motion. Operating in conjunction with these elements are the traditional principles of balance, stress, leveling, and sharpening, attraction and grouping, and positive and negative. Light is used as a medium in this chapter to create successful visual designs.

Light is one of the ways to create interesting effects on positive elements and negative space. Light also enables everything you do to be seen. If that seems rather basic, please realize that many display people forget to use lighting as a design element and many displays have faded into the walls because they can't be seen. Good lighting can make an ordinary display "pop" and become exciting. Whenever

Figure 2–27
Empty platform ends need to be defined by either props or mannequins and should be well lit. Customers tend to look at the merchandise rather than the floor and can easily trip over undefined risers. Visually, the design is more appealing when off-center.

a location is determined for a display, consider the lighting of the area, the source and the type of shadows that will be created from that light, the type of lighting (fluorescent or incandescent; check Chapter 8 for definitions), and whether it is warm or cool. Warm lighting is a warm white or pinkish light that is very flattering to people's complexions, ready-to-wear departments, and all softwear. Cool light is more like direct sunlight and is excellent for all hard-line departments where the merchandise should look sharp and clean, not soft or gentle. If you are doing a display in a housewares department and the lighting is all warm in the area, you can instantly create a different effect by changing the lighting in the display area to cool lights. This works particularly well if the area is removed from other sections of the department by architecture. Be careful not to change the lighting under a valance so that some of the fluorescents are cool and some warm. All that is created is a mottled look with no noticeable returns other than an unprofessional feel. Within a housewares department a gourmet section would be a good place to use cool spotlights. Often, within the same department kitchen-wearable accessories are sold and soft pink light on the aprons and mitts may give a homier feeling to that particular section. Only in rare instances should cool light be used in a soft wear department. Possibly in a new-wave shop or a shop devoted to vinyl merchandise cool light would give a more slick effect as opposed to the softening nature of warm light.

Incandescent lighting is most often used for spotlights because it is too expensive for general lighting in a large area. Fluorescent lights, on the other hand, are generally inexpensive for a large area. Incandescent spotlights are usually combined with the fluorescents for highlighting effects. Fluorescents light up a general area, but nothing stands out. Spotlights will make things "pop." If you're setting up a display on the selling floor, check in the immediate vicinity to see if there are any spotlights in the ceiling to highlight your design. The existence of lighting is as important as the finding of appropriate floor space. If you work for an organization where there is an electrician ready and willing to install spotlights wherever you desire, congratulations! If, in reality, you have to wait forever to get the lights you want installed or you have to do minor electrical work yourself, consider that problem in your presentation. There may be a floor plug in the area so that small spotlights can be anchored onto the platform and focused upward to highlight the necessary areas. Make sure that any floor spots you decide to use have a protective coating around them so that customers won't burn their hands if they happen to touch them accidentally or on purpose.

A spotlight will pick up a certain area and highlight it. By lighting a certain area, you determine where you want the customer to look. The light acts as a guide to what is important within the display and can intensify colors or wash them out, depending on how direct or indirect the light beam is on the object. Color filters can be used over the spots to create different color effects. These colored spots can liven up negative space and often make a display much more exciting by either echoing the primary object's color in the background or using an opposite color to create a tension between the two. Remember that color and shape are nothing if there is no light to see them.

COLOR

Color is the reflection of light. If you hold a prism up to the sun you'll see reflected onto a wall or floor a rainbow of colors known as a spectrum. Most often the spectrum is broken down into a color wheel so that the artist using it can determine which colors are complementary, which colors create a monochromatic color scheme, and which colors, when combined, create a vibration.

Complementary colors are those that are opposite from one another on the wheel (Figure 2–28). Complements can either tone down the other color or vitalize that color by its contrast. In painting, in order to tone down red, green can be added and the red will retain its integrity as red, but will have a lesser intensity. If primary red is painted next to green, a vibration is set up between the two colors

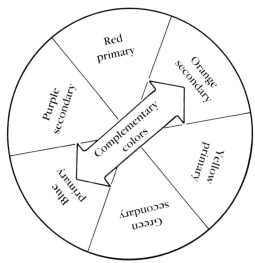

Figure 2–28
The color wheel showing primary and secondary colors. Complementary colors are those colors that fall opposite from each other on the color wheel. Close colors run next to each other. A close color combination may work well in a display presentation.

that equally intensifies both of them. Rather than using just the pure colors of the spectrum, effective results can be achieved by using complements on either side of the primary red, blue, and yellow.

Monochromatic color schemes consist of one color used in many different tints or hues. If you take blue and add white in progressively larger amounts, the blue's hue will become lighter. If black, is added, the blue will get much darker. Lighter or darker hues constitute the basic monochromatic concept. If, however, the complement of blue is added (red), the blue will be toned down in a different way and could be an interesting addition to a traditional monochromatic scheme.

Certain colors create intense vibrations when used together. Bright red and yellow create a hot, festive atmosphere that suggests a celebration or circus. Too much of any vibrating color scheme will detract from the merchandise and irritate the customer after prolonged exposure. Using different gradations of the color (such as a lighter yellow with a pinker red) will still set up a warm, friendly color scheme, and will be less intense and offensive over the long run.

Some of the most effective window and interior displays are monochromatic because a large area of any one color can be seen from a great distance and will create an impression of strength in that color. A common retailing expression is, "We believe in. . . ." If a monochromatic color scheme is done in a window, the store is saying we believe in red or whatever color is used. The customer becomes immediately aware that red is an important color for fashion, clothing, housewares, or makeup. Red becomes a statement on its own, and the merchandise takes a second place to the importance of the color. Color is a valuable tool in design and, if used for the right merchandise, can be very effective. To achieve a monochromatic color scheme with meaning and integrity, the merchandise should also relate in other important elements of design and price besides color. That means if a $150 skirt and an $80 blouse are in a window, a $20 blouse and skirt should not be shown in the same window even if all the items are the same color. Items should be grouped by price and design as well as by use. If there is a desire or need to show merchandise that is the same hue but of a different price point or use, a separate display can be set up to use this merchandise. That way the monochromatic color story is intensified even further by repeating it somewhere else. This strengthens the "we believe in red" feeling.

A display purposely set up to create a disturbance and vibration will work well in many departments for a limited time. Bright colors are exciting in a children's department or junior area. If they're overly strong and are not broken up by an eye-relieving area of a solid neutral or light tone, they will begin to tire the customers' eyes, who will then leave the department sooner than intended.

The use of the spectrum when colorizing merchandise will help achieve a harmonious feel to the department. Dark colors should be placed on the ends of a spectrum and light colors should be in the center. The brights work best on either side of the lights, e.g., Navy-purple-magenta-red-orange-peach-yellow-light yellow-white-pale green-green-turquoise-royal blue-brown-black. The merchandise colors rarely fit the light spectrum exactly but can be loosely interpreted so that a feeling of nature is achieved.

On fixtures there is no rule as to what color to begin with. Sometimes a "red" statement (or any other color) is desired in a department. In these cases, start the fixtures with the requested color and then continue the spectrum from that color, e.g., red-orange-yellow, etc. From towels to men's sweaters can all be colorized with the use of the color spectrum.

Color psychology becomes very important when designing a display. Many theories have been espoused on the effects of color on people and their moods while shopping. What seems to work is often based on what a customer is used to seeing. There are certain colors that have been used over and over for the same thing and have become synonymous with as well as symbols of that holiday, event, or place. Memories may be awakened by certain colors that will stimulate the imagination of the customer.

- Red and green for Christmas

- Red alone for Valentine's Day

- Yellow and purple for Easter

- Green for St. Patrick's Day

- Orange and black for Halloween

- Orange and brown for fall

- Warm colors for sun shops (warm colors of the spectrum: reds, yellows, oranges)

- Cool colors for swim shops (greens and blues)

- Cool colors for winter shops

- Beige tones for ready-to-wear departments

- Purples and oranges, or other brights, for junior departments

- Pastels for infants' and children's with splashes of bright color

- Browns, greys, and rusts, and wood for men's departments

- Dark tones for china and glass areas (china and glass show up better against a dark background)

- Natural wood, white, and brown for housewares departments

Certain combinations work for the customer because they've been traditionally accepted for many years. New color combinations have to be carefully thought out to avoid shock or offense through an inappropriate use of a familiar color. A slightly different shade or tone of a color, or using it in an unusual manner, may work very well. An example is the use of a bright purple in a man's area, which would be offensive, whereas a deep purple could work well. Black or very dark tones in a children's area are inappropriate unless a special effect is being created in a limited area. Pastels in housewares will work only in a section devoted to pastel merchandise. Light tints often soften the clean hardware effect of the merchandise and make it look less professional. Many shades of green or blue are difficult in a women's dress area. The reflection of the green or blue combined with the yellow-green fluorescent lighting makes the customer and the merchandise look sallow. Warmer greens, such as very soft celery or celadon, may work when broken up with warm accent colors.

The best way to learn about color in retailing is to go to the newest stores in your area and see what color combinations have been used in the different departments. Usually, when a new, better priced department store is built, much time and research is put into the choice of colors for each department. The newest trends are considered and usually used. Peach and melon tones for lingerie are very popular now but may be passé in three years. The best research is through careful observation. To try and determine new trends, the magazines *Interior Design* and *Abitare* will give a feeling for the latest color trends in architecture.

Color, like light, can make or break a design. Learn which colors work together by experimenting with paint, colored paper, or colorful towels. Ask people whose taste you respect how they feel about color combinations. The most important learning tool in visual merchandising is the experienced person whom you admire and respect. All you have to do is swallow your pride and ask what that person thinks. Most of the time, people are more than happy and flattered to be put into the position of teacher, advisor, or mentor, and will help you to learn why some colors work and others clash or fail.

FLOW/RHYTHM

If your eye travels from one area on a display to another, so that it eventually sees the entire design, a flow exists. The eye should be able to flow from one thing to the

Figure 2–29

Notice the connecting board at 5A-C. This board carries the eye from the background to the foreground. It acts as a tool or bridge to permit flow and rhythm within the composition. Although this is a black and white copy of the painting, the concept that is important to understand is the use of the board as a connector of the two areas of the painting.

next without getting bored or losing track. A classic example of an artist creating flow within a painting is Degas in 1876 when he painted *Absinthe* (Figure 2–29). A zig-zag pattern is created by the table tops and the piece of wood in the lower left that connects them. The piece of wood is totally the artist's invention yet it makes the painting flow from the bottom table to the figures in the upper right. In design this is typically called rhythm.

People who read English tend to read from left to right. When you look at a newspaper, the most important news is always in the upper left hand corner. As most people are creatures of habit and are accustomed to colors meaning certain things, they also read a display design from left to right. It's important to create a visual need for the observer to want their eyes to travel across the entire design. Degas lead the eye with a plank. A display can lead the eye with color, repetitive shapes, shadows created by light placement, lettering, and texture. Rather than allowing the viewer's eyes to hop all over a display with no discernible pattern, it's the job of the designer to lead the eye from place to place in the pattern desired.

TOO MUCH/TOO LITTLE

It is not easy to create a design that flows perfectly in the beginning. First you have to know when to stop. How many elements can be in a design before it becomes overcrowded and loses its flow (Figure 2–30)? A riot of color unless it is perfectly placed and balanced can keep the eye hopping. Too many textures will do the same. Several unrelated objects confuse the design and the customer because the point of the display is lost. Examples of good and bad design flow and rhythm are given in Figures 2–31 through 2–37. There are thousands of ways to create flow and good design and even more ways to do it wrong. Again, through observation and practice, the talent for flow can be learned. Try to create a sense of flow/rhythm through the use of light and dark patterns, a repetition of a major color throughout the design, or spotlights in a well thought out pattern (Plates 5 and 8). Don't take a piece of ribbon and wind it through a display in the hopes that the eye will travel the same path. It will, but the observer will never understand the purpose of the ribbon, only that it's there—and the eye will leave the display without ever having seen the merchandise and what you're trying to sell.

BLANK SPACE/OVERLAPPING

Objects placed together in the same area should not be separated by too much blank space. Overlapping is one of the most effective tools for creating a good flow. If a mannequin is placed against a wall with several objects or lettering on the wall, the mannequin's head should overlap at least one of the objects so that a feeling of flow is created from the base of the mannequin to the wall. With too much blank space, the eye has to jump from the mannequin to the wall, and because customers don't wish to have to concentrate, their eyes will never get past the mannequin or the wall.

ARTISTIC/VISUAL THEME

When designing a display, try to develop a singular visual/artistic theme to tie and unify the design. In 1981 the military look became very popular and camouflage fabric was used by many display designers to get the proper military feeling across at first glance. This fabric was used, usually across a wall, to give an overall feeling to

Figure 2–30

The problems with this design for a window start with the sloppy, thrown together look. None of the items work together for mutual enhancement of each other. The colors are all different as are the shapes and fabrics. The bamboo displayer suggests summer but the floor merchandise is for fall. At F-4, note the small sign tacked to the side of the fixture. If it is important, it should be large. If unimportant, then it should not be in the window at all. The elements at war in this design are color, balance, signing theme, proportion, and flow.

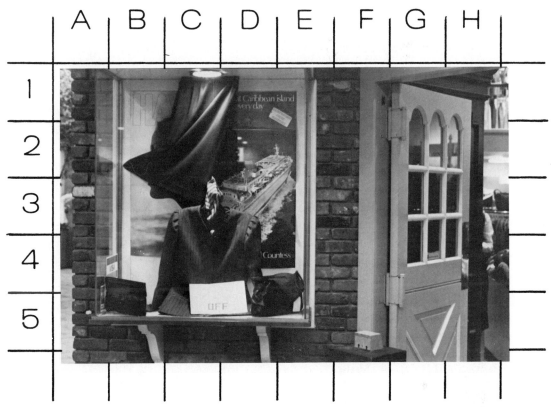

Figure 2–31

This photograph of a mall store window in southern Connecticut is an excellent example of an attempt at flow/rhythm that failed. To begin with, when presenting a coordinated outfit, the top belongs on top and the bottom goes below. The posters are left over from a summer bathing suit window and have no relationship to the business suit on display. The composition is balanced and dull. A straight line of darkness runs down the center of the window with the two dark handbags balanced on either side of the suit. Note the sloppy placement and look of the sale sign (C-D-4–5).

a department of military goods. The pattern of the camouflage material set up an automatic flow. When Indian patterns became popular in fashion at about the same time, Indian fabric was used for the same effect: unity and flow. Sometimes using one basic color can create rhythm in an area and identify a merchandise statement. The most obvious choice is red for Christmas. To the customer, red symbolizes Christmas. (Red is also the symbolic color for Valentine's Day.) A red stripe immediately sets an area apart as a holiday department. Of course, wreaths and other traditional elements will enhance a basic red stripe, but the impact of the color is what will create the subconscious impression on the customer.

Figure 2–32
This bank of windows works as both an excellent design and as a selling display. Each group also has a prop in common. The first group (Armani) all wear Sony Walkmans. The second group wear hats. Note how the faceless heads relate to the balls on top of the columns. The lights are trained on each form equally. The strong horizontals are balanced by the oversized vertical columns.
Credit: Colin Birch, V.M.D., Bloomingdales, N.Y.C. 1982. Photo by: Jerry P. Melmed.

PROPS

Props can be used to achieve flow and rhythm within a display. They can be an expensive alternative to color or fabric but can be exciting to the eye and imagination. Props may create bridges between mannequins and/or merchandise. They can provide an interesting resting place for the customers' eye. They often "bridge" the gap between two or three related areas or items.

If props are used to create a feeling of flow/rhythm, they should relate to each other through proportion, size, color, and basic meaning. Using an oversized pencil with an oversized apple will indicate back-to-school in a dramatic manner. Using the oversized pencil with little apples, wood chips, birch poles, or other items that indicate fall—but not specifically school—will confuse the design and the customer. When using props to create flow, often an effective method is the repetition of the prop. This doesn't have to be very expensive if initiative is used in finding the props. Colin Birch, a well-known visual merchant, revamped the busy display style of the 1970s into a clean, design-oriented look occasionally using inexpensive items (normally found in the yellow pages) in profusion in windows to create a sense of drama. In the late 1970s he posed one or two impeccably dressed mannequins with a prop that corresponded to the feeling of the merchandise. A swimwear window with an all white background was filled with beach balls—all the same kind—in a feeling of organized profusion. The mannequins were in their own "white" space, so that the feeling of negative space was as important as the

Figure 2–33

An interior photograph of a very successful housewares store. They merchandise ordinary and design-oriented household objects in a special way. Each item is treated as a design object. Things are placed together by classification. Some items are merchandised by use, others by material, and the rest by their combined uses. The balance and flow of the presentations combined with the rhythms that are set up by the different materials make the total display of this store successful.

Credit: Greg Turpan-David Sanders, Turpan Sanders, N.Y.C. 1982. Photo by: Eileen Freidenreich.

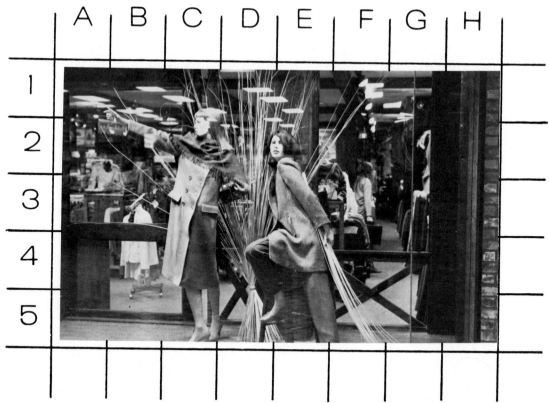

Figure 2–34

This window is a good example of flow and rhythm. From the dried stems on the floor at 5-G to the mannequin's outstretched arm at 1-A, the eye travels over the entire display in an easy path. The movement created by the angle of the dried stems is echoed in the knee of the seated mannequin and in the angle of the shawl of the standing mannequin. The standing bunch of dried stems also carries out the movement. The colors compliment each other in a monochromatic scheme. The window is as good as its counterpart (Figure 2–35) is bad.

positive colors and repetitive shapes of the beach balls. For little girls' party dresses he hung masses of streamers from the ceiling of a bank of windows and threw confetti on the floor with a grouping of little girls all dressed up off-center in each of the windows. The choice of the multicolored confetti and streamers offset the solid-colored dresses and created a strong party feeling from the street level. The wistful looks on the mannequins' faces gave a slightly different feeling to the scene on second glance and a sense of the excitement and the trials of childhood was created.

REPETITION OF TECHNIQUE

Flow can be created by a repetition of a display technique, e.g., flying. The term *flying* is used for merchandise that is either pinned on a wall or hung from the ceiling on an angle with other merchandise criss-crossing it to give a feeling of movement. This type of display has been prevalent for many years and has come to be identified with lower to moderately priced junior merchandise (Figure 2–38). The growing trend in better shops is the cleaner architectural feeling of folded or perfectly stretched merchandise creating geometric forms, such as squares, rec-

Figure 2–35

This window is next to the good example of 2–34. It employs the same props and two mannequins made by the same manufacturer. Unlike 2–34, this composition is balanced and boring. The center of the composition falls between the two bundles of dried stems and (D-3) say "Fall Suit Sale." The merchandise seems secondary to the central visual impact of the sale sign. The poses suggest a visual separation of the mannequins. This could have been improved by placing the mannequins closer together and offsetting the composition with the dried stems angled like the mannequin's body on the left.

Figure 2–36

A very simple display that creates a sense of excitement and flow without the use of props. In this case the merchandise is used as props and the chairs that are tied together form a strong vertical image. The window area is very tall and the display can be seen from both inside the store and out on the street. The rope acts as both a visual tie and a literal one. The tie/rope in this case serves the purpose for which it was created. It is not used purely as a visual element. It does create a sense of motion and suspense that highlights both the merchandise and the store.

Credit: Greg Turpan-David Sanders, Turpan Sanders, N.Y.C. 1982. Photo by: Eileen Freidenreich.

Figure 2–37

Another example of an outside prop being used to tie in a display presentation. In this case it is a failure. Both crepe paper and playing cards (taped together) strung around the window in an attempt to create a sense of rhythm or flow. The viewer's eye immediately travels from 2A to 2G with the strip of crepe paper. As there is nothing of value in these two corners the rest of the display has to be taken in on a second glance—if the viewer bothers. The scarf that is hanging in mid-air at B-1 seems to have no connection with the rest of the display. Only light colored clothing should be shown against a backdrop that is this dark (C-D-1–5). The eye is traveling around this composition in no definite direction and with no place to land.

tangles, circles, triangles, etc. These are occasionally framed and hung on a wall. A very trendy store that has branches all over the world—Fiorucci—framed their unusual merchandise in antique frames with Lucite. The feeling was more like abstract splashes of color on a clear ground rather than hard-edge geometric—and made an exciting contrast to the usual purity of either geometrics or flying. Depending on the store and its clientele, using the concept of contrasts working together to form an interesting entity can work well if executed with professionalism and style.

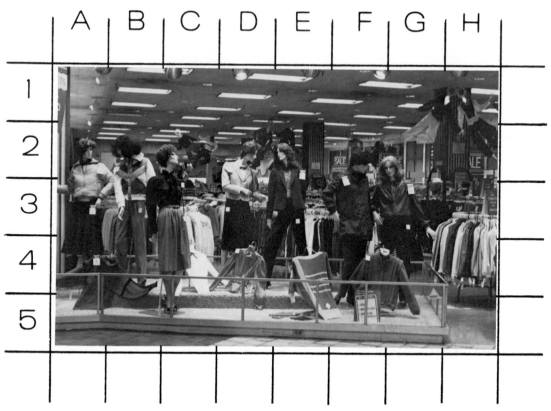

Figure 2–38

An example of flying merchandise in a junior-oriented store. The area from 2A-H has forms suspended from the ceiling to better define the flying merchandise. Before these forms were bought, the visual merchandisers used clear fishing tackle attached to the ceiling to "fly" these garments into their positions.

SIGNING

Signing or lettering can create a good flow through repetition or style. An entire display can revolve around the lettering and name of a department. In New York City a designer named Norma Kamali was given a shop in the arcade section of a famous store. Along with massing out (using large quantities) the merchandise and using five fantastically dressed mannequins on metal tube platforms, the department was named "Hot Kamali"—a takeoff on hot tamales and on "hot" meaning new, exciting, and different. The lettering was custom made in New York and was the major shop expense. Its impact was immediate. The unusually large size and depth of the mirrored letters made the name stand out and an image was created first by the lettering, then the merchandise. One backed up the other so there were no visual letdowns. Often repetition in signing is used to create visual excitement. This can work if it's not overdone in a store. If one wall says "mugs . . . mugs . . . mugs

. . . mugs . . . mugs," the customer knows immediately what is in that area. It can be a very graphic way of identifying a department. If this same concept is used again within the store, the customer doesn't see it anymore. It works once because it's original within its environment, but doing the same thing over and over is inviting boredom on the part of your customer—and yourself.

The color spectrum, repeating the merchandise hues in a row above the goods, creates a strong impact. It is an example of a concept which has worked so well that it has often been repeated. This popular method of display should be creatively varied to avoid obvious repetition and boredom.

Creating a flow can be accomplished by using a variety of design techniques. In summary, these techniques are as follows:

1. Creating a left to right "reading" in the display

2. Using like elements that mean something together and relate to the merchandise

3. Creating a pattern through the use of light and dark, either with color or light

4. Overlapping

5. A fabric or color that unifies the theme

6. Props that are repetitious either in form or in theme

7. Using a type of display to create flow, e.g., flying merchandise

8. Using lettering either with repetition or with dominance to create flow

PROPORTION AND BALANCE

Everything has to work together in a good design. If one element is wrong, the design fails. Proportion and balance are so closely related to flow that it is difficult to separate them without giving the impression that one is more important than the other. All three work together to create harmony. When the proportion or balance fails, the display looks lopsided. When all three work together, it looks right and works as a successful design.

Balance is based on the theory of equals. If something large is placed on one side, then an equally large item should be placed on the other side to balance the composition. Traditional balance calls for this strict adherence to large/large, small/small thinking. Informal or assymetrical balance can create a more fluid and exciting feeling. Something large can be balanced by several small items, a larger expanse of negative space, a bright color, a shot of light, or something equally large. Several soft colors in a large space can be balanced by one small bright color because the intensity of the bright color will compensate for its small size. If the bright color is too large, it will overwhelm the pastels. If the several small objects are more exciting than the large object, they will also overpower the larger item. If you're trying to sell the pastels or the large object, e.g., an outfit on a mannequin or

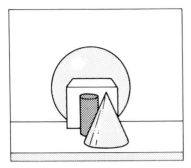 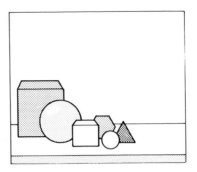

Figure 2–39
(A) With uncentered merchandise or props the pieces should be placed heading towards the center of the composition. Keep the larger items in the rear. (B) With centered pieces the larger items again belong in the rear. Placing the smaller front items slightly off center is more interesting.

pastel cookery, attention has to be paid to the surrounding objects to make sure they don't become more important than the saleable items. Large expanses of negative space will call attention to a singular object placed within it. If this object is placed on an angle, or to one side or the other, the space on either side of that piece becomes important. If the object is centered, the negative space loses importance because its shape is predictable and therefore has less recognition as its own element (Figure 2–39).

Proportion is linked to balance by scale. If a very tall object, such as a mannequin, is placed next to several short baskets, there is no proportion or flow. If dried flowers are massed into the baskets, the height of the smaller objects is raised so the eye flows more easily from the head and neckline of the mannequin to the baskets.

If all the objects are large, there is nothing to break the monotony and the sameness of that large feeling. Adding an off number of smaller, related items to the large pieces will create more interest and balance. The proportions will then take on more meaning when the items define one another. An example of that concept is a man standing next to an elephant. The elephant's size is defined by the known size of the man next to it. Proportion and balance can be achieved by paying attention to the articles within the design and allowing them to play off each other through their size, shape, and color.

SUMMARY

Good design works by selling image and merchandise. Bad design doesn't work at all. To make it work, more than the the artistic aspects have to be taken into account. Attention and thought have to be given to the five questions asked earlier in the chapter:

1. What is the image of your store?

2. Who is the customer you are trying to attract?

3. What is the concept of the merchandise to be used in the display?

4. Where is the display being set up and how will the location determine the design?

5. Why is this merchandise being put on display and how does this reason determine the design?

After asking these questions and using all the resources available within the store, such as the sales manager, buyer, advertising department, store manager, and operations department, to determine whether a questionable area will take a certain display in terms of weight or fire laws, the visual merchant is ready to design the display. Breaking the element of display design down to six basic concepts helps us to understand each more thoroughly. These six concepts will create a design that works only when they interact together. If one of the six is forgotten, the design will miss being good. Although good design is arbitrary, the designer can tell if it works or not by noting if the elements and principles listed are included in the design:

1. Positive and negative space

2. Light

3. Color

4. Flow

5. Proportion

6. Balance

7. Theme

8. Props

9. Signing

Reading trade and fashion publications, such as *Interior Design, Visual Merchandising, Inspiration, Vogue* (for excellent ideas about fashion presentation and mannequin placement), and *Architectural Digest* (for placement of objects and trends in interior decoration) will broaden an understanding of design and all its possibilities. Visiting stores known for their good design will also develop an appreciation for the proper usage of design elements.

SUMMARY CHECKLIST

Major Concepts

1. Design enables the visual presentation to work.
2. Stores select an image that they want to be uniquely their own.

3. Know your customers and community when designing displays.
4. Display merchandise, not merchandise a display.
5. Location is an important aspect of a visual display.
6. The display and the location must work together through the use of the elements of design.
7. The existence of lighting is an important aspect of display.
8. Color psychology is very important when designing displays.
9. A variety of design techniques can be utilized to create positive flow.
10. Proportion, balance, and flow are utilized to create harmony.

KEY TERMS

1. Image
2. Outpost display
3. Negative space
4. Complementary colors
5. Flow
6. Balance

DISCUSSION QUESTIONS

1. What are the primary points to consider when designing a display? Why is each important?
2. What is the purpose of utilizing a design image throughout a store?
3. What is meant by the statement, "Display merchandise, not merchandise a display?"
4. List the six questions that should be asked before you begin designing a display. What is the relationship between the six?
5. What are the six basic types of display locations that are found in a retail environment? Which type of location do you feel would best sell merchandise? (give examples)
6. What is meant by the statement, "The display should identify and support the merchandise?"
7. Explain how an outpost display could be used to sell merchandise.
8. Describe how negative/positive space is utilized in display.
9. Explain the purpose of utilizing a monochromatic color scheme in a display.
10. Flow can be accomplished using a variety of design techniques. Discuss each technique.

STUDENT EXERCISES

Number 1

Choose a product with which you are familiar. Using a large sheet of paper and a pencil, sketch a display that will feature the product. Upon completion of the design, complete a self-evaluation based on the major design components discussed in the chapter. After your evaluation is completed, color the display using a monochromatic color scheme. Assume you are preparing a small window display.

A. Are you pleased with the design?
B. What design changes would you make?
C. What color changes would you make?
D. What could be done to improve the total design?

Number 2

Utilizing three retail businesses in your community, determine the image that each is attempting to portray. Prepare an analysis of each business's image by answering the following questions:

A. What type or types of customers is the business trying to attract?
B. What color scheme is being utilized?
C. Is there an underlying theme?
D. What type or types of merchandise are being sold?
E. Is the location appropriate for the image?
F. Is lighting, color, signing, and flow utilized in the displays?

CASE PROBLEM 1

The Changing Line

Klinmans is a small women's and men's apparel store that is located in a college community of approximately 30,000. The store has been at the same location for 15 years and the customers are generally middle class to upper middle class.

During the past five years, the store owner, Mr. Ralph Johnson, was against selling any type of jeans or jean products. In January of this year, the store was sold to Ms. Sue Wyatte, who had been the store manager for the past three years. After consulting with the store employees, she decided that jeans would be a good-selling item. But where should they be displayed? The store was already at capacity. The only space available was a 14' × 30' basement room that has been used for storage since the store opened.

On Monday morning, Lisa Notting, a qualified and knowledgeable apparel and accessory salesperson who had worked for the store for six years, asked to talk to Ms. Wyatte. Lisa presented Ms. Wyatte with a proposal that she be allowed to design, decorate, and purchase all merchandise for the new jeans department which would be located in the basement. In return, she would be made assistant store manager, and her salary would be based on the profits of the new jeans department.

Before Ms. Wyatte would agree to the proposal, she asked Lisa to provide her with more specific details on basic design procedures, such as signing, lettering, color, lighting, image, and merchandise display.

Questions to Discuss

1. How would you attract attention to the jeans department in a way that would be consistent with the image of the store?
2. What type of customers are you trying to attract?
3. How should the merchandise be displayed?
4. What type of lighting and color should be utilized?
5. What signing or lettering should be utilized? What could this new department be called?
6. What kind of fixturing will be needed?

CASE PROBLEM 2

The New Image

"What should be done?" This is the question that Sue and Randy Hobbing are presently asking themselves. For the past 10 years, Sue and Randy have been the proud owners of a men's and women's apparel and accessory store called the Clothing Shoppe. Until recently, business was good and a reasonable profit was being made.

Merchandise carried by the Clothing Shoppe includes men's suits, sportcoats, pants, and such accessories as shirts, ties, underwear, socks, and belts. The women's department specializes in dresses, skirts, business suits, and casual wear. Accessory items include blouses, hoses, and jewelry. A complete line of winter coats is available for both men and women.

During the past year, two other clothing stores opened and immediately business began to decline. Even steady customers were starting to purchase their clothing at the new stores. During a conversation one evening, Randy asked one of his long-time customers, Rich Simpson, why he no longer shopped at the Clothing Shoppe.

Rich responded that he felt the employees, prices, and customer services presently offered by the Clothing Shoppe were very good. However, when he entered the new clothing stores, he had a good feeling inside.

After speaking to Rich, Randy and Sue discussed the problem with several other friends and customers and came to the conclusion that their store no longer had any buying appeal or excitement. There was no motivating force to entice a customer to purchase merchandise.

After giving the problem serious consideration, Randy and Sue decided to adopt a new theme for the store—a theme that would be based around the 1900s and the years of prohibition. How should they carry out the new theme? The store is large, having over 6,000 square feet of selling space, and is already an established business.

Questions to Discuss

1. How could the store front be changed to reflect the desired image?
2. What lighting/color patterns could be utilized?
3. What various types of props, fixtures, display cases, etc., should be utilized to display merchandise?
4. Should the pricing structure be affected?
5. What specific types of signing or lettering should be utilized? What should it say?

CHAPTER 3

Tools and Materials of the Trade

LEARNING OBJECTIVES

At the completion of this chapter, you will be able to:

1. Discuss the importance of in-house production of display props.

2. List the reasons for having an organized tool section in the display shop.

3. Analyze the importance of preplanning as it relates to visual merchandising projects.

4. Utilize proper tools in the completion of visual merchandising projects.

5. Argue the importance of safety when working with display tools.

6. Identify the various types of tools that are used to build displays.

7. Recognize miscellaneous hardware items and evaluate their importance.

8. Name the various types of flat materials that are available for building displays.

9. Discuss the importance of tools in the visual merchant's daily activities.

We all grew up thinking that Scotch tape and rubber bands could hold the immediate world together. As we matured, we added nails, glue, and staples. Walking through a department store rarely brings to mind the question, "What do they build all these things with?" We tend to look at the finished product—the prop or display presentation—and ignore the literal nuts and bolts. This is the nuts-and-bolts chapter—tools that are used to help accomplish almost anything that is seen in a retail display. We'll ignore Star Wars effects for the present as well as elaborate light shows. Those fit more into the prop category and are rarely done in-house. "In-house" is the term for anything that is produced within the confines of the store. In-house production is done through either a production staff experienced in both aesthetics and construction techniques or by a visual merchant with a rudimentary talent for production but with a strong aesthetic sense.

Often in a large-city department store there will be a production staff that can build almost anything. They will occasionally build props for the branches but usually the suburban stores have a staff of two to four individuals who are allowed from time to time to use the carpenter's shop or the carpenter's time for short periods. The basics of construction can be learned from courses given in local technical schools, or by watching and helping craftspersons or cabinetmakers. Basic skills are essential for visual merchants whereas advanced skills are necessary for production persons. Advanced skills are an asset in any area of visual merchandising but take a lot of time to acquire. Advanced skills consist of cabinetmaker techniques as well as braising, soldering, and welding techniques. A knowledge of painting techniques also qualifies as advanced skills.

The tools of a visual merchant's job are usually kept in the shop—hopefully in an organized manner. Many display people, however, find it easier to carry all their tools in a tool box and replenish supplies as needed. An organized tool box ensures that almost everything needed for most jobs will be available to the visual merchant while in the work area. There are few things more frustrating than working within a deadline and discovering that essential tools needed for finishing a project are back in the shop—three floors away. An organized tool box, cart, shopping bag, or canvas bag all work for the visual merchant while disorganization impedes accomplishment.

An understanding of tools is necessary before any decisions can be made as to which are needed for each job. Tools can be broken down into three main categories: tools that cut, tools that join, and tools that attach. Materials that are cut, joined, and attached are also tools of the trade and are explained in this chapter.

TOOLS THAT CUT

Scissors

Different types of scissors are made to cut fabric, paper, and metal. They should be bought for the VM department and used only for their original purpose; otherwise they dull quickly and lose their effectiveness. Labeling them by use is helpful.

Wire Cutters

Wire cutters are often combined with pliers and are a necessity. Pliers will open or close metal as needed. Attached wire cutters save time and cut wire easily.

Cutawl and Blades

A cutawl is a classic saw that can cut tiny scrolls and circles. It is ideal for letters or intricate patterns but terrible for straight cuts. It takes time and practice to learn how to use the cutawl, but skill at working it is a tremendous asset to any display department. Having a good selection of blades handy can strongly aid in proper usage. The cutawl works directly on the table surface and the blade is adjusted to go through the thickness of the material to be cut—but not to the point of cutting the table top.

Hack Saw

A hack saw is best for cutting metal and hard woods.

Regular Wood Saw

The classic saw works best when you put your strength into the pulling part and go easy on the push. The bite of the teeth is in the pull, not on the push.

Sabre Saw

The sabre saw is used for curved line cuts. The blade is long and the material's edge to be cut must hang over the edge of the table. This is a hand-held saw and has a variety of blades available to cut through different materials.

Mat Knives

Mat knives are best for straight cuts. The safest kind are the ones that have a retractable blade. The blades must be changed often, so buy a lot of spares.

Exacto Knives

Exacto is the cutawl of knives. It is good for cutting intricate, rounded edges, but is very fragile. Again, it's necessary to keep extra blades handy.

Blades should be disposed of by sticking them into the edge of a piece of discarded cardboard up to the dull edge so that the person emptying the garbage doesn't get cut.

In a well-equipped workshop you will also find the following:

Scroll or Band Saw

The scroll saw has a stationary blade that moves up and down while the material is maneuvered by hand. This is limited only by the distance from the blade to the point where the arm is attached to the body of the machine. This is usually a 2' span.

Table Saw

The table saw is excellent for straight cuts of all materials. Blades can be bought to cut through most materials. The height of the blade can be adjusted to cut many different material thicknesses. A bar along the blade is also adjustable to guide the material through the saw on a straight line. There is usually a built-in ruler to determine the proper width cut.

Drill Press

A stationary electric drill is a drill press. The drill bit is raised or lowered by hand while the other hand steadies the material to be drilled.

Electric Hand Sander

An electric hand sander allows the operator to sand a piece of wood in a third of the time it would take by hand with a wood block and sandpaper.

TOOLS THAT JOIN

Tapes

Masking Tape

Masking tape comes in many varieties and is used mainly for temporary attachments. Masking tape is very sensitive to changes in temperature and can lose its grip in too much heat (it dries out) or cold (it softens and slides). Masking tape left on a surface too long will eventually dry out and become very difficult to remove. The two varieties that would be most useful for the visual merchant are the paint-masking tape for creating hard edges on surfaces to be painted, and drafting tape, for attaching paper to wood without ruining the paper's surface. There are multiple uses, e.g., rolling several pieces of 2" paint-masking tape and sticking them to the bald head of a mannequin will help keep the wig on and render it easier to comb.

Cellophane Tape

Cellophane tape also works, but be aware that it leaves a sticky surface once pulled up. It also has the same temperature sensitivity as masking tape and is best for temporary displays. Transparent tape will hold balloons to the ceiling by their strings or any other extremely lightweight display. Double-stick cellophane tape will hold up hems in skirts or slacks. It can also be used to create a feeling of wind when the skirt is attached to the legs of the mannequin by the tape and then pulled out on the other side by wire woven through the hemline or by fishing line attached to the floor.

Double-Stick Tape

Double-stick tape is most often used in a display department. Double-stick comes in many sizes, widths, and colors. The white tape is the best kind and the practical size for general use is ½″ wide. Double-stick will leave the bottom half of its surface on whatever it's been stuck to and its top surface will stick to the other object. It rolls off easily but it can pull up loose surfaces, e.g., homasote, old plaster, fome-core.

Glues

Hot Glue

Hot glue is most often a wax pellet that is pushed through a "gun" that is a heating unit with a "cool" handle. As the wax is pushed through, it melts and comes out a small hole creating a line of hot melted wax. This wax cools quickly, so any gluing must be planned for and executed within 5–10 seconds. Hot glue is very effective for attaching almost anything. However, it pulls up loose surfaces such as old plaster or homasote, but is cleanly removed from baraboard and other hard surfaces, e.g., Masonite, glass, and metal.

If hot glue (wax) gets on any part of your body, as difficult as it will be, resist trying to brush it off. Spreading it will only extend the burned area and will also burn your other hand. If possible, allow the wax to cool on your hand and then carefully peel it off your body. If a burn occurs after the wax is off, quickly put the burned area under cool water. Resisting screaming or cursing in public when this happens will probably be one of the biggest challenges of your career. Obviously, screaming or cursing in public will not only make the store and yourself look bad, but will probably result in your being fired. Burned and broke in one day can be very discouraging. Not getting burned in the first place is an obviously important goal. The glue gun is too convenient and useful as a tool to avoid because of its possible danger. Never glue something that is thin, e.g., fabric, and try to press down on the glue and fabric with your hand. The glue and heat will seep through the fabric and dually stain the fabric and burn your hand—a double problem! Gluing Styrofoam only works on some foams. The hot glue will most likely melt through most Styrofoam surfaces and possibly burn your hand. Always remember that you're working with heat. While temporarily away from a department, do not leave your gun hanging from a ladder or lying on the floor in an area where employees or customers can get burned.

Don't leave the hot gun on a flammable surface for obvious reasons. The extension cords necessary to use the gun in an area away from an outlet should be out of the customer's path or a yellow tape should be used to attach the cord to the floor. Another solution would be to use a "spotter" to warn customers of the electrical wire so they don't trip. This is fine for quick, five-minute jobs, but longer jobs should use yellow tape or somehow find a closer outlet.

Hot-glue guns are the most useful attaching tool for letters, small props, some pads, and numerous other jobs. Effective use of this tool requires thorough knowledge of safety considerations.

White Glue

White glue, such as Elmer's and Sobo, work well for paper, wood, and fabric. They dry clear and can peel off your hands. When applying these glues to a project, use a small amount on both surfaces and let it get "tacky" (slightly dry) before putting the two pieces together. Put weight on top of the pieces to help them join firmly or clamp them with appropriate size clamps until the glue dries. The drying times are directly affected by the room temperature. If the environment is warm and not humid, the glue should dry fairly quickly. Cool temperatures slow down the process. White glue when watered down works well for fabrics. Naturally, before using glue on fabric, test a small piece to make sure the glue doesn't stain the fabric. It is often used instead of paste (flour and water) for paper and fabric maché.

Fabric Glue

Fabric glue is available at most fabric and sewing centers. It actually works well, and for quick touches and emergencies is an excellent solution. Fabric glue is usually machine-washable (check the label) and works well for making emergency tablecloths when no sewing machine is available.

Epoxy

Epoxies are glues that have to be mixed together in order to harden. They are composed of a resin and a catalyst or hardener. The chemicals in the catalyst allow the resin to harden. When mixing epoxy, it's often a good idea to use disposable utensils, e.g., a carboard box and a tongue depressor for mixing and temporary storing. Epoxy hardens quickly on the surface and takes varying amounts of time to harden completely. Epoxies are stronger than white glue and are used when more joining strength is needed. This glue is highly flammable and should be stored with the paints.

Rubber Cement

Rubber cement is used most successfully as a paper glue. It is highly flammable and should also be stored with the paints. Because rubber cement has a tendency to thicken with exposure to air, there are thinners or solvents that can be used to make the glue more spreadable. Always add the thinner in very small portions and stir the glue at the same time so that it doesn't become too thin and lose its bonding properties.

For longer lasting bonds with rubber cement, use the dry-mount process. This process joins two pieces of paper together with rubber cement when the glue is evenly spread on both surfaces and then allowed to dry to the point of feeling surface-dry. Carefully, the two pieces are joined together, and then cannot be torn apart successfully for weeks or months, depending on the temperature.

Pliers

Regular and needle-nose pliers are used to open and close metal chain links and other metal fasteners. Regular pliers usually have a flat ½″ nose whereas needle-nose pliers have a long, narrow, pointed nose that works well in tight spots or for small objects (Figure 3–1).

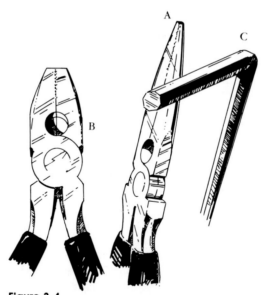

Figure 3–1
(A) Needle-nose pliers. (B) Regular pliers. (C) Allen wrench.

Allen Wrench

An Allen wrench is an L-shaped black metal rod that has a hexagonal end that fits into special bolts. The wrench works only for the bolts for which it was designed. Fixtures most often require Allen wrenches and these should be requested from the fixture company.

TOOLS THAT ATTACH

Nuts and Bolts

Nuts and bolts are used to hold two pieces of material together, i.e., wood or wood byproducts. When only one nut and bolt are used, 360° flexibility is achieved. (Figure 3–2), which works for the arms and legs of cutout mannequin forms. If two bolts are used there is no flexibility, but bolts are easily removed (they slide in and out) so that they become very useful for sandwiching merchandise between sheets of Lucite or between Lucite and an opaque material. Bolts can be made decorative by chrome-plating the nut and making it into a decorative element (Figure 3–3).

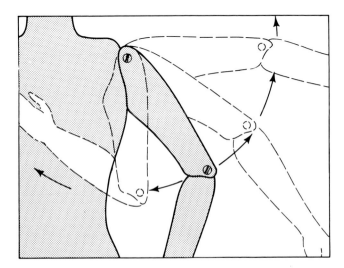

Figure 3–2
Bolts to achieve 360° flexibility.

Figure 3–3
Chrome bolt used for decoration.
Bolt is metal.

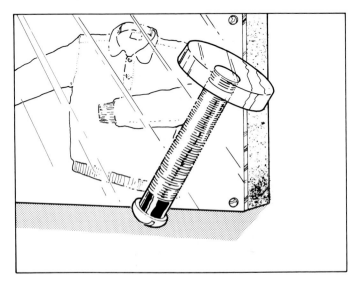

Always keep the same size nuts and bolts together when possible—and label them so the proper size drill bit can be easily selected to drill the correct size hole for the bolt. Washers should be used with nondecorative nuts.

Screws and Nails

Used most often to join wood, there are special types of screws and nails available to work with Sheetrock, metal, brick, and glass. Check with a well-stocked hardware store for the proper nail and/or screw for special projects. An assortment of different size nails should be in each shop. Sizes range from 16 penny (largest) to 4 penny (smallest) with 4 and 6 penny being the most common sizes used for display work. Nails come with or without heads. Headless nails are used for finishing work because they will not show on the surface. A finishing nail is usually countersunk into the wood, which drives it down about ⅛″. The hole that is left is then filled in with wood putty and sanded. When a finished wood product is going to be polyurethaned rather than stained or painted, the sawdust from the wood can be mixed with white glue to act as the wood putty or filler. This mixture will be the same color as the wood and blend well with the surface. A nail with a head is used for areas that won't be seen. Nails can have decorative heads for finishing upholstery leather projects. These decorative nails or tacks give an Old English, country feeling and will work in many different ways to achieve certain desired looks (Figure 3–4).

Figure 3–4
Decorative upholstery tack.

Figure 3–5
Regular wood screw.

Screws are used by carpenters to hold pieces of wood together firmly. They should be used whenever a display created of wood or metal will be on the floor for more than a few days. Screws have a much firmer "bite" or hold than nails. The breakdown of the prop (taking it apart) is cleaner and easier when screws are used instead of nails. The prop can remain in good shape, stacked neatly out of the way (screws in an attached envelope), while with nails, each nail has to be removed thereby damaging the wood and paint of the prop (Figure 3–5).

Screws also come with different heads. Two basic screw heads are those that take either a flat-head screwdriver or a Phillips head (Figure 3–6). Screws can also be bought with hooks or eyes on the end (Figure 3–7) for hanging things, e.g., a screw eye in a wood beam can hold a light display prop or the weight of a person in a hanging chair depending on the size of the screw eye. Screw eyes can go into

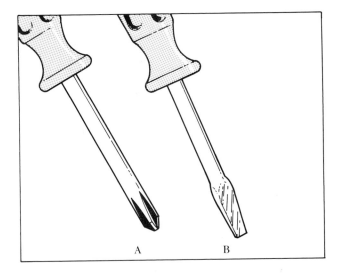

Figure 3–6
(A) Phillips head screwdriver. (B) Flat-head or regular screwdriver.

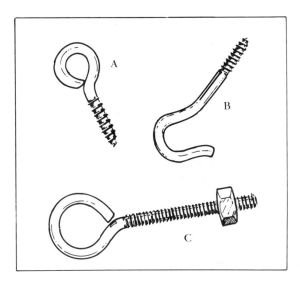

Figure 3–7
(A) Screw eye. (B) Screw hook.
(C) Eye bolt.

ceilings, but always test the screw eye by pulling on it with the same approximate weight as that of the hanging object. Do this for at least a minute. If it's going to pull out of the ceiling, it should happen while you're pulling on it and not when the prop is suspended in midair over people's heads.

Pins

Very heavy pins are often used in display in the same manner as light nails. Pins of all sizes are always needed in great quantities for display work. The most popular is the T-pin (Figure 3–8). Headless nails for finish work, nails with heads for hidden projects, decorative heads, heavy pins, and tacks are all necessary hardware for a display department. Pins are most often used to display clothing. The pinholes can damage merchandise if they're poorly placed. Pins should be used primarily in the seams of clothing where the holes won't show. When used to stretch merchandise, pins will leave holes in the material. Inform the sales manager of the potential damage to stretched merchandise. Silk pins are best for fragile materials whereas bank pins work for sweaters, loose knits, and heavy materials.

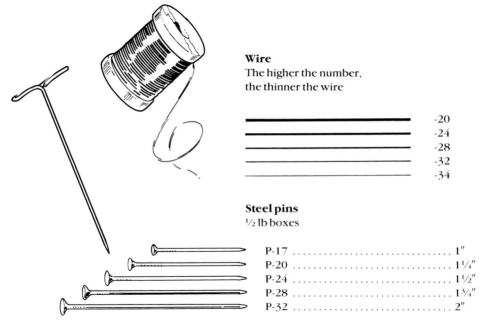

Wire
The higher the number,
the thinner the wire

-20
-24
-28
-32
-34

Steel pins
½ lb boxes

P-17 . . . . 1″
P-20 . . . . 1¼″
P-24 . . . . 1½″
P-28 . . . . 1¾″
P-32 . . . . 2″

Figure 3–8
A T-pin, wire and steel pins.

Toggle Bolts and Moly Bolts

Toggle bolts and moly bolts will be discussed in the chapter on safety but we will introduce them here.

Toggle bolts are used for hanging things from a hollow ceiling or wall. They are available with an eye on the end (Figure 3–9). Toggle bolts come in many weights and a large selection should be on hand in the shop. Moly bolts are also used for attaching things to hollow walls. Different moly bolts specialize in plasterboard,

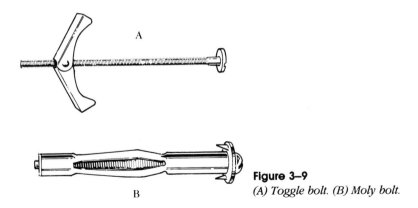

Figure 3–9
(A) Toggle bolt. (B) Moly bolt.

plaster walls, hollow wood doors, while regular molys will function with almost all other surfaces. Moly bolts are necessary for hollow wall hanging where nails will pull out.

Ceiling Clips

Ceiling clips are used to hang merchandise from the ceiling. When the bottom, rounded area is squeezed, the top pieces separate so they can fit over a ceiling grid. These clips should *only* be attached to grids. Never attempt to attach them to lights, fire sprinklers, pipes, or anything not built to handle weight.

Spool Materials

Wire, fishing tackle, string, and thread are all used to bind or hang objects. Black-annealed wire is most often used to stand mannequins in windows and for relatively heavyweight work. The most common and useful sizes to have in stock are numbers 28 and 30. If too much weight is pulling on black wire, it can snap after an hour, a day, or a month. When in doubt about a heavy weight, always double the wire (by twisting two pieces around each other) or, if the object to be hung seems too heavy for wire, use soldered link chain (so the individual pieces of chain won't unbend with the weight). The most efficient way to cut wire is with wire cutters. Scissors will be ruined if used for wire cutting but they will work in an emergency. Wire can be twisted until it breaks, which takes time but will work if nothing else is available.

Fishing tackle is available in many different weights (to catch different fish) and spools of 10, 30, and 60 lb are convenient to have in stock. The major advantage of tackle is its transparency. The disadvantages are the occasional difficulty in knotting and its tendency to stretch with weight pulling it over a few hours. If precision hanging is necessary, tackle can be very frustrating. Everything can be perfectly hung in the morning and by afternoon it can all look slightly uneven as the weights stretch the tackle to different lengths. Despite its two disadvantages, tackle is still the best way to hang things so they appear to be floating in air.

Rope and string are very visible and are used mainly when special effects are desired, e.g., western or nautical. Thread is lightweight and can hold very little bulk, but it is perfect for hanging lightweight cardboard displays, such as greeting card promotions or kites.

Staplers

Staplers come in many different varieties to perform different functions. The basic paper stapler is a desk necessity but is useless for much else.

The Hansen stapler—a display staple gun—is essential for every shop. The Hansen gun is lightweight and doesn't require much pressure to use. For constant stapling (such as pads), the Hansen is a necessity as its light weight requires less pressure and therefore the user does not tire as quickly. The handle is designed so that calluses and blisters won't form as rapidly as will happen with a heavier gun. When using the Hansen, have the plunger nearby to clean out the staple channel. The Hansen gun clogs easily when staples are inserted in small clumps instead of in a solid piece. The Hansen also comes in a tacker which is ideal for jobs that require deeper penetration with little staple surface showing (Figure 3–10). Covering walls or cubes with heavy fabric requires the tacker as opposed to a staple gun. The tacker holds better and shows less. Special staples are required for each Hansen gun and fit particular models. The most common sizes used are ¼″ for lightweight pad covering and stapling, ³⁄₁₆″ for stapling fabric or paper to walls, and ⁵⁄₁₆″ for heavier weights.

Heavy-duty guns are necessary when longer staples are required for more weight. The staples for these guns are a heavier gauge and go as long as ⁹⁄₁₆″. They're

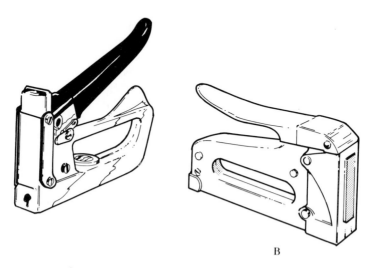

B

Figure 3–10
(A) Hansen staple gun. (B) Arrow staple gun.

used for work that doesn't require the staples to be pulled out easily or often.

An hour spent in a hardware store with a knowledgeable salesperson can be one of the most valuable hours in your training as a visual merchant. Knowing the different hardware available will inspire and aid you in developing and completing ideas for projects.

NECESSARY TOOLS

The tools that are listed below are necessary in any shop. A working knowledge of these basic tools is necessary before considering display as a profession. Actually, these tools are necessary on a daily basis for everyone.

Hammer. Regular and tack (smaller hammer)

Screwdriver. Flat head and Phillips head

Set of wrenches

Ruler. Metal edge yard stick and see-through

T-square

10′ retractable measuring tape/metal/cloth

Chalk line marker

Along with a working knowledge of the large variety of tools for cutting, joining, attaching, and measuring, the visual merchant must also be familiar with the selection of materials available to build displays.

FLAT MATERIALS

Plywood

Plywood is composed of layers of wood laminated together to form a thickness, e.g., ¾″ plywood means ¾″ thick (actually, slightly less) by 4′ × 8′. Plywood is used for the construction of anything that requires strength, rigidity of surface, and ease of cutting (with a saw). It comes with either one or both sides finished. A finished side has a smooth surface with no knotholes. An unfinished side has open knotholes. Only finished plywood can be used if the wood is going to be painted or stained. If the wood will be covered by a firm material, an unfinished plywood will work.

Because finished plywood is more expensive than unfinished, the use of the wood should be considered before ordering. When plywood is cut, the edges are not always solidly filled in as the different layers are composed of wood with knotholes. This should also be considered before using plywood as a material to be cut and painted. When plywood is painted by a water-soluble latex paint, the surface grain of the wood swells and has to be sanded before a second coat of paint can be applied. The advantages of plywood are its relative light weight, ease of cutting, and ease of drilling or hammering. Staples can be used on plywood.

Baraboard or Chipboard

Baraboard is made of wood byproducts. It comes in 4' × 8' sheets and its composition is wood chips and sawdust laminated together to form a heavy, compact, hard-surfaced board. Although baraboard is easy to cut, it is difficult in terms of nailing or stapling because of its extra hard surface. It is excellent to paint, and the edges when cut are uniform but rough looking.

Masonite

Masonite is another composition board that has a very hard surface. It comes in 4' × 8' sheets of varying thicknesses, but ⅛" and ¼" are the sizes used most often. Masonite has the best surface for painting. There is a right and wrong side to Masonite. The wrong side is unfinished and will absorb paint. The right side has a hard surface and accepts paint well, but is very difficult to staple into.

Upson Board

Upson board is a heavyweight compressed cardboard that comes in 4' × 8' sheets. It has paintable surfaces but will warp slightly with latex paints. Upson can be cut easily with a saw, but the edges may be fuzzy and need to be sanded. It is lightweight and comes in ⅛" width.

Homasote

Thick compressed cardboard makes up homasote. Normally it comes in a 4' × 8' sheet in a ⅝" or ¾" width. This is fairly lightweight, weatherproof, easily cut by a saw, nailed, painted, and stapled. Because the surface of homasote isn't smooth, paint doesn't look as finished as it does on Masonite or gatorboard.

Fomecore

Fomecore board is the most popular material in a display department. It is light-weight, paintable, can be covered with fabric, glued, and cut easily with a knife. Fomecore is a rigid board made of Styrofoam sandwiched between two pieces of paper. It ranges in width from ⅛" to ¾" and comes in white or brown. Fomecore can be structured and finished to resemble not only architectural elements but all kinds of display props. Overuse of fomecore can result in a cheap look, affecting the store image unless the fomecore is used with discretion and refinished so that it isn't always white or thin. Covered with fabric, nailed or glued over a frame so that it appears thicker, fomecore can appear to have more substance and depth. It bends easily and must be maintained carefully so that bent edges and fraying of corners doesn't occur.

Gatorboard

Gatorboard is the big cousin to fomecore. Gatorboard is based on the same principle as fomecore but has two rigid paintable surfaces that sandwich a much denser Styrofoam. This must be cut by a saw but, it is so thick (starting at ¾″ width and ranging up to 3″ in a 4′ × 8′ panel) and lightweight that it becomes the expensive (almost three times as much as baraboard) but versatile and preferable alternative to all the heavier materials. For temporary architectural elements and displays, gatorboard creates a feeling of permanence and quality.

Seamless

Seamless paper is a heavyweight paper used by photographers and visual merchants to cover large areas with color. It comes in more colors than Baskin-Robbins has flavors (40). Its width can go up to 14′ and the length of the roll is around 50′ yards. Seamless can be used for many different purposes including window backdrops.

Lucite or Plexiglass

A plastic derivative, Lucite can be either transparent, translucent, or opaque. It is available in 4′ × 8′ sheets and many different thicknesses. The most common are ⅛, ⅜, and ¼″. It is fragile and can crack easily, but is more durable than glass. The range of colors and finish are growing daily. Lucite can be cut with a special blade by most power saws. When drilling holes in Lucite, place a piece of masking tape over the area to be drilled. This will prevent the scratching and cracking of the Lucite by the drill bit.

SUMMARY

Quite a few basic materials and tools have been listed and explained but there are hundreds more to be explored by the visual merchant. The basics need to be understood, experimented with, and mastered before tackling the more complicated production techniques. A good working technique with the tools mentioned will take a visual merchant through almost any project.

A complete shop should have the following tools and materials:

Fastening

Wire, numbers 24, 28, and 30 black-annealed

Masking tape, 1 and 3″

Transparent tape

One dozen rolls double-stick tape, white

Fishing tackle, 10, 30, and 60 lb

Rope

String

Thread

T-pins

Silk pins

Heavyweight pins

Brads

Tacks

Nails, numbers 4 penny and 6 penny, finishing and head

Selection of bolts, nuts, and washers

Eye bolts

Screws, wood and metal selection

Screw eyes

Toggle bolts

Moly bolts

Toggle eye bolts

Hansen staple gun and staples (size selection)

Heavy-duty staple gun and staples (size selection)

Glues

Elmers or white glue, sobo glue

Rubber cement

Fabric glue

Epoxy

Hot-glue gun and wax pellets

Cutters

Scissors for fabric

Scissors for paper

Wire cutters

Mat knife and blades

Exacto knife and blades

Cutawl and blades

Extension cords, heavy duty

Hack saw

Wood saw

Sabre saw

Electric drill

Attachers

Regular hammer

Tack hammer

Flat-head screwdrivers

Phillips head screwdrivers

Assortment of wrenches (also Allen wrenches)

Pliers, regular and needle-nose

Measurers

Metal-edge ruler

10′ retractable tape measure

Yardstick

T-square

Necessities

Large broom

6′ wood ladder

Paints

Polyurethane, 1 gallon

Assortment of latex artist paints

Assortment of latex brushes

Assortment of Krylon spray paints

Gesso

Polymer gloss and mat medium

One gallon each white and black latex paint

Assortment of wood stains

Clean water

Turpentine/acetone

Silk-screening materials, e.g., wood, squeegee, silk, film, ink

Surfaces

White and colored poster board

Colored tissue paper

One carton white fomecore

One carton gatorboard

Six sheets each: upson board, Masonite, homasote, chipboard, and plywood with one side finished.

PADS

How to Measure

A pad for a case should fit exactly into the bottom of the case with no room around it for dust to settle in. The best material for a pad is homasote (but each store has its own ideas). Measure from front to back (a) and from end to end (b). Measure the standards (that hold up the shelves) (c) and note where they are in relation to the pad, e.g., 1″ × 1″ (standard's width) cutouts separated by 25″ (Figure 3–11). If two pads will slide in easier than one, discuss it first with the manager, then measure from the exact center to the ends. When you cut the pad, leave ⅛″ off each side for fabric width. For an angled pad, use large paper and make a template by placing the paper inside the case and folding it along the angles (Figure 3–12). Before cutting the pad out of homasote, cut a pattern out of paper to make sure it fits and the angles are correct. Mark the side to be covered with an X.

A pad for a wall should be centered over the merchandise and large enough to balance the area between the merchandise and the valance. This pad should cover bare standards whenever possible (Figure 3–13).

How to Cover

On a flat surface with the wrong side of the fabric up, place the front-side down on the fabric, making sure the placement will allow the best use of the fabric. For

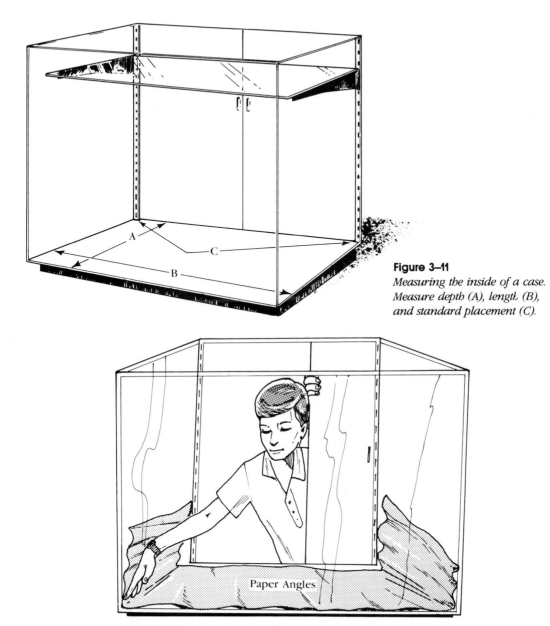

Figure 3–11
Measuring the inside of a case. Measure depth (A), length (B), and standard placement (C).

Figure 3–12
Measure angled cases with paper.

example, if your fabric is 56″ wide and the pads are 18″ wide × 22″ long, the pads should be placed lengthwise leaving enough room to cut and staple (Figure 3–14). Put one staple in one end, then in the opposite end, pulling the fabric taut. Then put one staple in the two opposite sides, again pulling the fabric straight to remove any wrinkles. Continue stapling one or two staples per side, rotating the pad until all

Figure 3–13
A wall pad placed to fill in the wall area and to hide the standard.

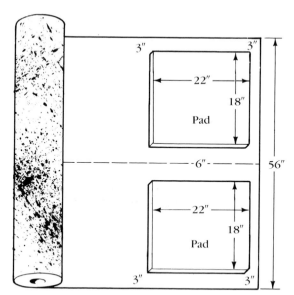

Figure 3–14
How to measure fabric to cover pads.

the wrinkles are pulled out. Corners can be overlapped, cut, or folded depending on the weight of the material. Corners should never show (Figure 3–15).

Canvas for paint is stretched in the same manner as regular fabric over a wood

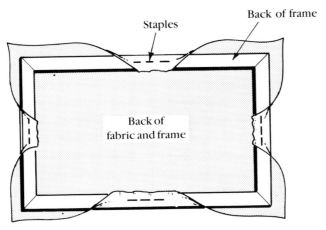

Figure 3–15
How to staple fabric over a stretcher frame.

frame. The rotating allows the fabric to be stretched or pulled evenly over the entire surface.

Make sure the back of the pad doesn't have extra fabric hanging down that will look sloppy from the front. Trim the fabric fairly close to the staples, as soon as you're sure the pad isn't too small (Figure 3–16).

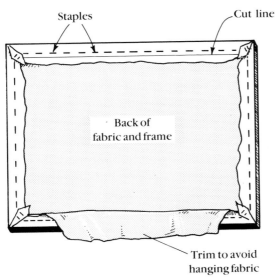

Figure 3–16
Trim the extra fabric in the back of the pad.

If you're covering a pad with a fabric that has a pattern, each line of the pattern has to be straight from the front. Staple the fabric on the front of the pad so the pattern is perfect. Then carefully remove the staples from the front as you staple

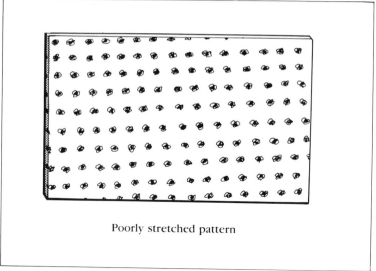

Poorly stretched pattern

Figure 3–17
This shows a poorly stretched pattern over the surface of a frame.

the excess fabric onto the rear of the pad. Always look at the front of the pad to make sure the pattern is still straight (Figure 3–17).

Often fabrics with definite weaves need to be treated in the same careful manner. When a pattern or weave is stretched carelessly, the pad looks warped from the front.

Problems to avoid are (Figure 3–18):

Puckers in the fabric

Sloppy corners

Fabric hanging down in the back

Uneven pattern

Uneven pad, wavy edges

Fabrics that are difficult to use for stretching are fabrics that have no stretch, e.g., moire, satin, heavy duck, and some vinyls. Fabrics printed badly off-grain should not be used.

Great fabrics for stretching include felt, polyester blends, terrycloth, 100 percent cotton, burlap, and lightweight vinyls

PAINT

When using latex paint, remember that it's water-soluble and dries quickly. Always have water readily available to wipe up spills or dip your brush in to thin the paint. Leave your brush in water if you'll be gone more than 10 minutes. Use water

Sloppy corners

Uneven edge

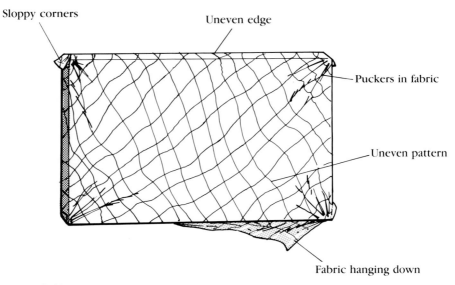

Puckers in fabric

Uneven pattern

Fabric hanging down

Figure 3–18
*This shows puckers in the fabric, sloppy corners, fabric hanging down in the back,
an uneven pattern and a wavy-edged pad.*

immediately on your clothes if the paint gets on them by accident. Once latex paint
dries, it is there to stay. Latex has a greater life span on fabric than on a flat metallic
or wood surface. For hard use, latex will chip and peel more readily than enamel
paint. Enamel takes a lot longer than latex to dry (from 4 to 24 hours). It is soluble
with turpentine or acetone, and smells—but is much sturdier for daily uses, such as
fixtures and furniture.

There are many different types of brushes available for painting. Brushes that
work best for latex paint are made of a nylon or acrylic fiber. Natural fibers, such as
sable or oxtail, are excellent for oil-based paints. For large areas, flat brushes are
made that range from ½″ to 6″ wide.

Rounded brushes are for detail work and work for both oil and latex paints. All
brushes and pads should be cleaned with the appropriate solvent (water or
turpentine) immediately after use.

Pads also work well for large surface areas. Pads are made up of a rubber
composite that slides into a plastic holder. These are also excellent for covering
rough surfaces.

Painting a Straight Line

Take regular masking tape and lay it along your measured and *very* lightly drawn
pencil or chalk line. Rub the edge of the tape that will be painted very hard and
thoroughly with a hard object (pencil end, penny, or the like). After the edge is
firmly attached to the surface to be painted, put a coat of clear polymer medium (a

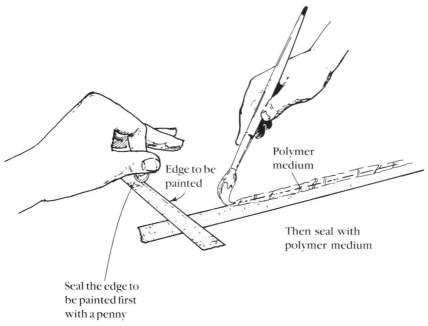

Polymer medium

Edge to be painted

Then seal with polymer medium

Seal the edge to be painted first with a penny

Figure 3–19
First, seal the edges of the masking tape with a hard edge e.g., a penny. Then seal the tape with polymer flat medium.

clear acrylic sealer and glazing agent) along the edge—about ½" on either side—to seal the edge of the tape so that no paint leaks down under the edge (Figure 3–19).

When the paint is 100 percent dry, slowly pull the masking tape up as evenly as possible. Pull *away* from the painted surface so that any extra paint that is attached to the surface and the tape will come away cleanly and not leave a gap on the painted area (Figure 3–20).

This works equally well for spray paint as long as all the areas not to be painted are covered completely with paper. Overspray from a can of spray paint will travel for at least 7'—so be careful where you spray, and cover everything that shouldn't be painted.

Cutting a stencil to spray over will work as long as the edges of the stencil are firmly attached to the surface. Experiment with rubber cement for sticking the stencil to the surface. Always spray on a 90° angle to the painted surface; this lessens the chances of the spray sneaking under the stencil.

If there is a spray booth to work in, use it! If that is unavailable, spray in a well-ventilated area and wear a mask. Spray paint is worse than cigarette smoke for your lungs. Nile green or gold metallic insides are attractive but potentially lethal.

Spray Paint Tips

1. If the can is in a warm *(not hot!!! It's extremely flammable!)* room, the paint comes out more evenly and dries more quickly.

Figure 3—20
Peel the masking tape up and away from the fresh paint.

2. Try to spray the first coat lightly and add coats of paint gradually as the first dries. This prevents paint runs.

3. Hold the spray can perpendicular to the floor so that the spray comes out parallel to the floor. This allows for the maximum amount of paint to be sprayed from the can.

4. When you're finished, hold the can upside down and spray until no paint comes out. This cleans the spray nozzle.

5. *Always* check the direction of the spray nozzle before pushing it down. It is easy to forget and thereby cover your face, body, or someone else through neglect. It is terrifying and dangerous when it gets in the eyes, and disgusting when it gets in the hair. Safety is a prime concern when using spray paint.

6. Mat black, white, gloss black and white, yellow, red, blue, green, and metallics are essential colors to have in stock. Extra hues provide versatility for future projects.

7. Metallic colors dry very quickly and will paint easily over regular colors, but regular nonmetallic colors, e.g., blue, red, will not cover metallics without separating.

8. Some colors when sprayed over others will cause the undercoat of paint to crack and ruin the surface of the new paint. Trail, error, and experimentation are the best teachers here, but be aware of this potential hazard. (Layers of spray paint on plastic letters are especially vulnerable because they will crack or separate easier due to the nonabsorbant surface.)

9. Don't *ever* spray paint on the selling floor.

INSTANT FLOWER ARRANGEMENTS

Although floral arrangements are more appropriately considered props, they are a fundamental to display and the materials that are used to create a floral display are materials that every department should own.

A basic floral arrangement in a store is most often seen "in the round" or as a 360° walk-around. An arrangement of this type should be attractive from all sides, and from the top if it is near an escalator or stairway.

To determine how to lay out the materials, first study the shape and size of the materials and how they relate to the pot. A basic symmetrical arrangement using formal balance starts by putting the tallest pieces in the center. Each flower, feature, or leaf should be placed individually. Trying to save time by jamming in several at once will look terrible and won't work.

Work in a circular pattern so that each section of the arrangement works from all sides (Figure 3–21).

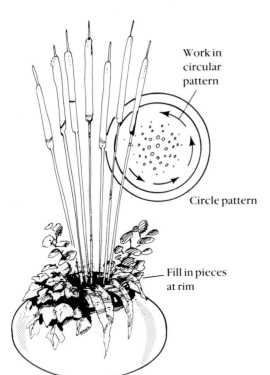

Work in circular pattern

Circle pattern

Fill in pieces at rim

Figure 3–21
Work the flowers and leaves in a circular pattern. Fill in the rim area with shorter or fuller leaves or flowers.

Around the rim of the urn, allow some pieces to fill in the stem area and fall over the sides slightly to break up the hard edges.

Spread the colors evenly so that the eye will travel over the entire arrangement rather than being drawn to one bright section. A traditional circular arrangement is an entity, a composition. Each flower, leaf, or feather should not stand out by itself but must work with the others to create a total visual image (Figure 3–22).

Figure 3–22
Spread the colors evenly throughout the arrangement.

A pyramidal arrangement is created in a similar manner, but the longest pieces are placed in the center and are not evenly fanned out from that point as in the circular floral, but progressively shorter pieces surround the tall ones to form a pyramid (Figure 3–23).

Hints

1. What you place the materials into is important. Styrofoam is great but it works best when hot-glued to the edges of the container so that there is no unnecessary movement or imbalance. If the container *never* moves, then the most stable holder for stems is sand, but sand is *very* heavy!

2. The Styrofoam or other holder should *never* show at any time. Cover it with pebbles, sand, swamp grass, anything attractive, but don't let it be seen from the floor.

3. Individual stems can be hot-glued into the styrofoam to prevent theft or movement. However, once glued they're there to stay. They can only be removed by cutting at the base or by considerable effort.

4. Air out dried materials before putting them into an arrangement. Statice has a tendency to mold in the box and smell terrible!

Figure 3–23
Pyramidal floral arrangement.

HANGING A PROP, TEMPORARY VALANCE, OR BANNER FROM THE CEILING

An easy way to ensure that the object will hang straight is to attach eye hooks to the frame or pole (banner) and thread fishing tackle or wire through both hooks so that it forms a large U-shape. Attaching one end to the ceiling clip, pull the other until the object is at the desired height. Then attach the other end to the second ceiling clip and adjust the object by moving it from side to side until it is parallel to the floor and ceiling lines (Figure 3–24).

An easier way is to use rods that can be bought from a display vendor. These are easily hooked through eye hooks and ceiling clips and will hang evenly. These must be kept neatly on long hooks in the display shop because when they get tangled you can easily lose a half-hour trying to untangle them (Figure 3–25).

TOOL PLANNING SEQUENCES

Tools should be planned for each job so that all the necessary tools can be brought to the project to save time. An easy morning's work sequence for an assistant visual merchant is as follows:

1. Change the junior mannequin on corner 4.
2. Clean off the platform in the area.
3. Put up pads over shelves in accessory area.

Planning for these three jobs takes a few minutes but can save an hour of wasted time searching for tools.

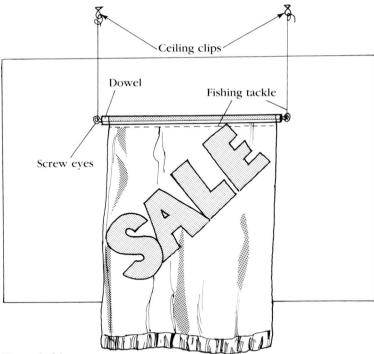

Figure 3–24
This shows the use of continuous filament to hang a banner. Thread the filament through screw eyes at both ends of the dowel and then attach them to ceiling clips.

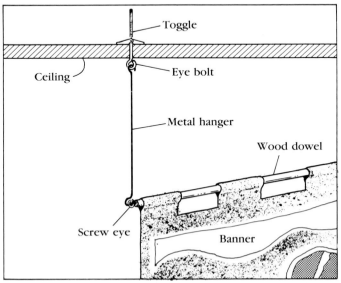

Figure 3–25
Chrome hangers—used instead of filament.

1. *Change the junior mannequin on corner 4.* This is a simple job that requires certain tools, e.g., hairbrush, hair accessories, extra stockings, sign-out book for shoes and accessories, screwdriver, masking tape for wig, transparent tape for hems, pins, and a rag for cleaning off the platform. This job is usually done early in the morning when few customers are present.

2. *Clean off the platforms in the area.* Depending on the store, this falls either to display or to the maintenance department. Either way it is necessary to keep these areas clean and fresh. All that is needed are a few rags and some ammonia and water in a plastic spray bottle.

3. *Put up the pads over the shelves in the accessory area.* This can be more complicated. Pads are pieces of board, either painted or covered, that are attached to a wall (or placed in a case) to add color or definition to an area. How heavy are the pads? What will be placed on them? Will the nails show? What are the walls made of? Is a full ladder necessary or will a stepladder do? If the pads are very heavy, e.g., baraboard or very large sections of homasote, they will need to be held up with moly bolts or toggle bolts if the wall is a hollow wall. If the pads are smaller sheets of homasote, upson, Masonite, or fomecore, headless nails will hold very well. Extra touch-up paint should be brought to the job to repair any scratches as well as to cover the nail heads. On fabric-covered pads it may be possible to pull the fabric out and over the nail heads. Or the nail head can be painted to match the fabric. If the nails will ruin the appearance of the fabric or pad, alternative hanging methods must be taken. Hanging the pad like a picture, with screw eyes and wire, will work for a hard-surface pad such as wood, baraboard, or thick Masonite. Homasote needs to have the screw eyes glued into it, and even then it may not hold. Fomecore and small sheets of upson board can be put up with either hot glue or double-stick tape. Of course, the pads should also be brought along to save the extra trip. For fabric-covered pads a staple gun would be useful to have along in case some staples pull out or there is a wrinkle not seen in the shop.

Another sample sequence that may be encountered during a typical work day is as follows:

1. The domestics manager requests that the sheet patterns displayed above the sheet bins be changed because the merchandise has been rearranged.

2. Several towel displays have been torn apart in the same area and need to be restored.

3. The bath shop needs to be spruced up with some accessories to make it look more exciting.

1. *Change the sheet panels in domestics.* Sheet panels are created by cutting a sheet, stretching it over a frame or board, and hanging it above the packaged sheet bins. This allows the customer to see the pattern from a distance and in a larger size than the small packages reveal.

This can take longer than a morning depending on how many sheet panels have to be changed and how they are displayed. Panels nailed or screwed to a wall will take an extra 15 minutes each to unscrew, take down, and put up again. Panels hung like paintings on the wall are easier because it is a one-person/one-adjustment job and no effort is required beyond restapling the sheets. Panels suspended from the ceiling require a ladder plus a "spotter." A spotter is the person who stands on the floor and tells the person on the ladder when the frame is hanging straight. The spotter need not be another visual merchant. Any person with an accurate eye (and not settle for "it seems okay") would be helpful. Don't leave the project until the hanging object is perfectly straight. Weeks of passing the offensive crooked panel without a handy ladder is a mistake that should never occur.

The tools that are needed to accomplish the job of changing the sheet panels depend first on how the sheets are attached to their frame. Staples, hot glue, or tape can all be used effectively, depending on the surface of the frame. Staples are the quickest, most efficient, least expensive method of attaching fabric to a board. A stapler, stapler dejammer, extra staples, scissor, ruler, and tape would be the first items to take. A screwdriver for screwed-on panels with touch up paint for the screw heads and frame (if needed) may be necessary. Logic dictates that the visual merchant check the project first in order to assess tool needs.

2. *Restore the towel displays.* Several types of towel displays exist in a domestics department. Towels can be displayed like sheets stapled within a frame which is hung to show off large patterns (such as oversized beach towels), or towels can be displayed above the bins in vignettes.

   Again, the displays that are to be renovated should be assessed beforehand and the tools needed should be determined at that time. Often the towel department is adjacent to the sheet area because many manufacturers create matching sheet and towel lines.

   Tools for this project include those needed for the sheet panels, clear fishing line, wire, short nails, or a hammer. Dried flowers, depending on the vignettes or baskets, may be used as props to liven up the area. Just the addition of a countertop fixture to give height to the displayed towels can contribute color, height, and recognition to a towel department.

   The tools for towels should be packed along with the sheet tools to save time.

3. *Accessorize the bath shop.* The bath shop, often located next to the towel department, can be reaccessorized in the afternoon if no time is left in the morning. Again, look over the area and plan the job in the morning while checking sheets and towels. If an existing display is slightly torn up, see what was done before and how to repair it. Allocate appropriate tools to repair the existing display. (Possibly a decorative toilet seat is hanging unevenly due to a missing screw or nail. Bring along an appropriately sized screw, nail, and hammer or screwdriver.)

   If the area comprises mainly the usual Lucite or metal bath accessories, e.g., tissue boxes, cups, toothbrush holders, soap dishes, and glasses, look first to the existing merchandise within the department to create the accessories. Small towels can add color and movement to a basic display. Using these may require some double-stick tape or bunched up newspaper to give height in a small wastebasket.

These are two very common sequences encountered in a department store, but they can't possibly give an idea of the myriad of different problems and jobs that arise every day. What is important is the thinking process before leaving the shop and starting a job on the selling floor. What do I need? What if . . . then what do I need? Prepare for emergencies; be a scout!

Often a sloppy display results when a needed tool is unavailable. Rather than going all the way back to the shop, the visual merchant "made do" with something that wasn't quite right. It shows!

Plan ahead!

Thinking out your tool needs before leaving the shop can help to ensure a good display. Always take extra staples, extra tape, pins, nails; you never know!

Tools are purchased out of the visual merchandising department budget. A good idea for any visual merchanding department is to label their tools or individualize them by painting the handles a certain color, e.g., red. Often a display person will hop from job to job, leaving a tool on a fixture, planning to pick it up later—and lose it for life. Department managers love tools. They can do their own displays with your tools, at their own taste level. This is extremely common and makes the necessity for early morning stockroom checks even more viable.

A safety factor that cannot be overlooked is the problem of leaving unattended tools on the selling floor where children and adults can use them for play or destructive purposes. A hammer is a weapon, as is a staple gun, screwdriver, or awl. A can of spray paint can damage not only merchandise and the physical plant, but eyes as well!

The most important points to remember about using the tools of the trade are to think ahead, plan your projects, consider all the possibilities and anticipate problems, remember safety, and always try to use the best material for the job.

Beyond that, look to your tools and materials for inspiration. They can surprise you!

SUMMARY CHECK LIST

Key Concepts

1. In-house production staffs are an important part of the visual merchandising process.
2. Display jobs should be planned ahead so that all necessary tools can be brought to the project.
3. A sloppy display job is sometimes the result of a tool that was needed but not available.

4. Safety is an important factor to consider when building displays.
5. Tools are broken down into three categories: tools that cut, tools that join, and tools that attach.
6. You can use wire, fishing tackle, string, and thread to bind or hang objects.
7. Knowing different types of hardware will aid in the development and completion of ideas for projects.
8. A working knowledge of basic tools is necessary before considering display as a profession.
9. Quality fabrics to use for stretching include felt, polyester blends, terrycloth, 100 percent cotton, burlap, and lightweight vinyls.
10. It is important to plan your projects in advance, and to consider all possibilities.

KEY TERMS

1. In-house
2. Work sequence
3. Sheet panels
4. Epoxy glue
5. Toggle bolt
6. Homasote
7. Latex
8. Pyramidal arrangement

DISCUSSION QUESTIONS

1. Why is it important that visual merchants have an understanding of in-house production techniques?
2. What is the importance of planning ahead when preparing to complete a visual display project?
3. When changing sheet panels, what are important items to remember?
4. Why is safety an important factor when using tools to build displays?
5. What major tools would you normally find in a well-equipped display shop?
6. Indicate the advantages/disadvantages of each type of flat material.
7. Explain how you measure a pad for a display case.
8. When stretching a fabric over a pad, what are five problem areas to consider?
9. What are important points to consider when using spray paints?
10. What is the best procedure to use when attempting to hang an object?

STUDENT EXERCISES

Number 1

Obtain an empty picture frame, fabric, nails, staples, and any other tools necessary to cover the picture frame. Stretch the fabric over the frame utilizing the proper methods outlined in the chapter. Have your instructor evaluate your finished product to determine if the work has been properly completed.

Number Two

Utilizing two retail businesses in your community, determine what display tools are available for use by the visual merchants. List the tools available under the following major headings: (1) cutting tools, (2) joining tools, (3) attaching tools, and (4) tools necessary for any display shop. Analyze your results to determine why one business is better equipped than the other. Are there tools that should be purchased?

CASE PROBLEM 1

Planning the Work

Roger Larson entered the hardware business in Afton during the early 1950s. Mr. Larson's store is located on one of the main arteries in the shopping district. Larson's Hardware offers free delivery service, and they handle all bookkeeping services including credit applications and charge customers.

The hardware store is divided into eight different departments as follows:

1. Carpenter tools
2. Plumbing supplies
3. Garden tools
4. Electrical supplies
5. Building hardware
6. Carpet
7. Paint/miscellaneous
8. General home repair

Each department has a manager responsible for selling, buying, and stocking. The store also employs two general salespersons and an assistant manager, Gail Burrton, who is also responsible for all visual merchandise planning.

In a meeting with Gail and John Petersen, the carpet manager, Mr. Larson noted that the carpet sales had decreased during the past two years. In Mr. Larson's opinion, the department needs a total visual reconditioning. Gail and John agree. Mr. Larson stated that the department would be increased in size to 30' wide by 70' long or 2,100 square feet. The department is located in a corner which will allow for display on two walls. The ceiling is drywall board nailed to ¾" studs. It is presently January 15 and Mr. Larson has requested that all remodeling be completed by February 15.

Questions to Discuss

1. What should be included in a work sequence outline for this particular project?
2. What major tools would be needed?
3. What types of flat materials would be utilized?
4. What hardware should be used to suspend display items from the ceiling?

CASE PROBLEM 2

What to Purchase

In the fall of this year, Mr. Glendon, the manager of High Fashions, was faced with a problem due to a good sales year. The sales for the past three years have increased consistently with this year's increase being 12 percent. The increase in volume of business has necessitated that departments be remodeled to handle the new styles and quantity of clothes.

High Fashions is a moderately large store appealing mainly to middle-class customers. The store is open six days a week from 10 A.M. to 6 P.M. The store offers a full range of apparel and accessory merchandise.

While walking through the store, Mr Glendon noted that the departments were crowded, merchandise was displayed improperly, and wall displays were totally inadequate for the newly purchased merchandise. In reviewing the situation, Mr. Glendon made the decision to hire a visual merchant.

Applicants interviewing for the position questioned the fact that there was no display shop available within the store for building displays and storing tools and materials. Al Latterson, the best candidate for the position, accepted the job on the condition that a display shop be provided. Mr. Glendon agreed.

Questions to Discuss

1. What major tools should be purchased for the newly established display shop?
2. What types of display materials should be purchased?

CHAPTER 4

Safety and Loss Prevention

LEARNING OBJECTIVES

At the completion of this chapter, you will be able to:

1. Name the appropriate hanger used with each type of ceiling configuration.

2. Explain the proper safety procedures related to working with ladders.

3. Identify the safety hazards that are present when working with mannequins.

4. Analyze the safety problems that exist when fixtures are left empty.

5. Describe the importance of having a clean work area.

6. List the proper procedures for hanging materials on the walls.

7. Discuss the major safety policies that are found in a display workshop.

8. Explain basic safety laws that should be followed by all visual merchandising employees.

9. Explain the importance of security as it relates to visual merchandising.

10. List various security precautions which should be considered when setting up displays.

11. Discuss the importance of honesty when purchasing visual merchandise from vendors.

SAFETY

The assurance of safety is in the unwritten contract between a retail establishment and its customers. Customers do not want to have to worry about their safety when they enter an establishment because the question of safety rarely·occurs to most people on a shopping trip. Nor should it! The purpose of this chapter is to stress the importance at all times of safety as a primary concern of a visual merchandiser.

That concern for safety must become second nature.

This chapter discusses many methods for ensuring safety in display as well as compliance with basic fire and insurance regulations.

Safety precautions are a necessary evil as they take extra time to observe when time is most valuable. However, as with security measures, it is essential to take every precaution. In security you're dealing with merchandise while in safety your concern is human life. Skimping on one wire could cause a permanent disability or death to another person or yourself.

In a large New York City store, an elderly woman walking into a department slipped on loose nails that were scattered around the base of a mannequin display. Her hip was broken in two places, she was bedridden for several months, and she proceeded to come down with pneumonia. She sued the store for medical expenses and damages in a suit that asked for approximately $1 million. She won a large settlement from the store in court.

For an 80-year-old woman to live a perfectly healthy life until she entered this store is a sad and typical case of safety precautions being ignored.

The visual merchandising department was directly responsible for this accident. The VM person who failed to pick up the nails has personal responsibility for this woman's pain.

"What goes up must come down"—ideally, when it is planned. Much of display and visual merchandising has a short life expectancy, but following certain safety precautions can ensure that nothing will come down until so desired by management.

What can come down? People from ladders, signs, mannequins, entire structures, props, valances, windows . . . anything. Fire can bring down an entire building as well as pose a most serious hazard to life.

Things That Hang

Anything that hangs from the ceiling must be 7′ above the ground. An object to be hung from the ceiling can be attached in the following ways:

Ceiling Clips

Ceiling clips attach to the grid structure that holds the acoustical tiles in place. Wire, filament (fishing tackle), rope, metal ceiling hooks, chain, or Lucite rods can be attached to the ceiling clips to give the desired length to a hanging object. The weight of the hanging object cannot be more than the ceiling clips or the ceiling grid can withstand (Figure 4–1). The maximum weight per ceiling grid is 15–20 lb.

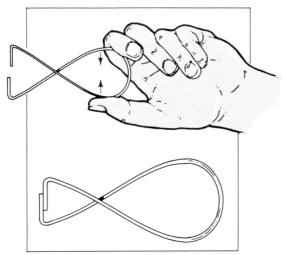

Figure 4–1
Ceiling clips attach over suspended ceiling grids.

Usually ceiling clips are used for hanging lighter objects. The most common of these are posters, canvas banners, light wood or plexi signs, gatorfoam valances, and lightweight props, such as 6′ fiberglass pencils, hoops, or bicycles.

Pins (2" Length)

These heavyweight pins can hold up very light items when pushed into acoustical ceiling tile on an angle. The head of the pin should be pushed in away from the weight of the object so that when it's pulled on, it catches and holds. Lightweight means nothing heavier than paper, light cardboard, gauze, or ribbon. Don't take chances by thinking it "might work." Be sure.

Toggle Bolts

Toggle bolts are designed to fit into a plaster or plasterboard ceiling where there are no grids and where screws will pull out easily. A toggle for hanging has an eye hook on its end. In older buildings without lowered grid ceilings, permanent holes must be made when hanging signs, banners, and the like. For promotions, locations for hanging signs are usually predetermined by the existing placement of eye hooks.

When installing the toggle, make sure that the location of the hole is correct. Installing a toggle bolt is simple, *but check the available weights to make sure that the toggle is heavy enough for the proposed hanging weight.* Toggles are available in all sizes. Usually, when making a hole in plaster, using a heavier than needed toggle will provide hanging for future projects without the temptation of using the existing lighter weight eye bolt because it's there and convenient. If possible, when installing a toggle, bring a small baby jar of ceiling paint up the ladder with you and

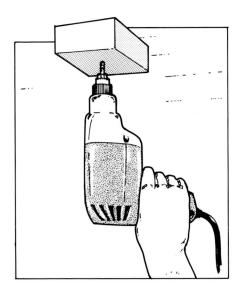

Figure 4–2
*Drill through a box so the sawdust or
plaster will not fall in the eyes or on the merchandise.*

immediately paint the eye bolt so that it blends into the ceiling color. The
customer's eye will be less likely to be drawn up and away from the merchandise.

Another tip for installing toggles is to drill the ceiling using a box around the
drill bit to catch the plaster dust so that it won't fall in people's eyes or on the
merchandise (Figure 4–2).

The toggle has a wing that acts as a brace to keep the eye bolt from falling out
through the hole in the ceiling. The wing also evens out the weight of the hanging
object by distributing the stress evenly over a larger section of the ceiling. Test the
toggle by pulling on the eye bolt before hanging anything from the ceiling. Often
the toggle is put on backward and the bolt will fall through the ceiling with the
slightest pull. This may sound simplistic, but carpenters as well as displayers make
this common error (Figure 4–3).

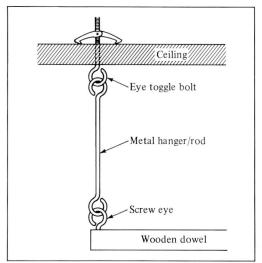

Figure 4–3
*Note how the toggle faces down and grips the ceiling.
The metal rod hooks through both the eye bolt and
the screw eye that is attached to the end of the dowel.*

Hangers

The same hangers for length that are used with ceiling clips can be used with toggle bolts if the bolt end of the toggle is an eye hook (as mentioned above) as opposed to a regular hook. Eye bolts are 100 percent safer than hooks because of their closed circle that allows less chance of movement. To further strengthen the metal hangers, use pliers to close the hooks on their ends. For fishing tackle, simply doubling the weight of the line provides an extra margin of safety. Tie all knots securely to make sure that they hold. For Lucite, check to make sure there are no hairline cracks that could break under stress. Wire snaps easily when too much weight is pulling on it. Use a heavier weight if you have the slightest doubt as to the hanging strength of a lesser weight. Wire should be double-knotted—twist it around itself twice, over and under (Figure 4–4). Rope should be checked for fraying and chains checked for loose and unclosed links. As solid as chain seems, unsoldered links can pull apart easily when the weight is too heavy for the metal. If you need to use soldered links, a special tool is needed to cut through them. Security departments often own these cutters for security chains and will loan them if you and your department have established a reputation for returning tools promptly.

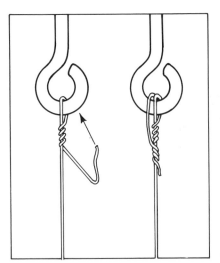

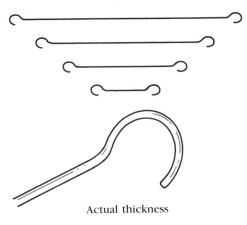

Actual thickness

Figure 4–4
Double and tie the wire to prevent snapping or slipping.

Threaded Rod

When extremely heavy objects must be hung from the ceiling, and clips or toggles aren't strong enough to do the job, threaded rod should be used. Anything over 25 lbs needs the extra safety that threaded rod provides. To use this method, ceiling tiles in a dropped ceiling must be removed so that the rod can be attached to the roof or superstructure of the building. One method is to drill a hole into the metal support, push a rod through it, and screw a large washer and bolt on the end to hold

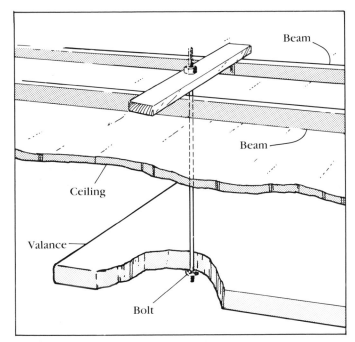

Figure 4–5
Threaded rod holding up a valance.

it from slipping through. If there is no metal to drill through in the particular location needed, a piece of metal can be used in a similar way as a brace (Figure 4–5). This will distribute the weight evenly on two struts. Be very careful where the hole is drilled, or over which pipes or supports the brace is placed. Hot-water pipes, sprinkler systems, electrical conduit would all be potential disasters if they snapped from too much weight.

Wood Beam

If a wood beam is available, a good-size screw eye will work well. Wood ceilings are scarce but they provide the ideal hanging situation as screw eyes stay in place and screw in easily. Squeeze some white glue into the hole before screwing in the screw eye for safety's sake. It helps to keep the screw eyes from pulling out of the wood.

Things That Stand

Ladders

Ladders are made to stand when needed and collapse when not needed. If the reverse occurs, a display person could be injured as can other people in the area of the ladder. Ladders can be very dangerous if used improperly and are one of the foremost occupational hazards of visual merchandising. Several rules to follow when climbing ladders are:

1. If any screws are loose, tighten them.

2. If any steps are missing or loose, do not use the ladder until it's fixed.

3. If the ladder is too short for the job, don't compensate by standing on top of the ladder or putting the ladder on another object; get a taller ladder. It's a violation of federal labor standards to use a ladder that is too short for a project, as well as to extend its height in an artificial manner such as putting it on top of a table.

4. If the ladder is placed improperly so that you have to stand backward or stretch precariously to reach the project, the risk is too great and the ladder should be moved to make the job safer. Don't work backward!

5. If you feel faint or have an inner ear problem, don't go up a ladder at all.

6. Don't carry too much up the ladder. Make two trips if necessary. You need one free hand for grabbing and balance at all times.

7. If the weight of the object to be carried up is excessive, share the weight with another person on another ladder.

8. Don't leave *anything* on top of a ladder—ever! Nine times out of ten you'll forget that your hammer, paint, staple gun, pins, or glue gun are up there and an unsuspecting bystander could jostle the ladder slightly and be permanently stained or even injured by a falling object.

9. For work involving electricity, such as lighting, use a wood ladder.

10. When using a hot-glue gun on a ladder, loop the cord loosely around a top rung of the ladder leaving enough room to manipulate the gun. That way, if the gun falls off the ladder, it won't burn anyone or break.

11. To raise or lower a ladder, walk it up or down with your hands on the rungs. For a ladder over 12' high, lay it on the floor on its side and open it on the horizontal. With two people, lift it up from the side (Figure 4–6). Lower it the same way.

12. Transporting a ladder around a store is easiest on a rolling rack. The old racks are best for transporting all kinds of long props (Figure 4–7).

13. Never leave unattended ladders propped up or open on the selling floor or in trafficked hallways where people can trip over them or they could fall on someone. Ladders are considered by the courts to be attractive nuisances to children. By "attractive nuisance" is meant a clear and present danger to the health and safety of the public that appears, at least to children, to be fun.

14. When not in use, carry the ladder to a non-fire exit hallway and carefully prop it up against the wall at an angle so that the legs are firmly on the floor and won't slip and fall if bumped. By law, ladders should be chained or tied in place to the wall for safety.

15. Shoes should be low-heeled and preferably rubber-soled for flexibility, comfort, and grip.

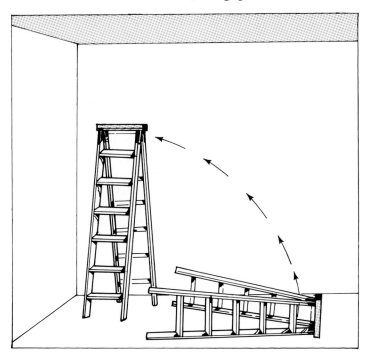

Figure 4—6
To stand up or raise a tall ladder, lay it on its side and bring it up as shown.

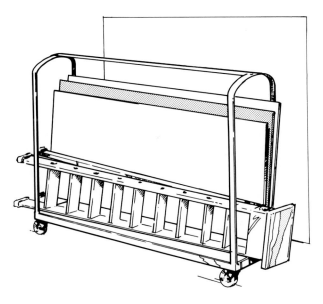

Figure 4—7
Rolling rack used as ladder transportation.

Mannequins

Mannequins are a tremendous selling tool. They are fascinating to all ages although children are the most curious about these large "dolls." A mannequin that is not properly on its base can tip over fairly easily. Make sure that the base and rod number for the mannequin match the number tattooed on the buttocks. If the mannequins are old and the rods and plates makeshift, get the best combination possible, the sturdiest and most balanced, and mark all the pieces with an identifying number so that the combination can be kept intact. To save time when dressing a mannequin and to ensure that it is on its rods properly, mark the back bottom of the rod (while the mannequin is standing correctly) and the back of the base plate. This acts as a guide for future dressings and undressings (Figure 4–8).

Wired mannequins should be used only in windows or formal display areas that are inaccessible to the public. Vibrations from street traffic can make mannequins fall even in formal, protected windows. Many New York City stores often have problems with this. Their windows require constant maintenance because of the unceasing traffic on the midtown streets. This problem applies to many major

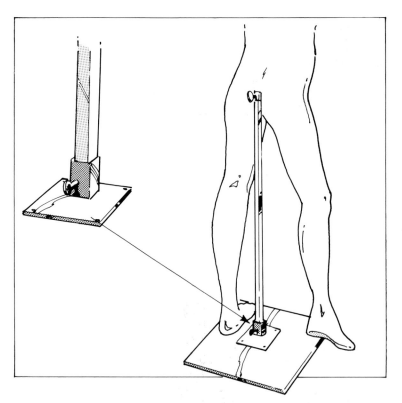

Figure 4–8
Base plate and rod attachment for a mannequin. Mark the back of the rod and the rod holder.

city stores around the country. Double or triple wiring is necessary to help prevent this because it maintains stability. (Triple wiring would be three wires extending from the buttocks of the mannequin to different places on the floor for balance.) A mannequin broken by falling is expensive to repair. It can break a show window, which is extremely costly and dangerous to pedestrians on the street as well as potentially hazardous to persons within the store.

Platforms

There are many different ideas as to how high a mannequin platform must be to prevent accidents. Often customers are so absorbed in shopping that they ignore their immediate path and trip over a platform on the floor in front of them. Clearly delineated aisles must be maintained and mannequin platforms should fit into one of the fixture aisle patterns so as not to physically confuse the customer (Figure 4–9). The platform should be high enough to allow the display to be seen (not

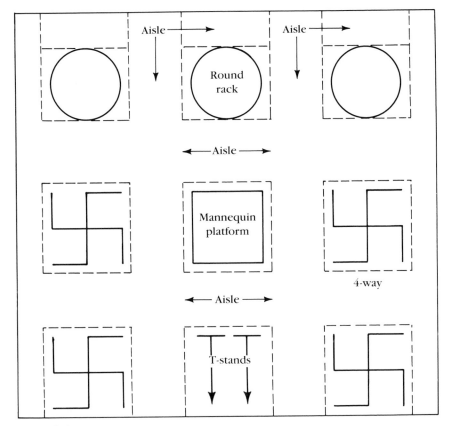

Figure 4–9
Fixture aisle pattern encompassing a mannequin platform.
⊞ *quad rack/4-way;* ⌐ *t-stand;* ○ *round rack;* ▣ *mannequin platform.*

necessarily completely) above the racks. The platform should not be overly large unless it's filled with mannequins and/or props or is visually balanced with open space between the solid areas. There should not be long, empty stretches of platform to confuse the customers. Allied Stores Inc. require an 18″ high platform for safety when the platform is in a customer's walking area. Leaving the end of a platform bare is inviting people to trip over it and hurt themselves badly. Whenever possible it is a good idea to have the platform color different from the floor color to better identify the platform. Law suits in this type of accident are very common. Also, an overhang on a platform is very dangerous.

Fixtures

Visual merchandisers work less often with the actual setting up of merchandise on fixtures. Nevertheless, it is their responsibility to constantly remind sales managers and staff not to leave empty fixtures on the floor. Even one empty arm of a rack can poke out the eye of a preoccupied customer. Hanging one garment on the end of an empty arm can act as a flag to prevent a potential accident from occurring. Make sure all fixtures are sturdy and won't fall down when touched. Check often.

Electricity

Anything electrical on the selling floor must be checked and approved by a licensed electrician. If a store is unionized, an electrician must install all wiring. If not, it must be approved so that no building codes and laws are broken. Any behind-the-scenes wiring falls under the same regulations.

Sharp Objects

All blades should be removed from food processors, e.g., Cuisinart. Knives and scissors should be locked in a display case at all times—even during promotions. A demonstration for a baking promotion must have a Lucite or glass shield around it at least 16–18″ high so that children cannot burn their hands on the electrical appliances.

Things That Hang on Walls

Pads

When hanging things on a wall, e.g., pads, paintings, props, make sure the nails used are heavy enough and are in securely. When in doubt, use toggles or screws.

Standards

When designing a wall with standards (Figure 4–10) to be used to hang clothing, use the heavier weight standard unless you're 100 percent certain that the area will

Standards

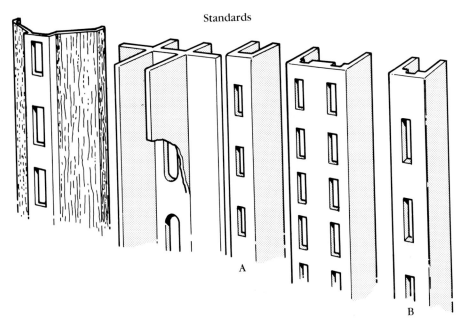

Figure 4–10
(A) Regular weight standard. (B) Heavyweight standard.

never be used for anything heavier. If lightweight standards are used and the department is eventually converted into a china or gift area where heavy items are merchandised, the standards may not support the brackets and the whole area might fall. When heavy items, such as coats, are hung on standards designed for bathing suits, the same problem can occur. Use a heavier weight for the future, just as a heavier weight toggle or eye bolt is used. The difference in looks to the customer is minimal, the cost factor is negligible, and the difference in future time, energy, and safety to the merchant is tremendous.

Valances

Nonhanging valances are often attached to standards on the walls or toggle-bolted through metal brackets into the walls. Often the solution to creating a new atmosphere for a department is changing the valance. Additions to valances are easily accomplished but be aware of the amount of extra weight that is being put on the valance and check to make sure that the valance brackets and/or standards can support the extra weight.

Letters

Signing on walls or valances is a regular part of the display job. Letters do fall easily and can badly injure someone if made of wood, mirror, Masonite, or plaster. There are several safe ways of applying letters. When letters are exceptionally heavy, drilling holes halfway through the back of thick letters and placing nails into these holes (Figure 4–11) will ensure that they don't fall. If the letters are metal or plaster, using hot glue combined with strategically placed brads (small, thin nails with no heads) will prevent them from falling. Double-stick tape is not a safe method on fabric but works well with homasote, baraboard, Masonite, or plaster-board—if the letters are normally light in weight. If one letter falls, assume the rest will follow eventually, so strengthen each letter quickly.

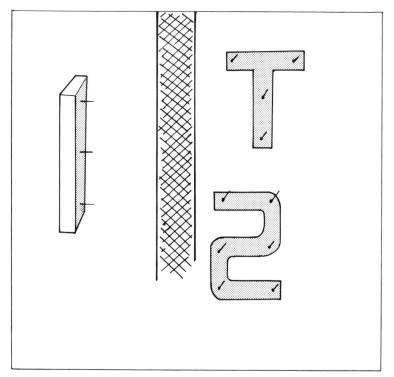

Figure 4–11
Nails embedded in the back of extra heavy letters so that they will stay up on a plaster board wall.

Things That Don't Show

The display workshop can easily be the most dangerous section of a store. Almost anything can go wrong, and will, if certain rules are not adhered to in the beginning by the entire staff.

No Smoking!

Although the laws for fireproofing are very strict, fabrics, tube paints, and the like are all highly flammable. Usually the garbage can is filled to overflowing with a variety of flammable materials. Smoking is the number one hazard in the visual merchant's area.

Electrical Tools

Unplug all electrical tools even for a minute to answer a phone. If the call is an emergency, it's easy to forget to go back and unplug everything before rushing out of the shop. A hot-glue gun or iron can cause a fire if placed next to a flammable object. Any power tool (saw, drill, etc.) must be turned off immediately. If another person enters the work area and is unaware that the iron or glue gun are hot, he or she could easily be burned. If unattended machines are left on, a person could lose a limb through inattentiveness. It sounds gruesome and it should; carelessness can kill.

Paint

Spray paint and paint removers are extremely flammable. By law these should be kept in a locked metal closet when not in use. The primary reason for this law is because spray cans and certain paint removers can explode when heated. In case of a fire, spray cans act as moving weapons and bombs. A fire can turn quickly into a mine field with spray cans and paint cans around waiting to explode.

Paint Booth

A paint booth should be set up in each display department. Very often this is ignored, but you as visual merchant should insist on a working booth. Inhalation of paint fumes can damage lungs as well as break down cells in the body and brain. Slight memory losses are common after inhaling spray paint fumes for any length of time with little or no ventilation.

Covers

All electrical appliances should have covers to prevent spray dust and small flammable objects from getting into the working parts and causing a short in the wiring. All wires and plugs should be replaced when worn.

Exits

There should be clear paths to the exits within the display shop. Ideally, and in most cases, the law demands two exits, both clearly marked and accessible. Paths must be clearly maintained.

BETTER SAFE THAN SORRY

It is the direct responsibility of visual merchants to clean the area in which they are working. Often the paging system will alert the visual merchant to an emergency or call somewhere else, and it is very tempting to leave an unfinished project as is "for a few minutes." Don't leave without storing the staple gun, hammer, nails, paint, unplugging the glue gun and putting it in a safe place, pushing the cart with or without the ladder off the selling floor, removing all items from the ladder rungs, and throwing something over a naked mannequin so customers won't be shocked or offended. This all requires a maximum of three minutes, yet such precautions make a tremendous difference in the safety of your customers and merchandise. Never underestimate the negative impact of an unfinished and messy display on the subconscious mind of your customer. You have no idea how long you'll be gone from the area, so it's much better to be safe.

Summary of Basic Safety Rules

1. Aisles to exits must be unobstructed at all times.

2. There should be at least one emergency exit from the display shop within a reasonable distance.

3. Check with local fire codes for flameproofing regulations. Usually these codes are strictest on the east and west coasts. Flameproofing adds an extra 10 percent to the total cost. Certificates can be obtained from the vendor certifying that the goods are flameproofed according to fire regulations.

4. Sprinkler heads must have at least 18″ of open space in all directions around the head to allow an unimpeded flow of water to the ground. A sprinkler will spray water over an 8–10′ circle. Usually 22 gal/minute will come out of the head at 15 lb of pressure. Painting sprinkler heads reduces their effectiveness and tampering with them in any way can set them off. Never hang anything from a sprinkler head. The newer ones now being installed have antivandal valves that are tamperproof. An alarm will go off if someone turns off the valves without the proper authorization. These precautions prevent an arsonist from making a store vulnerable by turning off the sprinkler system before starting a fire.

5. Use proper methods for hanging anything from a ceiling. Allow for sway caused by air flow to exert extra pressure on hanging objects. This sway may also cause movement alarms to go off in a store after it's closed, indicating to security that there's a prowler in the building. Close the O in all hooks so that unusual sway won't cause the prop to fall.

6. Do not climb a broken ladder. Don't leave an open ladder standing unsupervised on the selling floor. Don't leave anything on top of a ladder or on any step. Use wood ladders for electrical work.

7. Check store codes for proper platform height. If there is no code, use good judgment, and don't have empty edges where they can be overlooked and tripped over by the customer.

8. Let experts do what they're paid to do. If you're not an electrician, don't learn on the job. Your life and that of others may be at stake.

9. All paints and spray cans must be stored in a locked metal cabinet.

10. Always ask yourself the following: Is it tight enough? Will it stick? Is it high enough? Is it visible? Is it balanced? Is it secure? Is it too heavy? Will it sway? Can someone pull it down and be injured?

If an accident occurs, heed the following procedures:

1. Wash out a cut immediately with cold, clean water. *If there is a nurse or medical department, quickly report the injury, no matter how minor.* Report any injury to the store as it happens. This way, if there is a need to apply for workmen's compensation, a record of the injury will be on hand for verification.

   Cover the cut with a sterile bandage.

2. For a fall, do not get up immediately. Carefully test each area of your body to make sure nothing is broken or sprained. Get up slowly and continue to check for injuries. Report the accident. If the pain is acute, have someone drive you to the emergency room of a local hospital.

3. For a sprain or strain, do not use the muscles that have been harmed. Request paper work or nonstrenuous activity if available, so that healing time will be shortened.

4. For spray paint in the eyes, quickly wash the eyes out with fresh, cool water until all traces of the paint are removed from the eyeball area. Vaseline will remove the paint from the eye/skin area slowly, but it is much safer than turpentine. *Do not use turpentine around the eyes—ever!*

Safety takes time and effort. If this chapter is gruesome, imagine living in fear every time you walk into a store. If basic regulations and laws are not followed, shopping could become far more dangerous than driving in any city. Display is fun, challenging, and fast-paced, but it can also be deadly if the basic principles outlined in this chapter are not followed.

LOSS PREVENTION

The loss prevention department is an essential part of the management team. When profits are calculated, excess shortage can make an exciting profit look very dim. Loss prevention, also known as security, affects every aspect of the retail environment. It is the responsibility of visual merchandising to consider security when planning displays. Assume from the beginning that anything you put on display will be open to theft. When planning a display, consider the following points:

1. Is the merchandise secured on the mannequin, e.g., handbags, accessories?

2. When putting expensive merchandise on a mannequin, make sure that the security regulations in your store permit that particular merchandise to be unattached on a fixture on the selling floor. Merchandise displayed on a mannequin should be found next to or near the mannequin platform.

3. Merchandise placed on top of a case must be within the limitations set by security, i.e., expensive scarves should be under glass while $10-and-under scarves should be self-service.

4. There is usually a sign-out procedure for items (such as accessories) to be used for display. It's usually time consuming and frustrating to fill out all the forms necessary and to get the appropriate signature for the merchandise sign-out book. It is vital that the display department adhere to these regulations.

No matter how much time you may feel is wasted by these procedures, your performance is judged not only by visual merchandising talent, but by honesty and adherence to rules and regulations. More employees are fired and talents lost from the visual merchandising team through recommendation by the security department for infractions of security procedures than for any other reason. The visual merchant must be above suspicion. Display people are often in the store before opening and have access to every piece of merchandise. From the beginning of a career in retailing one of the main considerations an employer has when interviewing or reviewing a person is honesty. One dishonest act will follow a person throughout his or her career. Emphasizing the importance of signing out merchandise in the proper manner and keeping current with all paper work cannot be overstated.

There are many store policies for buyers when they deal with their vendors (the manufacturers or jobbers from whom buyers purchase merchandise). Usually a buyer has to sign a paper promising not to accept any free favors or merchandise from vendors. A visual merchant buys from vendors also and is susceptible to the same pressures and temptations that face the retail buyers. As tempting as it may be to accept a free prop, television, calculator, or money for an exceptional order, it is not advisable to do so. Once you are in the position to buy display merchandise and have the responsibility for a budget, your honesty must be above question.

Important aspects of security to remember are as follows:

1. As a display is developed, security of merchandise must be considered.

2. Sign out all merchandise with the proper paper work and procedures. Don't think twice about the extra time it takes. Two major reasons for this

adherence to rules are (1) to remain above suspicion and (2) to keep an accurate record of the location of merchandise inventory and sales records.

3. Once you steal or accept kick backs (gifts from vendors), your credibility and honesty will be suspect for the remainder of your retailing career.

Security is important to remember, both for your good and for the good of the store.

SUMMARY CHECKLIST

Key Concepts

1. Safety is the primary concern of the visual merchant at all times.
2. Safety precautions must be considered when designing displays.
3. Display items that hang from the ceiling must be attached with proper equipment.
4. Improperly displayed mannequins are a major safety hazard.
5. The display workshop can easily be the most dangerous section of a store.
6. The visual merchant must be aware of all local and state safety laws.
7. Display is a pleasant way to sell merchandise, but it can also be deadly if proper procedures are not followed.

DISCUSSION QUESTIONS

1. Name three display items that could be a source of injury to customers and/or store employees.
2. Explain the difference between security and safety.
3. Why is it necessary that visual merchants take every precaution necessary to ensure the safety of the store's customers and employees?
4. What are some areas of safety concern within the display workshop?
5. What are the six major ways of hanging material from a ceiling?
6. What are the basic safety rules that should be followed when utilizing ladders? Why are ladders a safety hazard?
7. What is a major safety precaution when dealing with mannequins?
8. Visual merchants should be aware of potential hazards in several areas of their reponsibility. Indicate these areas and why you feel they are hazardous.
9. What is the number one hazard within the visual merchant's area?
10. Why is it important to store all paint and paint removers in a locked metal closet when not in use?
11. What major security precautions should you consider when planning a display?
12. Why is it important to sign out all merchandise with the proper paper work and procedures?

STUDENT EXERCISES

Number 1

Assume the role of a retail sales employee. You have been asked by your department manager to prepare a checklist that could be utilized in the store to evaluate the safety consciousness of each department. Prepare this checklist.

Number 2

Visit three community businesses with which you are familiar. Obtain a copy of the safety regulations that employees must follow while at work. Compare and contrast the three policies as they relate to employee and customer safety.

CASE PROBLEM 1

The New Policy

Mr. Alfred, the owner of Alfred and Sons Department Store, is excited. They recently built a new store in the new Othegon Mall which is being opened in the southern part of Livingston. Plans call for the new store to be opened in approximately four months. Alfred and Sons is presently having an inventory reduction sale, which hopefully will allow them to sell most of their merchandise so they won't have to move it to the new store.

Livingston is a large community of 400,000 and is located within 60 miles of a major metropolitan city. The new store will have approximately 150,000 square feet of selling space available. Alfred and Sons has dominated its market area for several years with a store that attracts the middle range of department store shoppers. It is a full-line department store that carries a quality line of merchandise. The new store will be two stories high, with the storage area located in the rear of the store on the main level. In talking to the store manager, Mr. Houston, Mr. Alfred expressed concern regarding the safety of both the employees and the customers. During the past six months, several minor accidents have occurred, but no one was seriously injured. All accidents dealt with some type of display.

Mr. Alfred is not sure if the accidents were caused by employee negligence or by faulty equipment and facilities. After all, the building which houses the present department store is 40 years old, and the store budget has not allowed for major renovation. Mr. Alfred does not want any accidents to occur in the new store.

Questions To Discuss

1. What are some hazards that exist in display areas?
2. What safety precautions should be taken when building displays in the new store?

3. What state safety laws will normally have to be followed?
4. What items could be placed in a "safety policy" that will apply to all visual merchandising activities within the new store?

CASE PROBLEM 2

The Fire

The store had just opened an hour ago and already several customers had entered the store looking at merchandise that had been advertised in the Sunday paper.

"What a beautiful way to start a week," thought Jane Sampson, visual merchandising manager for The Fashion Palace. It was the first day for the Christmas promotion, all the displays and shops in the store looked beautiful, customers were starting to purchase merchandise, and a light snow had begun to fall, adding to the serenity of the morning.

Jane was proud of herself and her employees. They had worked all week, day and night, to transform the store into a winter wonderland, and already several positive comments had been received from the customers and employees regarding how pretty and appropriate the displays were, especially the windows.

The Fashion Palace is a children's store with approximately 75,000 square feet of selling space located on one floor. In addition to clothing, two other major areas of the store are baby furniture and children's toys.

On her way back to the display workshop, Jane suddenly stopped. "Something is wrong", she thought! Then the odor reached her. "Smoke, there is a fire!" Quickly scanning the store she located the fire. Flames were visible from the preteen winter coat area. She knew she would have to act quickly.

Questions To Discuss

1. What steps should Jane take in this situation? (indicate in priority order)
2. What knowledge of fire and fire equipment should Jane already possess?
3. When building the displays over the weekend, what could the visual merchandising employees have done wrong which could have caused the fire?

CASE PROBLEM 3

The Check

Look At Her Now is a regional women's clothing chain that has thirty stores located in eight states in the western part of the country. The chain started out with one store 30 years ago, and due to excellent management, good employee morale, excellent employee benefits, and less than 2 percent employee turnover, the chain is continuing to grow with another store opening scheduled for next year.

All major decisions for the chain are made at the home office. This includes basic display approaches, buying, store decor, sales promotions, advertising, and so on. The individual store manager has very little input regarding major decisions of the chain.

Each store employs one assistant display manager, who takes orders from the home office display manager, Mr. Roffer. Mr. Roffer has been with company for 20 years. Every quarter, Mr. Roffer visits each store and discusses the next quarter's display approach with the assistant display manager. He also collects all purchase orders for display materials and props. All purchases must go through Mr. Roffer. The assistant display managers do not like this policy. Approximately 65 percent of all purchases for the display departments are from Anderson Distributing. The company provides a quality product at a reasonable price. They deliver on time and the service is excellent.

Mr. Roffer recently returned from a visit to the Appleton store. Upon opening his mail, he found a letter from Anderson Distributing with an enclosed check for $2,000 payable to Mr. Roffer. The letter stated that the check was a thank you for past business. The company does not have a policy against buyers receiving gratuities. To Mr. Roffer's knowledge, this has never occurred in the display department before.

At home that evening, Mr. Roffer and his wife discussed his options:

1. Keep the money.
2. Send the money back.
3. Put the money into the display budget.
4. Give the money to the owners of the company.
5. Divide the money between the employees.
5. Give the money to charity.

Questions to Discuss

1. What should Mr. Roffer do? Give a rationale for your decision.
2. Should there be a company policy against buyers receiving gratuities?

CHAPTER 5

Fixtures

LEARNING OBJECTIVES

At the completion of this chapter, you will be able to:

1. List the reasons fixtures are important in selling.

2. Name the types of fixtures available.

3. Give the advantages/disadvantages of each type of fixture.

4. Describe the relationship between security and fixtures.

5. Explain the importance of sign holders as fixtures.

6. Describe which fixtures work for different types of merchandise.

7. Describe the relationship between lighting and valances.

8. Develop a procedure to follow for storing all display fixtures.

9. Explain the importance of proper fixture placement within a department.

Merchandising in a visually appealing manner can be accomplished through the use of mannequins, props, lighting, and fixtures. Of the four, fixtures are the most important element in the merchandising aspect of the visual merchant's job.

A fixture is anything that is made especially for the presentation and sale of merchandise. Fixturing must relate directly to the specific requirements of the merchandise and the store. An attractive fixture that does not display the merchandise to its best advantage is a waste of space and money. A good fixture should complement the feeling of a department rather than compete with the merchandise being sold, and display the merchandise well.

Floor space is a primary concern of fixturing. One major way that sales are computed is by sales per square foot of selling space. If a fixture takes up a lot of space yet sells comparatively little merchandise, either the fixture or the merchandise is wrong for that particular spot. Essentially, each fixture must perform a sales function by itself by becoming a salesperson who hustles!

The different types of fixturing sit on the countertop and floor and hang on the wall.

COUNTERTOP FIXTURES

Countertop fixtures (Figures 5–1 to 5–5) are used to get more selling space from the counter area by putting the less expensive but related items within the reach of

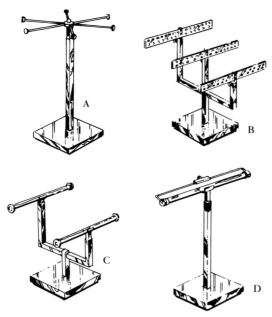

Figure 5–1

(A) Tie, jewelry or scarf fixture (6 arms, 9" long, revolving, adjustable 24–42"). (B) Earring fixture. (Theft resistant, clear plexi arms, all tiers adjustable). (C) Necklace or bracelet fixture (12" clear plexi arms.) (D) Necklace, bracelet fixture. (Security padlock device. Adjustable).

Credit: Edron Fixture Corp., N.Y.C., N.Y.

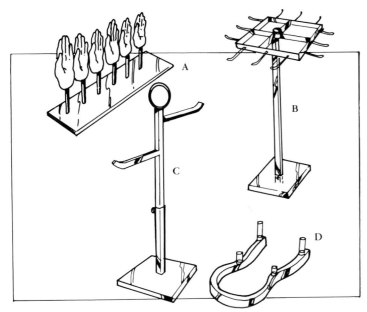

Figure 5–2
(A) Glove fixture. (B) Tie, 4-sided revolving fixture. (C) Towel/fabric stand,
adjustable height. (D) Cup/saucer/plate holder.
Credit: Edron Fixture Corp., N.Y.C., N.Y.

the customer. For example, one might put change purses in a fixture sitting on a case with expensive wallets and purses below.

Countertop fixtures are available in many different materials. The most popular materials are Plexiglas (which is usually combined with chrome or brass), chrome or brass alone, and wood (which is occasionally combined with any of the others). The material depends on the department in which the fixture is to be placed. Men's departments may use a lot of brass while women's accessories departments often utilize Plexiglas. All the materials listed require careful maintenance and respect for their relative fragility. Plexiglas as a fixture, disappears from view when merchandise is properly placed on it. Plexiglas is a good material for fixtures because ideally the fixture should not be primary in a customer's line of vision. The merchandise should be seen first. In some cases, when a certain ambiance is desired, visible fixturing can make the difference in the mood of the department. A feeling of expensive elegance can be created within an area through the use of antique brass fixtures if they hold merchandise that relates to the expensive feeling and the fixture itself is in good condition.

Chrome fixtures seem modern, and even more so when combined with mirrors for reflection. Wood fixtures, especially when stained dark, create a country, traditional feeling while other finishes create a variety of atmospheres ranging from country to European. A light wood stained with white gives a beach air, dark tones suggest masculinity, and medium tones, e.g., fruitwood, can appear antique or sophisticated. Wood fixtures are not as common as the metal or plexi

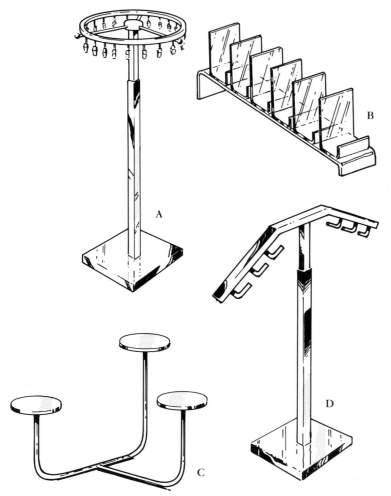

Figure 5–3
(A) Scarf fixture, revolving and adjustable. (B) Clutchbag fixture (C) Hat or wig fixture. (D) Shoulderbag adjustable fixture.
Credit: Edron Fixture Corp., N.Y.C., N.Y.

varieties. They are more expensive and are usually custom-made. When handled with care, they last forever, imparting a feeling of warmth like fine antiques that the others do not. Wood can scratch, dent, or split with mishandling. Chrome can chip or bend and plexi can crack. All fixtures should be handled with care.

Countertop fixtures come in all shapes and forms to serve all functions. Some common fixtures include those for hanging shirts or sweaters, handbags both shoulder and clutch, all small leather goods, sunglasses, scarves, gloves, hats, and bust forms for clothing.

Countertop fixtures are usually bought for each department on an individual basis to accommodate different needs. If the departments blend into one another,

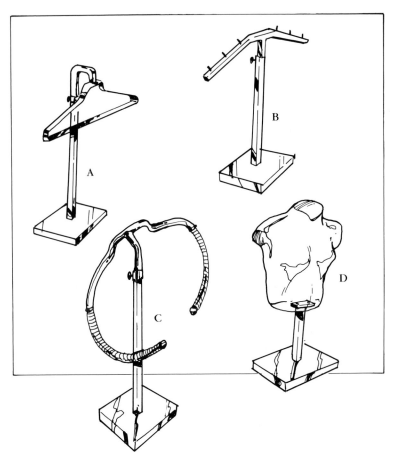

Figure 5—4
(A) Men's jacket fixture. (B) Pin stop/hanger holder for blouses, sweaters, etc.
(C) Flex-arm fixture for tops. (D) Clear plexi form, open back, for women's tops.
Credit: Edron Fixture Corp., N.Y.C., N.Y.

care should be taken to keep the basic fixture look consistent by staying with the same material, e.g., chrome, plexi, wood, brass. When a department is separated from the others by architecture, a different look in material and style can be used to create a different feeling within that shop if needed. Countertop fixtures are usually in short supply and high demand. Their life span (staying in one piece and looking new) is longer on the selling floor than when stashed away in a stockroom. Keep your eyes open when visiting a stockroom for unused fixtures. They are excellent sales agents and belong out on the floor to encourage impulse buying.

It is tempting to overdo the use of counter fixtures because of their selling power. Too many fixtures on a counter can look messy and crowded as well as effectively blocking the better merchandise that is below, under glass. A general rule that seems to work is to limit countertop fixtures to two per case. If the

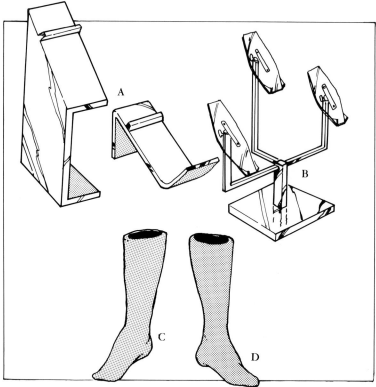

Figure 5–5
(A) Shoe fixture. (B) Ladies three-shoe fixture. (C) Ladies' knee-hi, self-standing weighted toe. (D) Men's crew sock, self-standing weighted toe.
Credit: Edron Fixture Corp., N.Y.C., N.Y.

fixtures are placed at either end of the case, there is still room for the customer to see the merchandise—and for the salesperson to write up a sale. The visual merchant is also a policing power in a store. It's up to you to keep the store looking good, and to enforce rules such as "two to a counter." Enforcing in a pleasant, understanding manner is an effective method of control. Make exceptions for the overabundance of Christmas merchandise—only!

Impulse buying and impulse stealing work well off the same fixtures. Security countertop fixtures that require a key to remove merchandise are available in the market. These also require alert and abundant sales help to aid customers. Security fixtures are best if placed near the cash register because salespeople usually gather around that location to chat and ring up sales. In this location the salespeople can easily aid customers in their choice of locked merchandise. Customers react very negatively when they are genuinely interested in looking at a piece of merchandise and find it locked securely against their honest attempts at shopping. Salespeople must be aware at all times of shoppers interested in locked goods.

FLOOR FIXTURES: SOFT-LINE MERCHANDISE

Round Racks or Rounders (Figure 5–6)

Rounders are the most common rack in many stores. The round rack holds more merchandise in the same amount of floor space than any other fixture. It comes in all materials: chrome, painted metal tubing, wood, and brass. There is usually a glass circle placed on top of the middle section so that a display or sign can be placed above the merchandise to better identify the clothes below. Round racks are used only with soft-line goods, such as clothing. Hard-line items, such as domestics, housewares, or appliances, are obviously never hung on round racks.

Round racks are not the glamor fixtures of a department and in a larger store they are usually placed to the rear of a department where they can hold the bulk of the clothing. The section of the round rack that faces the main aisle can be considered the front of the fixture. When being used for new goods, the most exciting merchandise should be in that section. This merchandise should be

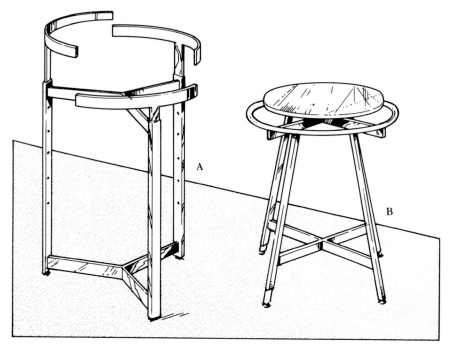

Figure 5–6
(A) Three-way adjustable round rack. (B) Basic round rack.
Credit: Edron Fixture Corp., N.Y.C., N.Y.

representative of the rest of the rack's content. Round racks are ideally suited for sale goods and are usually used exclusively for this purpose in stores with newer fixtures. Rounders are easily stored by removing the glass and placing them in an area that is reserved exclusively for glass rounds or glass shelving.

Tip: A small identifying letter can be marked on a hidden section of the frame and the same letter taped or glued to the glass so that the glass will match up with the frame once the fixture is ready for floor use again.

Rectangular Racks (Figure 5–7)

The traditional box-shaped rectangular rack is ideally suited for large quantities of like merchandise, e.g., similarly styled men's slacks that come in a large selection of sizes. These racks are rarely found in a new store as they are less visually interesting or efficient than the newer fixture styles. An advantage is their ability to mass out merchandise in a relatively narrow space while a primary disadvantage is their inability to show merchandise for optimal effect. Only the ends of the merchandise

Figure 5–7
Rectangular rack with adjustable height bars.

show, such as the sleeves or folded area of blouses and slacks. As with round racks, traditional rectangular fixtures are usually kept to the rear of a department to house the bulk of the nontrendy merchandise.

In an older store with a lot of rectangular fixtures, they may be placed around a column to create an island of similar merchandise. The column can then be used as a display area to show off merchandise on the fixtures below. Rectangular fixtures placed at right angles at the corners of a department can create a fence- or gatelike effect (Figure 5–8). Newer rectangular fixtures are manufactured in elegant materials, such as plexi and wood or chrome, and can lend themselves nicely to a contemporary environment. Additional attachments giving greater height or adding rounded sections and half-circles provide diversity to rectangular racks. As are round racks, these are excellent for sale merchandise.

To merchandise a rectangular rack in an interesting manner requires an understanding of the merchandise. Merchandisers employ different rules on merchandising. A popular choice of many stores is to group by classification. Classifications should be hung together on each bar by style, color, and size. An example would be a coordinate outfit that has a blouse, vest, jacket, and skirt. All the jackets work well when hung together, then the blouses, vests, and skirts. The colors look

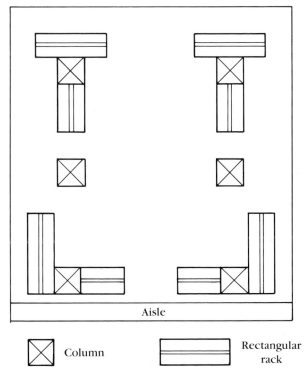

Figure 5–8
Department plan with rectangular racks defining the boundaries.

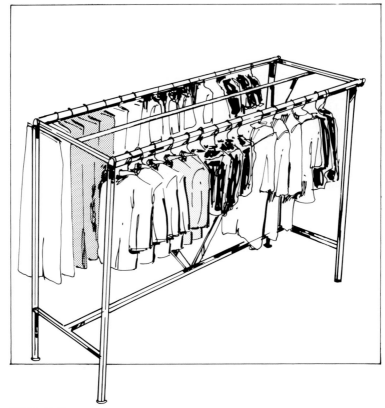

Figure 5–9
When merchandising a rectangular rack, hang by classification, color, size and style.

best when placed in the same sequence. Arranging sizes from small to large, left to right (Figure 5–9), make shopping easier. Rectangular racks usually have a long, narrow piece of glass along the top to display merchandise. Storage of these fixtures is similar to that of round racks.

Box Racks—or Four-Ways (Figure 5–10)

Box racks are excellent for showing off individual styles because each arm of the rack reveals the front of the merchandise. The four arms can come straight or waterfalled, i.e., on a downward slant to show all the pieces of the group. These racks are very popular and come in a variety of finishes and materials, yet all have the same concept of frontal projection. The best area in a department for these fixtures is from the front to the middle, which leaves the less attractive but highly functional racks (round and rectangular) for the rear of a department. Related styles of merchandise should be shown on these racks, e.g., a coordinate outfit, matching sweaters, shirts and slacks, and so on.

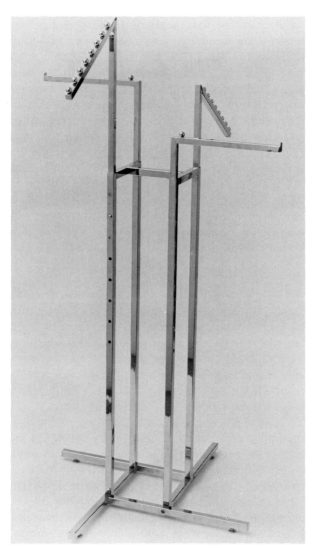

Figure 5–10
Box rack or four way.

Tip: One color group works better on a box rack than a large assortment of unrelated colors. Mismatched or unrelated merchandise looks jumbled and unappealing on this rack. Actually, unorganized merchandise looks terrible on any rack, but it's best in the rear of a department where less visible. Many customers are psychologically "turned on" to messy final clearance racks but regular sales do better with neat fixtures. If a department has to fall apart at all—in looks or organization—always let it happen in the rear or on the bottom. Better yet, with everyday maintenance, there is no need to become messy at all. It is the job of the sales staff to keep the department in shape and the merchandise displayed well.

Depending on the merchandising rules of the particular organization, the front hook of each arm is an ideal place for an accessorized or coordinated outfit to render the entire fixture sensible and exciting. Merchandising creativity comes into play with a box rack because all four arms should ideally be related so that the customer can put together an entire outfit from one or two adjacent racks.

Maintaining a box rack is not difficult, and yet such racks fall apart more quickly than any others, perhaps because they are in constant use. The arms of the rack can break, especially when tugged on by salespeople dragging the fixture across a rug.

The piece that allows the arm to adjust in height often is abused or structurally fails on its own, so that the arm will not adjust at all but will stay at one height only. Another problem is that the fixture will eventually sway as the screws loosen underneath. Allen wrenches should be ordered with every new fixture purchase. A set should be handy for fixture maintenance and repair so that a fully loaded rack does not fall over and hurt someone.

Bloomingdales or Quad Racks (Figure 5–11)

The Bloomingdale, also known as the quad rack, was designed for the store of that name to hold large assortments of merchandise in an attractive manner. Much bigger than the average fixture, Bloomingdales hold a large quantity of goods without looking dull. All the bars are adjustable and fixtures can be added to change the appearance and use of this rack to fit many needs. The problem is that they require a lot of floor space and the merchandise on these fixtures should, as on the box rack, be related. Often a store doesn't buy enough related merchandise groups to fill an entire Bloomingdale. When this happens, grouping the merchandise by style or color will achieve a unified look. As with all the fixtures mentioned, these are available in many materials and styles; however, the basic quadrangle shape or structure with four arms is characteristic of the Bloomingdale. Bloomingdales should be placed either in the center of a large department or toward the rear so that they don't block smaller racks from aisle vision. The Bloomingdale, like other fixtures, must be viewed from the main aisle. What the customer sees when approaching the fixture is the most important merchandise and should represent the rest of the rack. Always put new and exciting goods where they're most visible.

T-Stands or Costumers (Figure 5–12)

The T-stand is the mannequin of fixtures. This displayer comfortably holds up to twelve items and sets merchandising "stories" apart from the mass of merchandise on larger racks. A T-stand or costumer is usually placed in the front of a department highlighting along the aisle the newest goods that can be found in the rest of the area. T-stands should also be placed adjacent to mannequin presentations so that the merchandise on the mannequin can be found easily by the customer.

T-stands and costumers can have either straight or waterfall arms. The waterfall will show all the items at once and is ideal for a group of related but nonidenti-

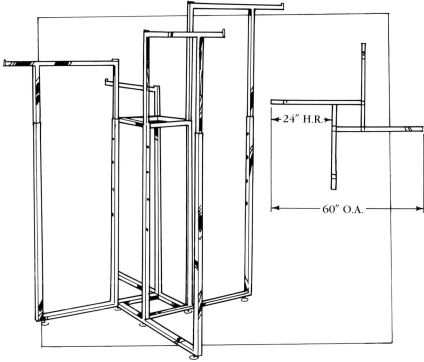

Figure 5–11
Bloomingdale or quad rack.
Credit: Edron Fixture Corp., N.Y.C., N.Y.

cal merchandise. When a T-stand is facing the aisle, the arm on the aisle should be lower than the back arm to allow total visibility of the merchandise. The best method of presentation is to have the "glamor" stock on the front arm, e.g., blazers, blouses, and all tops. The bulk items, such as skirts and slacks, work best toward the rear.

Customers like to create entire outfits from one T-stand. By putting certain items together on the costumer, you are telling the customer that these items can form an ensemble. Careful merchandising is required to make this concept work— and sell. (See Figure 5–13 for soft-line fixture floor plans.)

Sweater or Shirt Bin Units (Figure 5–14)

Sweater or shirt bin units are built out of glass, plexi, or wood squares with clips to attach the pieces; solid units are made from Lucite or solid units of wood. All of the above need a shelf to support the unit. This shelf should be made of wood or some other sturdy material that can support heavy weight. Glass can be used for a cube unit if the goods are lightweight. Showing the merchandise in a cube unit is difficult

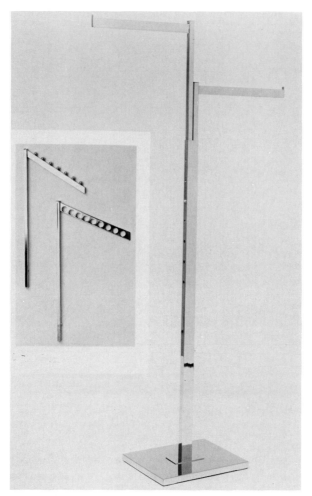

Figure 5–12
T-stand or costumer with alternative arms.

because folded items can't be seen by the customer. Colors can make the difference between an exciting merchandise presentation and a wall unit of dull, unidentifiable goods. Often, hanging the folded merchandise on either side of the cube unit or above the unit on display helps to identify the folded goods. The spectrum concept mentioned in Chapter 4 is used most often with folded goods in wall cube units. Cubes are also often used as floor fixtures. They are constructed of glass squares or Plexiglas, and are placed on bases made of wood/formica/baraboard. These floor cubes, like the wall variety, are merchandised with folded goods. They require a countertop fixture to show off the merchandise contained below.

A traditional setup
for ready-to-wear

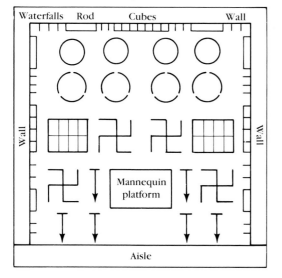

Setup for an angled
department

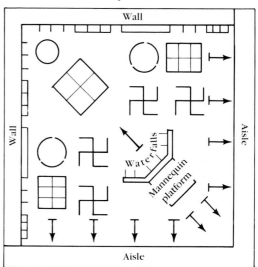

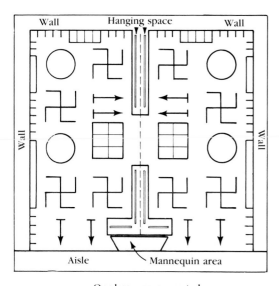

One large area separated
into two departments

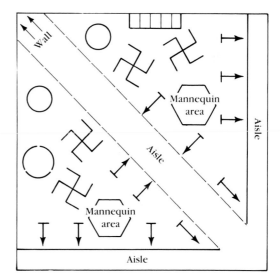

Corner area divided into
two departments

Figure 5–13

Floor plans for soft line fixtures. ↑ *T-stand;* ⊞ *Bloomingdale;* ⊞ *cube unit for folded items;* ▀▀▀ *rectangular;* 占 *quad;* ○ *round rack;* ○ *tri-round.*

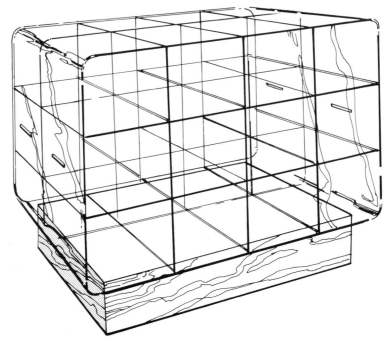

Figure 5–14
Sweater or shirt bin unit.

FLOOR FIXTURES: HARD-LINE MERCHANDISE

Gondolas (Figure 5–15)

A gondola is an upright unit approximately $4' \times 4'$ that is used primarily for shelving and has a built-in bottom shelf. Gondolas are not the glamor fixtures of a store, but they are extremely functional and hold a lot of merchandise. Most often towels, sheets, and cooking accessories can be found on their shelves. In most older stores that have not revamped their fixturing, the gondola is a staple fixture in domestics, housewares, and hardware. The flexibility of this fixture is the reason it is used so often. The shelves can be positioned to accept large amounts of merchandise and dividers can be added to sort the goods appropriately by color, style, or price. Older gondolas are usually an off-white formica with steel legs and a pegboard or plywood centerpiece. Newer styles come with a box base with a recessed kickplate, a formica base and centerpiece for durability, and matching shelves that are also formica. The old gondola formula still works well for most hard-line merchandise when the fixtures are well maintained and freshly painted.

Merchandising this fixture can be approached from several angles. The most important point to remember is to put the best items on top; the top row is the closest to eye level and the exciting merchandise belongs at that level. If your stock

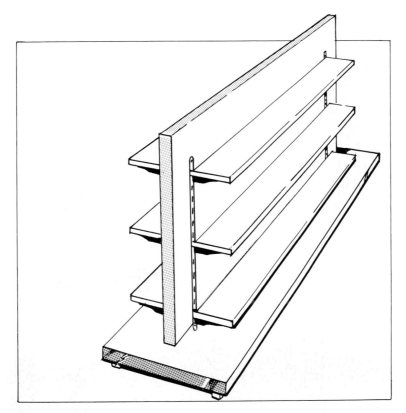

Figure 5–15
A basic gondola, older style.

selection falls apart, i.e., there are broken sizes, colors, and styles, let this happen on the bottom of the fixture where the mess will be less noticeable.

A popular method for merchandising these fixtures in the housewares department is to put open merchandise on the top row, so the customer can see it displayed out of the box, and neatly stack the unopened boxes below the samples, so the customer can easily buy the clean, unopened item yet see the product fully displayed before the purchase.

Flat-Top or Tub Tables (Figure 5–16)

Flat-top tables are used almost exclusively for sales. They are available in an infinite variety from folding tables to full, boxlike fixtures with a flat-top surface (with a lip) and shelves underneath for extra stock. They are usually unattractive and are used as a constant fixture only when a store has not yet remodeled and refixtured its selling floor. When used for everyday selling, the box and shelf fixture will often have risers added to it to create a feeling of height and to add to the merchandising capacity of the surface. A riser is a minitable with different levels to hold merchan-

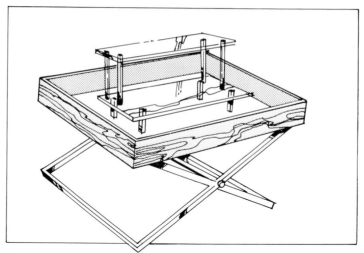

Figure 5–16
Tub table with riser table to add height and display space.
Credit: Edron Fixture Corp., N.Y.C., N.Y.

dise. The legs take up very little room and duplicates of the merchandise can be placed under the risers. When used for sales, the merchandise requires constant upkeep because customers have a tendency to paw through the goods on the top of the table. The flat-top folding table looks best with a tablecloth to cover the metal tubing legs. The tablecloths should be clean, pressed, and long enough to look professional. Granted, they won't necessarily remain that way for long, but every effort should be made to see that the image of the store is preserved throughout even the most incredible sale.

Cubes (Figure 5–17)

The most versatile of all fixturing, cubes are the building blocks of a department. Used mainly in hard lines, such as housewares and gifts, cubes or cubelike structures can flesh out a department and give form to the aisle structure while holding a lot of merchandise in an attractive manner. The cube can come in any size or finish limited only by the imagination and budget. The most common forms are the five-sided box (empty side down) and the same five-sided box with the empty side facing out so that extra stock can be stored within easy reach of the consumer. The most commonly seen finishes are raw wood for housewares departments (that try to look like sophisticated crating), formica finishes for durability (in an infinite selection of colors), and carpeted cubes that blend into the department so that only the merchandise shows.

Cubes can be arranged in many ways, but three or four cubes is the most common number used in a grouping. The cubes are usually of different heights and the smaller ones are placed in front with the taller cubes behind. When the

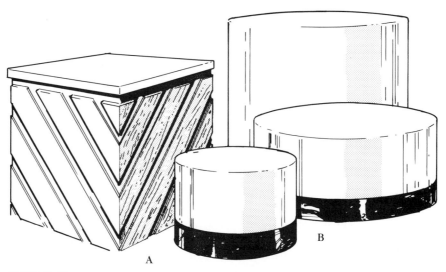

Figure 5–17
(A) Wood cube/decorative surface. (B) Drum tables, formica surface.
Credit: Edron Fixture Corp., N.Y.C., N.Y.

merchandise is placed on the cubes it looks "stepped." In a stepped arrangement the customer's eye travels from the goods placed on the lowest to those on the highest cube and therefore takes in the entire presentation. Although cubes don't hold large quantities of merchandise, they do have definite advantages. Each individual cube can hold one type of item and a cluster of three or four cubes can hold related items thereby creating a total merchandise concept (Figure 5–18).

Figure 5–18
The cubes in the foreground of the picture hold specific classifications of plastic merchandise.
Credit: Linda Cahan Schneider, 1980.

The merchandise flexibility of cubes makes them very desirable fixturing. Experimenting with different cube configurations and merchandise presentations will encourage the visual merchant to create solutions to a myriad of merchandising problems.

WALL FIXTURES

Anything that holds merchandise and is attached to a wall is considered a wall fixture. This includes shelving, cubes, rods, standards, and all the attachments to rods and standards as well as entire wall systems, such as pegboard and slotwall.

Standards

Standards are used to hold up almost everything that is placed on a wall. Standards are metal runners with slots to accommodate bracket ends. The ends fit into the slots and are then pushed down to lock in place. Standards come in a range of weights from light to heavy and will accept a lot of merchandise weight when properly attached. Hollow walls require that standards be attached with toggle bolts.

It's often best to put up a heavier weight standard in the beginning so that the merchandise capacity of the wall isn't limited by the standards. When the weight of the merchandise is not considered, the standards can sag or buckle and the brackets will then pull out, collapsing the entire rod structure. No customer or salesperson will ever forget the experience of removing one hanger and having an entire winter coat selection fall on his or her head. The danger is obvious, the potential for law suits is high, and the inconvenience of repairing all the damage is a nuisance. The toggle bolt must also be of a heavier weight to accept the strain of the merchandise.

Standards can be either mounted on the wall or recessed into the wall for a sleek and finished look. The advantage to a wall-mounted standard is the ability to move it easily to different locations when needed. The disadvantage is that this mounting is obvious and the eye is drawn to the standard and therefore detracts from the merchandise. The recessed standard is more difficult to install and requires detailed planning to ensure that all the standards are in the right position and at the correct height before the sheetrock is placed on the wall. The look is very clean with a recessed standard because only a slight gap can be seen from the selling floor. The standard itself is behind the gap and the holes for the bracket ends cannot be seen. If recessed brackets have to be moved, the entire section of wall must be removed. An alternative to tearing down a wall in a newly built shop or store is to use removable panels so that the wall section can be screwed off the wall struts and replaced as needed.

Brackets

Brackets (Figure 5–19) are used to hold up bars, shelves, and cube units by slotting into the standard's holes. Each type of bracket will hold different weights and only

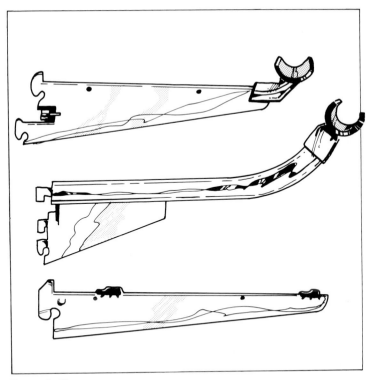

Figure 5–19
Three different brackets that fit into different types of standards.

the manufacturer or thoughtful experimenter will know how much weight a particular bracket will hold. A maintenance person in an older store will know each bracket and its capabilities, and will be able to assist you until you know the different weights and styles. Brackets have end pieces that attach to holes in the end of the bracket. These end pieces have suction cups to hold glass firmly in place. When shelving with glass it's important to remember to place these suction cups on the brackets so the glass won't scratch or slide off.

Shelving

Shelving is as versatile as cubes. Materials used for shelving range from glass to wood and all kinds of laminates. The most frequently used materials are glass and wood, but plexi, Masonite, baraboard, and marble/stone are also used. To be effective, a glass shelf should have a thickness of at least 1/4". For holding heavy merchandise, a glass thickness of 3/8" will ensure that it doesn't crack under pressure. Another form of insurance with glass shelving is to always place the heavier merchandise over the brackets and keep the lightweight goods in the center. If you check the gift department of your local department or specialty store, you may find that glass shelves are bowing under the pressure of too-heavy merchandise. Glass can "give" for just so long—and then will give out, causing a lot of damage and possible injuries.

Wood Shelves

Wood shelves are durable and rarely crack under pressure (unless they're too thin or already cracked). The ends must be sanded well to avoid splinters and all sides of the shelving should be painted before placement on the wall. Wood doesn't allow light to pass through, so the darkness below each shelf should be taken into consideration. Spotlights need to be trained on a wood-shelved wall to highlight the merchandise.

Rods and Rod Accessories

Rods and their accessories are attached to brackets for hanging merchandise from the wall. Ninety-five percent of merchandise seen on a wall in a store is hung on rods held up by brackets that attach to standards that are screwed into the wall with toggle bolts. ("The knee bone's connected to the thigh bone. . . .") Rods need end-caps to keep the merchandise from falling off. All parts, such as end-caps, brackets, etc., can and should be ordered from the manufacturer of the standards. If you can get a better price from a different manufacturer for the accessories, make sure that their parts will fit the existing standards. Measure not only the length and width of the slot holes but also the space between each hole and how many drilled out spaces there are for screws or toggle bolts and their distance from one another. This may seem like a lot of work and it is! Proper fixturing is necessary and takes time to accomplish. Knowing that, once displayed, merchandise will stay up and look good makes the extra effort worthwhile.

Waterfalls can be attached to rods to break up the look of a department and to give frontal projection to merchandise that won't sell by just the shoulder being seen. Waterfalls will usually handle six to eight pieces of merchandise. They should not be used for heavy assortments but rather they are to be merchandised similarly to a T-stand. Tell one story per waterfall, and don't overload the fixture.

Other attachments to a rod are hooks to hang only one garment, hanging rods that attach to the regular rod, and screw eye pieces to attach entire wall segments to the rod to blank out sections of merchandising space. Rods can be cut to size with a metal hack saw. However, it is advisable to label the rods by department so that when selling areas are moved around the original department rods can be reused with the standards that were bought for them. (See Figure 5–20 for wall-mounted waterfall fixtures to use when there is no rod.)

Pegboard

Pegboard is not used as often today as in the past. Pegboard tends to look old and outdated, and it scratches very easily. However, it is still the best item on the

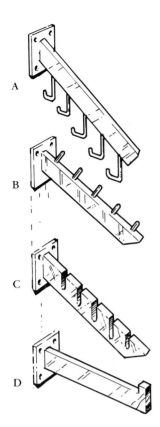

A

B

C

D

Figure 5–20

Wall-mounted waterfall fixtures to use when there is no rod. These can be attached to walls or columns with toggle bolts or screws to create hanging space in areas that won't take other types of fixturing. (A) Rear-facing hooks. (B) $1/2'' \times 1^{1}/2''$ tubing with five pins. (C) $1/4'' \times 1^{1}/2''$ bar with five notches. (D) $1/2'' \times 1^{1}/2'' \times 6''$ tubing.

market for small kitchen accessories, hosiery, and anything that is small and requires varied spacing. If pegboard is painted the same color as the surrounding wall area, so that it blends in, or in a high-gloss bright color with an exciting frame treatment, it can look good and not take away from a normally exciting and new department. It is only when it becomes scratched and chipped looking with frayed edges (which happens easily) that pegboard begins to detract from the looks of a department.

Slotwall

Slotwall (Figure 5–21) is a fairly recent innovation that is taking the place of pegboard. It is a paneling with slots or grooves to accept certain fixture attachments so that merchandise can be either hung or shelved against the wall (Figure 5–22). The fixtures are made in either plexi, metal, or wood, and are made to fit the slots in the panel. Both the slotboard and the fixtures have become somewhat standardized by now and almost all fixtures will fit different manufacturers' slotwall. One important measurement to note when ordering fixtures is the width of the pieces of board between the grooves. The fixtures are made to fit over several widths and must be custom-ordered by width.

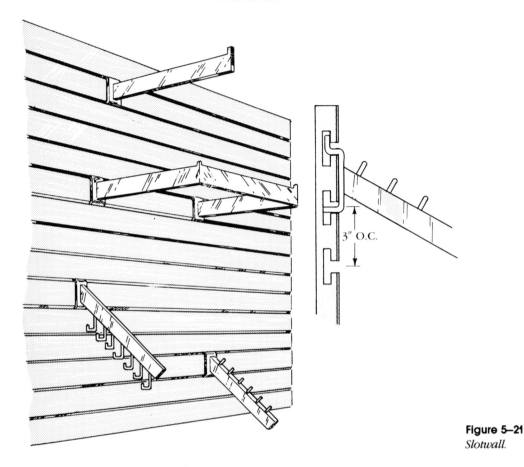

Figure 5–21
Slotwall.

Slotwall comes in many different finishes. As this paneling is being used to cover entire departments, it is necessary to take into account the different looks that the finishes can achieve. Natural wood is still the most popular finish and comes in a variety of woods. Natural wood gives a masculine as well as sporty look to a department. It is very appropriate for a boys' area, casual shoes, sporting goods, and housewares. For a dressier finish, mirror, plexi, brass or metal, wallpaper-covered, and painted slotwall can all give a more elegant or feminine look. Suede for a casual men's area can also work well for a dressier masculine atmosphere. Slotwall can be covered in any material that can be attached to wood. Its finish is limited only by imagination and budget.

Figure 5–22
Slotwall accessories. (A) Pin front-on waterfall. (B) Hook water fall. (C) Waterfall with holes for scarves. (D) 6" hook. (E) Shelf support. (F) Wood Shelf. (G) Clear plexi shelf. (H) Bracket. (I) Hang rod or shelf support. (J) Belts or ties. (K) Hat holder. (L) Plexi bin.
Credit: Edron Fixture Corp., N.Y., N.Y. .

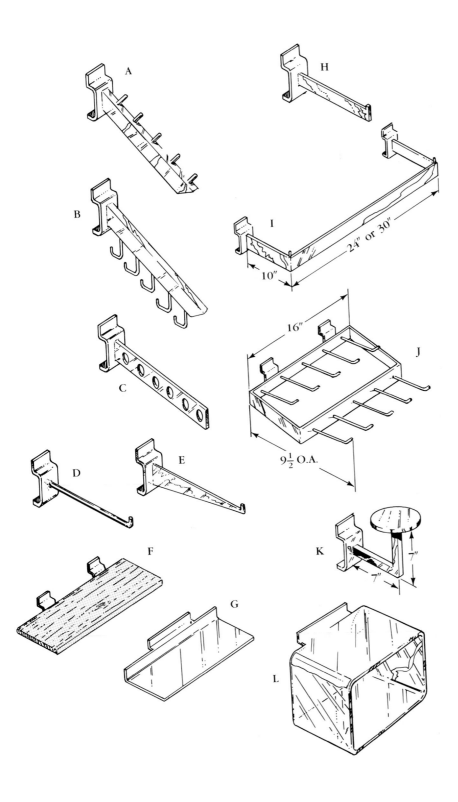

A

H

B

I

24" or 30"

10"

C

16"

J

D

E

$9\frac{1}{2}$ O.A.

F

K

7"

7"

G

L

Metal Grid

Metal grid, an outgrowth of the high-tech look, is quickly becoming a staple in housewares departments. Its professional look complements the hardware. Generally coming in standard 4' × 8' sheets, the grids are made up of 1/8" round metal rods with a grid pattern of custom sizes from 2 to 4". Many fixtures that are designed for slotwall have been redesigned for the new metal grid. The grids come in a large variety of metal finishes and colors.

SIGN HOLDERS

Sign holders (Figure 5–23) are fixtures that identify merchandise rather than

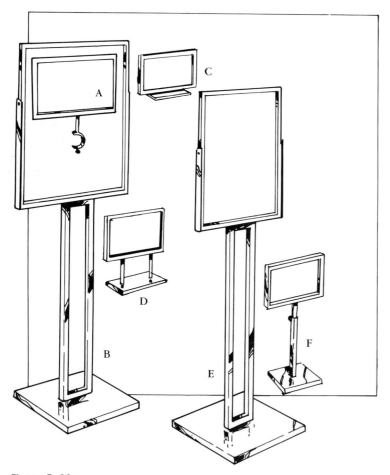

Figure 5–23

(A) Sign holder that attaches to hang rod. (B) Floor-standing sign holder. (C) Low-standing sign holder. (D) Higher standing sign holder (E) ½-sheet floor-standing sign holder. (F) Adjustable standing sign holder.

holding it. They will be discussed further in the chapters on signing and design, but several points are important to remember.

1. Sign holders and signs are usually the responsibility of the display department.

2. Continuity is essential when delegating sign holders to a department.

3. Each department should have the sign holder that best fits its decor. Generally, plexi works best because it's least visible. However, if there is a wide variety of sign holders and not enough of any one style to go around, the various materials should be kept together, i.e., the men's area all chrome, women's all brass, and accessories all plexi.

4. The sign holders should be double-signed when they can be viewed from all sides. There should be no blank spaces or empty sign holders on a floor. Outdated signs are even worse! A Valentine's Day sign on February 16 is laughable.

Fixturing is not what visual merchants think of when starting out in the field. It doesn't have the glamor of mannequins, windows, or exciting theatrical props— yet it is the backbone of a store. The right fixture in the right place can sell merchandise better than almost anything except a half-price sale. It's necessary for a visual merchant to understand how to use and merchandise fixtures in order to make a department work as a selling unit. Remember that each fixture has to act as an independent salesperson as well as working within a whole department to create a unified feeling.

TIPS TO REMEMBER

1. When ordering fixtures, ask the manufacturer to send the Allen wrenches for the fixture with the order. When the fixtures arrive, keep the Allen wrench in an envelope with the name of the fixture on the front of the envelope, so that if screws or bolts need to be tightened, the proper wrench is readily available.

2. Before attaching brackets to standards in the wall, check the length of the bracket to make sure that the length will accept hangers. If a bracket is 12″ long (from the wall) and the hanger is 14″, there will obviously be a problem. Also make sure that the bracket doesn't extend further than the valance. The lighting for the merchandise is often hidden in the valance and should shine evenly on the goods. If the merchandise hangs out beyond the light, it will appear dark and unappealing.

3. The clips for glass cube units are made of plexi blended with acrylic, Lexan (GE), or other substances. These clips are clear and look great, but can eventually stretch and lose their grip on the glass. Old clips should be stored together so as not to be confused with the new ones. When new clips

have to be ordered, the amount needed can be obtained by counting the old, collected clips. Since the clips cost up to 80 cents apiece, an accurate count can save a lot of money.

4. Glass shelves should be stored in an out-of-the-way space. Walls should be labeled by size and the shelves should be stacked by length, width, and depth for easy spotting. Rods and brackets should be stored the same way. Many hours are wasted trying to locate the right size fixture for a space.

5. If there are several types of standards used in a store, an inventory list of location and type is essential when brackets have to be ordered to fill in a department. Each department could be listed with the type of standard used in the different areas to facilitate ordering brackets.

PLACEMENT

The placement of fixtures help determine the amount of sales. There are several rules and years of experience on which to base fixture placement.

1. There must be at least 3′ between fixtures.

2. Major aisles must be (depending on the state) 4–8′ wide with 6′ being the most common width required.

3. No fixtures can block an exit or fire door and the aisle to that door is considered a major aisle.

4. Geometric aisle patterns within a department work best both visually and for customer sales. It's easier to follow an aisle than to skip all over a department.

5. Interest can be created by placing displays instead of a fixture within an aisle pattern. A display can also create an island to separate areas of a department.

6. A general floor plan for fixtures would be to have T-stands on the aisle, four-ways next in line, Bloomingdales behind the four-ways, and round racks as the last fixtures in the department, near the back walls. The progression is from small (size and capacity) in front to larger in back.

   In hard goods, cubes are in front while gondolas are toward the center and in the rear of the department.

7. Better (higher priced) stores will use fewer fixtures, show less stock, and tend to use T-stands and four-ways predominantly. An illusion of space and selective merchandising is required by these stores to sell higher priced goods.

   Mass merchandisers rely on fixtures with a higher item capacity to show as much stock as possible. They want to create excitement through quantity and color. To accomplish this they will "mass out" the merchandise on the selling floor using primarily quads, Bloomingdales, rounders, and T-stands for show up front. Cube units for folded merchandise are used in all stores.

8. Cube units are for folded items. Items that sell well folded are T-shirts, dress shirts, basic sweaters, flannel or novelty shirts, basic blue jeans, and the like. Naturally, the unfolded merchandise should be displayed on a countertop fixture on top of the cube unit.

9. Fixtures that are perfect for sales are tub tables, regular $3' \times 6'$ folding tables, round racks, and rectangular racks. Rolling racks (used to cart merchandise from one area to another) are occasionally used in stores for large, end-of-season sales.

SUMMARY CHECKLIST

Key Concepts

1. Fixtures are the most important element in the merchandising portion of the visual merchant's job.
2. Each fixture should perform a sales function by itself.
3. Security is an important consideration when utilizing fixtures.
4. Anything that stocks merchandise on a wall is considered a wall fixture.
5. The difference between an exciting merchandise presentation and a dull merchandise presentation is color and the placement of classifications.
6. Proper fixturing is necessary and takes time to accomplish.
7. Sign holders are fixtures that identify merchandise rather than display it.
8. Sign holders should be purchased with the department's decor in mind.

KEY TERMS

1. Quad rack
2. Stepped arrangement
3. Riser
4. Standards

DISCUSSION QUESTIONS

1. What are the advantages and disadvantages of Plexiglas as a countertop fixture?
2. How can the staining of a wood fixture provide the feeling or look desired?
3. List the various types of floor fixtures and the advantages/disadvantages of each.
4. In what situations would you use a gondola as a display fixture?
5. Why are standards considered one of the most important types of wall fixtures?
6. What precautions are necessary when working with glass shelving?
7. What are the advantages of slotwall over pegboard?
8. What considerations should be taken into account when using sign holders?

9. Why is fixturing an important aspect of the visual merchandising field?
10. Prior to attaching brackets to standards in the wall, what things should be considered?

STUDENT EXERCISES

Number 1

Assume the role of a visual merchandising assistant in a small department store. Utilizing an interior display case and several countertop fixtures, prepare a display that will emphasize an upcoming holiday season, such as Christmas, Easter, etc.

Number 2

Identify two retail clothing establishments in your community. Identify the display fixtures that are utilized throughout the store. Compare the two stores using the following questions as a guide:
A. What types of floor fixtures are utilized?
    1. Which floor fixture is utilized in most shops? Why?
    2. Are the floor fixtures appropriate for the store's image?
B. What type of wall fixtures are utilized?
    1. Which wall fixture is utilized in most displays/shops? Why?
    2. Are the wall fixtures appropriate for the store's image?
C. Do the sign holders identify the merchandise and fit the department decor?
D. What fixtures would you change? Why?

CASE PROBLEM 1

The Appropriate Fixtures

The McWhinney Company has operated a small, general-merchandise store for the past 30 years. The store is located in a rural setting in the southern part of the country. The store has a yearly sales volume of $625,000 and employs twenty to thirty salespersons. The merchandise is medium-priced and the store owners make no attempt to carry either higher priced or discount merchandise.

During the past three years, several competitors have opened stores in nearby communities, and the McWhinney profit has decreased accordingly. Mr. Ralph Appleton, the store manager, has been with the company for the past 10 years and is becoming very concerned about the decrease in profits.

Linda Smith has been employed as sales manager/visual merchandising manager for the past six years. Linda is very knowledgeable in the area of retail sales and has refused several job offers in order to continue working for the McWhinney Company.

Over coffee one morning, Ralph and Linda were discussing the profit decline when Linda suggested that maybe the problem was not the operating expenses but rather the image conveyed by the old fixtures in the store. She noted that customer traffic has also decreased. Linda suggested the purchase of all new fixtures to change the image of each department. Ralph said he would think about it.

One week later, Ralph presented Linda with the new store layout and told her to begin purchasing the appropriate fixtures for each department!

Activities for Completion

1. List by department the types of fixtures that should be purchased.
2. Describe the types of merchandise that will be utilized with each specific fixture by department.
3. Prepare a rough sketch of each department, showing the placement of major fixtures.

CASE PROBLEM 2

The Small Store

The Unique Shop is a newly established business scheduled to open during the summer of next year. The new store is owned by Ted and Alice Sample. Neither Ted nor Alice has ever had any previous retail experience. The Unique Shop is located in a small college town with a population of 40,000. The majority of the people living in the community have college degrees and the university is the main industry.

The store is small, measuring 20×20 with 400 square feet of selling space. Through research conducted during the past years, Ted and Alice decided to sell various types of novelity items, such as:

Cards	Small collector items
Small gifts	Woven baskets
Humorous gifts	Pottery
Small games and puzzles	Brass
Stuffed animals	University spirit items

With the business scheduled to open in approximately six months, Ted and Alice developed a summary checklist of all activities that had to be completed. In reviewing the checklist, it became obvious that one major decision had not been made—what fixtures to buy.

Activities for Completion

Develop a list of all display fixtures that will be needed in the store. Assume the building is presently empty, the floors are carpeted, walls are of a dry-wall material, and the ceiling is a suspended variety hung at a height of $8'$.

CHAPTER 6

Mannequins

LEARNING OBJECTIVES

At the completion of this chapter, you will be able to:

1. Explain why mannequins contribute more to the image of a store than any other prop or fixture.

2. Describe the evolution of mannequins over the years, from the first wax figures to the present fiberglass forms.

3. List the types of mannequins that can be purchased.

4. Cite the importance of using "movement" in mannequin presentations.

5. Explain the basic principles to follow when utilizing mannequins.

6. List the proper sequence for dressing and undressing a mannequin.

7. Analyze descriptive information prior to purchasing mannequins.

Mannequins have been called props, fixtures, silent salespeople, and dummies. They are actually a combination of all four. Mannequins, more than any prop or fixture, contribute to the image of a store. Realistic mannequins are looked on as people. They have names (given by the manufacturer) and different attitudes depending on their faces and stances.

Mannequins have evolved over the years from large-scale wax figures that melted in the heat to paper maché bodies that shrank when they dried. Plaster forms so heavy that they had to be lifted by two or more persons were next. Today's incarnation is lightweight made of durable fiberglass forms, sprayed with a thin plaster coating to give the look of human skin. Only the removable joints contain metal that is embedded into the fiberglass. The rest of the figure is hollow.

All adult, full-form mannequins have removable arms, legs, hands, and a torso that can be separated from the legs. This is to aid in dressing and undressing the figures. Forms of small children will usually have only the arms removable.

All mannequins are designed to express an individual personality or attitude. An attitude comprises pose, facial expression, posture, and total personality of a form. Each face and/or stance relays a message to the observer. The faces can be pouty, sullen, mischievous, sexy, happy, or the ever-popular bored look. The figure poses range from fashionable to arrogant, diving to seductive reclining. The range is limited only by the natural boundaries of human movement.

Attitude, another word for personality, is the most important aspect of a mannequin's look. Mannequins should be bought and used in a specific area because of their attitudes. Fashionably bored and haughty personalities are suited to higher priced designer fashion departments. Wild, sexy looks add excitement to contemporary up-to-the-minute fashions while conservative poses and faces are appropriate to traditional departments. Logic dictates which mannequins will work best for each area.

Mannequins come in different categories:

- Full-adult realistic and abstract forms—standing—male and female

- Full-adult realistic and abstract forms—seated—male and female

- Full-adult realistic and abstract—sports figures—male and female

- Full-adult realistic and abstract—reclining—male and female

- Full-adult realistic and abstract—standing—petite—female

- Full-adult realistic and abstract—standing—large-size—male and female

- Junior male and female versions

- Children's versions

- Preteen versions

- Full-adult realistic male or female—duo—two mannequins designed to work as a combo, and

- Abstract parts of body forms, including ½ torso—male or female; Legs—alone; Heads—alone; Headless bodies; Hands; and Feet

These abstract partial forms are characterized as fixtures because they have no attitude or personality. Rather than create a feeling, they serve only to show merchandise on a full-rounded form. These forms are important because they demonstrate the function of the merchandise, e.g., leg-warmers on a leg form, while taking up less space and budget than a full-form mannequin.

Half-figures, e.g., torsos without heads, heads without torsos, and legs alone, are made to show specific items and should be used accordingly. The clothes shouldn't droop or look unnatural on the short-form body (as in the cutoff legs of some male forms, or the bust forms for female and male sweaters). The merchandise can be folded under itself so that it hangs on the body in a natural way.

Moving mannequins and figures, known as animated figures, have been used for years for Christmas windows. Usually only animals and small figures are animated, but recently larger scale human forms have been devised for realistic movement.

Simple mechanics have been used as well as sophisticated computer technology to create robotic mannequins. A combination of pneumatic valves (using air pressure), pistons, and a computer program has been developed to make full-scale mannequins move with the fluidity and irregularity of human movement. The computer program can regulate how and when the movements occur. The valves regulate how far and how fast each piston's rods move. The entire range of human movement can be imitated by the exact placement of the pistons and the clever programming of the computer board. The computer can control a wide range of movements that are not necessarily limited to a human form. A piston can move any inanimate object to which it is connected. One company in Japan has developed lifelike mannequins for department stores. In the United States three companies are in the robotic business so far. Only one markets (identifies where it wants to sell its product) to the retail industry. This new field predicts an exciting future for mannequins. Although computerized mannequins are more expensive, their range of movements make the extra expense worthwhile. Regular mannequins are designed for one movement. Any change in that posture makes the form look awkward and unnatural.

A computer may eventually run not only the mannequins and displays, but also the lights, air or heat conditioning, and the sales registers. The future of computer technology is today!

Traditional fiberglass and plaster will continue to be important in the future as the "attitudes" and "personalities" evolve to reflect changing roles in society.

HOW TO USE A MANNEQUIN

Basic principles work for every style of mannequin. In the beginning of your career in retailing all mannequins may look the same. The differences between misses and juniors, contemporary and traditional, men and young men will seem both slight and inconsequential. When mannequins are bought for a department it's because their expression and image convey the message of the particular area. Switching mannequins around can cause visual and conceptual confusion in a store. Customers react subliminally to a junior figure and identify the department because of the mannequin. Often it's difficult to tell the difference between a junior and misses department judging by the merchandise content alone. The mannequin's face and body stance as well as the size range (odd numbers) may identify a junior department if a department sign isn't visible.

The confusion that could arise from the incorrect placement of mannequins can be easily avoided. Don't move mannequins from area to area until you can judge their "attitude" and age accurately. A demure missy next to a sultry and sexy missy looks like the odd couple. The merchandise statement is confusing because it's a contradiction of attitude and image. Why are those two "people" standing together? Only a grocery or movie line would attract two such disparate types.

Mannequins' personalities can clash as do persons' in real life. Always judge the attitudes that are being combined before placing figures together.

Keeping mannequins from the same manufacturer together is one way to ensure harmony. If this isn't practical or possible, related attitudes and skin tones will help create the desired relationship.

THE NUTS AND BOLTS OF MANNEQUINS

Along with knowing where to set up mannequins, it is equally important to understand how. Each mannequin has a fulcrum, a center of balance. Usually this balance is centered between the legs. In the case of some male mannequins the balance point is located in the back of the calf. The hole at the point of balance (either in the leg or crotch) accepts a pole that slips into it supported by a base plate to stand the mannequin upright (Figure 6–1).

The base plate is usually constructed of metal and shatterproof glass. The metal holder bolts into the glass. The pole fits into the metal holder and is secured by a small screw that goes through the holder to the rod. When a mannequin arrives in the store or when it is standing perfectly balanced, mark the back of the rod where the screw hits it. As explained in Chapter 4, a properly balanced mannequin will stay upright much longer than one that is balanced in a hit-or-miss fashion.

Mannequins may also be wired to the floor. This will only work effectively in untrafficked areas. Windows and other areas removed from the customer's reach and path are appropriate for wired mannequins. Wiring is done with a heavy-gauge, black-annealed wire. This is attached to the screw at the fulcrum and stretched to the floor. It is then wrapped around a nail that is driven into the floor at an angle. Sometimes two wires stretched in opposite directions will be sturdier. The wire should be stretched so tight that it "twangs" when touched.

In Chapter 3, a sample of the tools necessary for changing a mannequin was given. The items most often used are:

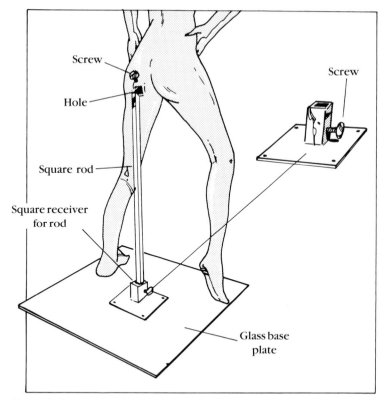

Figure 6–1
A rear rod and the entry area into the mannequin and the receiving base.

1. Hair brush (wire or plastic teeth)

2. Bobby pins (in different colors to match all wig colors)

3. Covered rubber bands and barrettes

4. Masking tape (2–3″ wide, rolled and placed on the head to help secure the wig)

5. Flat-head screwdriver (for the base and rod)

6. "Fantastic" spray (to remove old makeup)

7. A selection of makeup: powdered rouge, powdered eye shadows, pencils, and lipstick with a brush

8. Rags (to clean off makeup and any smudge marks on the mannequin's skin)

9. Ammonia and water plus rags (to clean off the glass plates)

10. False eyelashes (if used in the store)

UNDRESSING AN ADULT MANNEQUIN

Undress an adult mannequin as follows:

1. Take the wig off gently and put it in a safe place, out of the flow of traffic.

2. Remove both hands and place them to either side of the mannequin. They will either unscrew, pull out, or twist off.

3. Remove both arms by either twisting carefully (Figure 6–2) or pulling out, and place them also on either side.

4. Take off all the upper body clothing and either hang it up immediately or give it to the sales manager.

5. Twist the torso off the legs (or pull it off) and place it near the arms and hands.

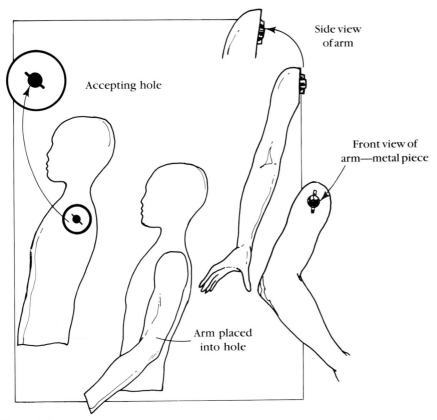

Figure 6–2

Twisting an arm off a mannequin allows the metal pieces to line up so that the arm can be gently removed from the torso.

6. Remove the legs by untightening the screw at the top of the pole and lifting the legs off the stand.

7. Remove the shoes, socks, and slacks or skirt, and return them to the sales manager. The shoes may mean a trip to the shoe department. Kill two birds with one stone by returning the used shoes and borrowing new ones for the new outfit.

8. Since the mannequin is now dismantled and in pieces on the floor, start immediately to dress the form to avoid customer visual distress resulting from viewing a nude and dismembered body and the possibility of theft of any loose parts.

DRESSING A MANNEQUIN

After the mannequin is dismantled, start by making sure all the clothes are pressed and wrinkle-free. The pressing should be done *before* the mannequin is initially undressed.

1. Put on panty hose or socks if needed.

2. Put on the skirt or slacks by taking the legs off of the rod and base and turning them upside down.

3. Put the shoes back on the feet and place the mannequin back on the stand.

4. Slip the rod back into both holes—the fulcrum and base plate.

5. Twist or slot the torso back onto the leg section.

6. Slip the top merchandise over the torso. Make sure the sleeve holes are lined up so the arms can slip through easily.

7. Add the hands to the wrists. Make sure the hands are in the position for which they were designed.

8. Place the styled wig onto the head.

9. Check the mannequin to make sure the clothes are on straight and all the tags are tucked in.

10. Check the entire mannequin area to make sure that the platform and surrounding area is clean.

1. *Put on panty hose or socks if needed.* Panty hose can either have a hole poked through the crotch (to allow for the balancing pole) or be pulled up half-mast under dresses and skirts. Make sure that the half-mast does not show through slinky clothing. If a smooth look is needed, the hose should be pulled up all the way to the waist. A medium size is needed for most full-adult female mannequins, although small may better fit others. If a run develops in the toe, or if only

hose with reinforced toes are available in the necessary color (and you're using sandals), knot the toe and push it under the foot. The knot will prevent the run from ruining the total stocking and will create a more attractive and stylish look for sandle-toed shoes.

Panty hose are a strong fashion statement. Always talk to the hosiery buyer and look through fashion magazines to find out the current trends in color. There are four basic panty hose fashions: textured legs, colored legs (opaque or translucent), natural color, and very pale or dark sheer tones.

The fashions change yearly from dark hose with dark shoes, to light or white hose with dark or light shoes. Just like hemlines, panty hose fashions change in order to stimulate more sales.

Panty hose usually must be bought by the visual merchandising department and goes on the VM budget. Check on the procedure before taking anything out of the department.

Socks for male mannequins should match the suit color. For sportswear, check the fashions of the times via *Gentleman's Quarterly* or *L'Uomo.*

Women's sock are usually sport socks, knee socks, or leg warmers. Leg warmers are worn *over* the pants and knee socks are worn under slacks or with preppy skirt looks.

2. *Put on the skirt or slacks by taking the legs off of the rod and base and turning them upside down.* The balancing rod will either fit up one of the legs or have to go through a slit in the seam of the crotch. Examine the undressed mannequin while it's supported on its rod to determine where the rod enters and if it's closer to one side or the other (Figure 6–3).

Some unfortunate and thoughtless mistakes have been made in the beginning of a display career. In a real-life incident a new VM (in the first week of her first job as a display assistant in a large department store) slit the back of a pair of designer wool slacks with a knife in the back. Told to "cut the pants"—and not knowing what the visual merchandising department did with the window merchandise after taking it off display—the new person assumed that the Anne Klein slacks had to be cut at the rod and ruined so that the rod would fit properly. Never considering the possibility of slitting the seam in the crotch was an example of uncreative and impractical thinking.

When confronted by a problem, think out all the alternatives before ruining the merchandise or the mannequin. Twisting the support rod into a different position so it fits down the leg of a pair of pants will throw the mannequin off balance. It will start to tilt unevenly on its stand and look drunk. This is much less amusing to a visual merchandising director than it is to the assistants.

Make sure to have the proper size pants. Too large pants look unfashionable and when belted, like the figure is wearing diapers. Pants too small won't close or zip and will frustrate the visual merchant as well as potentially ruining the merchandise. Rather than "waste the time" going back for the proper size, many visual merchants will try to make a pair of pants fit by stretching them until they close. Obviously, the cost in time and money makes this laziness foolish. One year

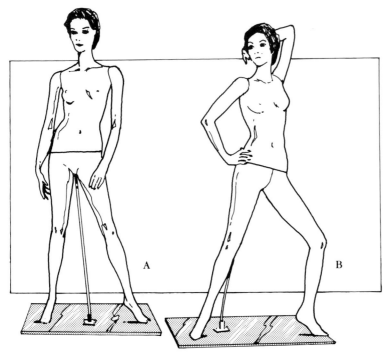

Figure 6–3
In A, the rod is positioned such that if pants are put on the mannequin, they will have to be split in the seam. In B, the rod is close to the balancing leg and will fit up a pant leg. No seams will need to be split with this positioning.

transparent plastic jeans came out in the market and were first shown at Bonwit Teller. Not only did the pant sizes run small, but they didn't stretch at all. A mannequin that would normally wear a size 8 jean needed a size 12 plastic jean. Before taking merchandise from a department, ask the salespeople how the size of the chosen garment runs. Is it running large, small, or just right? That way you can determine in advance what size to sign out to avoid extra trips and wasted time.

Some male mannequins have their support rods going into a hole in the calf of one leg. Both male and female mannequins can be dressed most easily while the legs are upside down. Flip up the proper pant leg on the male's slacks so that the rod fits into the leg hole more easily (Figure 6–4).

3. *Put the shoes back on the feet and place the mannequin back on the stand.* Sounds easy? This can be very difficult if you're unsure of the mannequin's foot size. If you've received new mannequins, call the manufacturer to find out the proper shoe size. Trial and error work best for old mannequins. Usually someone within the VM department will know by heart the shoe size worn by each mannequin. If you're unsure, always use the larger size. A lot of time and effort can be wasted trying to squeeze a small shoe on a large foot (remember Cinderella?). The shoe

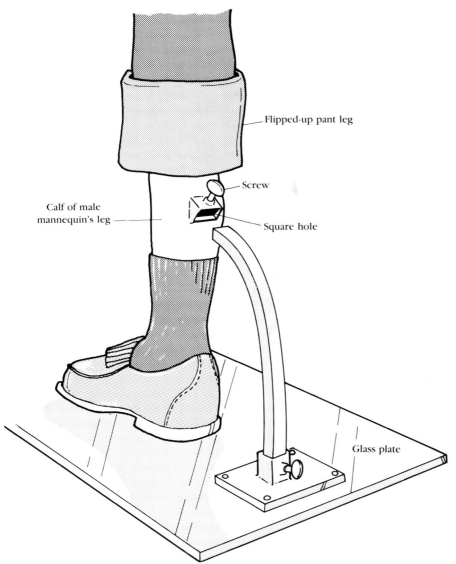

Flipped-up pant leg

Screw

Calf of male
mannequin's leg

Square hole

Glass plate

Figure 6—4
Flip up the pant legs of male mannequins so the rod installation is easier.

can be ruined so that it cannot be sold and is then charged to the display
department budget. Marking the correct shoe size on the bottom of the foot or on
the back of the base plate (lightly) is helpful for future reference.

If a mannequin is standing in a position that requires one or both feet to be in a
flexed position, creases will develop along the toe of the shoe thereby ruining it for
resale. Obviously, this can get very expensive and mannequins with flexed toes

should be avoided when buying them new. If you're stuck with several, make the best of a difficult situation. If and when shoes are ruined by the flexed toes and have to be bought by display, try to use the same shoes over and over. Buying a good basic stylish but classic shoe each season will help solve this problem.

If the mannequin is primarily with a misses dress department, a light-colored taupe pump will be appropriate from spring to fall. A darker colored taupe will be nicer from fall to spring. Sandals will sometimes fit and bend with this type of foot—if the straps fall in the right places.

Boots are also easily ruined by the unyielding nature of mannequin feet. Considering the high cost of boots, obviously much care must be taken to avoid ruining the merchandise. Use a boot size two to three sizes larger than the normal shoe size. This way, the foot will not touch or stretch the inside of the boot at any point. It will also be a lot easier to get a larger boot on a resisting foot than a correctly sized boot.

The basic rule for shoes or boots is to never force them on. Always use a shoehorn instead of breaking (creasing) the back of the shoe. Once the shoes or boots are in place, carefully slip the mannequin over and place it on its rod and plate.

4. *Slip the rod into both holes—the fulcrum and base plate.* If the rod has been marked properly to indicate where the back is, it should slip easily into both holes (the mannequin's and the base plate's). Now, the legs are standing—dressed with stocking or socks, pants, and shoes. If a skirt is desired, now is the time to slip it over the hips.

5. *Twist or slot the torso back onto the leg section.* Try to hold all the mannequin parts in places where grease and dirt from your hands won't show once the form is clothed.

6. *Slip the top merchandise over the torso. Make sure the sleeve holes are lined up so the arms can slip through easily.* Slipping the top merchandise over the torso is a step that has to be thought out in advance. Remember, the arms have to go through all the layers at once. Assume that a male mannequin is wearing a shirt, tie, sweater vest, sportjacket, and light overcoat. The sequence would be to put the shirt on—leaving the first four buttons undone, then the vest, jacket—pulling the sleeves through both so they go naturally into the sportcoat's sleeves, and then pulling all the sleeves of the sportcoat through the sleeves of the overcoat. It's logical, but it sounds confusing. The three buttons are left undone because both arms now have to slip in through the open neck of the shirt, through the sleeves of the shirt, jacket, and coat, and slip into the armholes in the shoulder. This is a two-handed job for the visual merchant. One arm keeps the neck of the shirt open while the other slides one arm of the mannequin in at a time. Then, feeling for the armhole with one hand, the other hand tries to fit the arm's hardware into the slot. Experiment several times to get the feel of this procedure while the mannequin is undressed before attempting anything as complicated as the given example.

After tucking the shirt into the pants and pulling the vest down, knot the tie. Some people learn to knot ties on themselves and can only approach ties from that angle. Others can easily knot ties on a mannequin's neck. Either way, learn a good knot by asking the best-dressed man in the store how he knots his tie. A tie salesperson should know what knot is stylish that year and how to tie it.

Straighten the vest and shirt collar. Adjust the sportcoat and overcoat. Never button more than one button on a sport or suit jacket. The middle button is the only button ever closed. On a man's suit vest, the bottom button is never buttoned. To button it is considered poor taste.

7. *Add the hands to the wrists. Make sure the hands are in the position for which they were designed.* Add the hands to the wrists of the mannequin's arms. Adjust them so they appear to be in a natural position. The wrist sections should match. It's very tempting to move the arms and hands into positions that fit a specific situation. An example would be twisting a hand up to hold an apple or clutch bag when the hand is supposed to be facing down. Mannequins are sculpted from human figures. The position it is in is physically correct. Any variation of the form makes it look awkward. Shoulders change their shape with each arm movement and tendons in the forearms move with different hand movements.

Realistic mannequins are designed to parody humans. Try to see the movements with a choreographer's eye. If a position looks inhuman, the subconscious impression in the customer's eye will be that of a dummy. The theory and purpose of a mannequin's attitude influencing a customer's impression of a store will be destroyed. No one wants to look like a dummy!

8. *Place the styled wig onto the head.* Think twice before automatically placing the same wig back on the mannequin. Look at the new outfit and judge what color and style hair would best compliment the new clothing. Try switching wigs with another mannequin, if necessary, to achieve a fresher look. Using a wig brush, gently comb the wig out to a desired style. Using hair spray on the selling floor is dangerous and annoying. Hair spray can be used if the wig is styled in the shop before coming onto the floor.

9. *Check the mannequin to make sure the clothes are on straight and all the tags are tucked in.* Make sure clothing is straight, falls properly, and merchandise tags and tickets are tucked out of sight. Always hide the tickets and vendor tags. Vendor tags can be removed and put into a pocket, or hung down the inside back of a garment. Sales tickets should never be removed for any reason. On a hat or jewelry the tags may hang in unattractive places. In these special cases, remove the ticket and carefully pin it or tape it (don't put tape over any printing) into the crown of the hat or with jewelry, slip the tag where it's not as visible, e.g., the back of the neck, under a wig, behind an ear, or on the underside of a wrist.

10. *Check the entire mannequin area to make sure that the platform and surrounding area is clean.* Is the platform clean? Is the mannequin secure on its base? Are any tools left around? Are any pieces of clothing scattered? Has everything been signed out that requires signing?

Although this seems like a lot to do in order to undress and dress a mannequin, it's really basic—just mechanics compared with understanding fashion and making a strong fashion statement with each figure.

WIGS

Wigs were mentioned briefly in the dressing sequence. A person who understands wigs is very valuable to any display department. As with any skill, practice makes better. There is no perfection with wig styling, but creativity goes a long way toward imaginative styling. Every six months a new "look" is in. Sometimes short, cropped hair is fashionable; the next month, wild, loose manes of hair are "in"; then classic page-boys that are worn by Breck models come into style. A large variety of wigs should be available within the visual merchant department. Good mannequin wigs are priced depending on length of hair, style of cut, and quality of fiber.

There are three main fibers used today for soft-style mannequin wigs: Kanelkalon, Elura, and Luraflex.

Kanelkalon (olefin, generic classification) is the softest fiber and the most like human hair, yet it can only be set once. The style and curl are heat-set (baked) into the thermoplastic synthetic polymer fiber used for wigs at the factory. The fiber is rolled over different widths of pipe and then baked to set the curl. The size of the pipe, the temperature, and the length of baking time determines how curly the fibers become. Kanelkalon will keep its original style after repeated washings, but it can never be changed to another style. It is the least expensive fiber of the three.

Elura can be reset after washing but is less soft and natural looking.

A new fiber, Luraflex combines the best qualities of each fiber. Created for Jacqueline Wigs (New York City), this fiber—like Elura—is less affected by hot lights, is as soft as Kanelkalon, and can be set and reset in many different styles.

The Luraflex is a new fiber in an industry where the biggest changes are normally in fashion. Styles change so quickly that the wig industry has to constantly be a year ahead to have the desired wigs for sale when they're needed.

Hard, lacquered wigs were used exclusively in early mannequin displays. They are still occasionally used by some stores and manufacturers depending on the situation. Hard wigs are horsehair and can be set into outlandish styles and then lacquered. These wigs are made to fit specific heads (the soft wigs are elasticized and fit almost all heads). The major problem with hard wigs is their lack of versatility. Once they're shaped and lacquered, that's it. When they start to fall apart, nothing can really save them. Glue will work for a while but can look unprofessional and patchy.

New wigs have been introduced with strands of gold and silver metallic fiber woven in for a very dressy look.

A mannequin should receive a wig that fits its face and body as well as its image. The wig can change the entire appearance of a mannequin and should be selected carefully.

To keep a wig selection fresh, repackage every wig not in use in a ziplock or plain plastic bag. Brush the wig well before storing. Fold it as neatly as possible to keep the original shape.

Soft wigs made of Elura or Luraflex can be lacquered and then washed out and reset. Wig stands are used to hold the wig in order to style it properly. Ideally, the wig stand should be clamped to a table so that vigorous brushing won't lift the head off the surface. The wig itself should be joined to the stand by T-pins. On the selling floor, as mentioned earlier, masking tape rolled into 2″ pieces will hold the wig onto the head.

Combs, barrettes, braids, ponytails, and other hair ornaments should be worked into the wig before placing the wig on the mannequin's head, if possible. If accessories are attached in advance, they can be put in more securely.

For a final touch, use hair spray in moderation, but the wigs will have to be washed more often when they've been sprayed.

MAKEUP

When a mannequin is bought from a manufacturer, the face can be ordered in several ways: full-face makeup, very light makeup, or just features, e.g., eyes, mouth, and darkened nostrils painted on the surface.

In larger stores that have an extensive staff of visual merchandisers, the luxury exists of individually making up each mannequin before placing it in the window. The mannequins for this purpose are purchased with just their features painted on so that eye makeup, blush, and lipstick can be applied in the shop. This way, makeup promotions can be displayed along with the clothing, e.g., Estée Lauder's collection for Missoni. Estée Lauder's cosmetics line collaborated with Missoni (Italian manufacturer of fine knits known for their quality of colors, fabric, and design) for advertising purposes. Both reestablished their exclusivity in the eyes of their customers by identifying with each other in large magazine campaigns. Estée Lauder created colors that worked well with the new Missoni line. In a window presentation, all the mannequins were made up with Estée Lauder Missoni makeup and wore Missoni's new clothing line. The window copy explained the promotion in a few well-chosen words: "Estée Lauder and Missoni—a colorful combination."

Makeup should be applied in the shop and off the selling floor. It's tempting to apply makeup directly as needed, but merchandise can easily be ruined if proper care isn't taken.

To remove old makeup, squirt the bare face (no wig or clothing on the torso) with Fantastic. Rub the makeup off with a terry cloth rag—but don't rub the painted eyes or mouth too hard.

Different quality and brands of mannequins have different skin finishes. Some are grainy and rough while others are exceptionally smooth and nontextured. A little texture is needed for the makeup to appear the most natural. If the skin is completely smooth, the makeup doesn't "set" in spots and begins to look smeared and streaked. Since human skin has a light texture, cosmetics are made to work best with texture.

Makeup from the cosmetics department can be applied with care directly to a mannequin's face. Powder blushes will usually work well if slightly moist. Cream rouges work best, but use a cosmetic sponge to spread the color on evenly. Gel rouges will stain the VM's hands and the surface of the mannequin. They are very strong and must be applied perfectly the first time. It may be best to avoid their use. The aggravation isn't worth the results.

Creamy-powdered eye shadows are best for the upper and lower eye. Hard pencils will skip over the slight bumps in the surface of the plaster and are more difficult to blend. New eye color pencils have been introduced that combine cream and powder that work well on mannequins. Frosty eye shadows will catch the lights and will either be very effective for a dressy outfit or seem inappropriate and tacky. Makeup should be chosen carefully to compliment the merchandise. Unless a sign indicates otherwise, the makeup isn't being advertised—the clothes are!

Lipstick should be put on with a brush and reapplied every day to avoid having dust stick to the lips. If this is not feasible for the size of your department, leave the mannequin's original lipstick color. An unfortunate choice of mediums for lip color is nail polish. Don't use it—ever! Even though it goes on smoothly and stays glossy, it looks very unnatural and is difficult to remove. Any errors made when applying nail polish to the lips can be damaging to the surface of the plaster when corrected. Acetone nail polish remover is a solvent that also dissolves the paint on the surface of the mannequin so that the entire torso needs to be repainted. Nail polish belongs on the nails, in clean, nonsmudged strokes.

Following are some makeup tips:

1. Always ask for touchup paint when ordering new mannequins or when sending them out for repair. Mannequins chip very easily and need constant maintenance.

2. Removing makeup can eventually wear away the face paint.

3. Rather than going to the expense of having the entire form resprayed, touch up paint can be used in-house in a spray gun or brushed on lightly with a straight-cut, natural-bristle brush.

Study *Vogue* for new makeup styles. Experiment on an old mannequin in your spare time before attempting to make up a new one.

Again, look closely at the mannequin's face. Is it a junior, missy, preteen, preppy, high-fashion, sexy, or new-wave look (Figures 6–5 through 6–10)? Analyze what look or image the mannequin has and what she will be wearing (male mannequins rarely, if ever, need makeup unless it's a special promotion or an avant garde look). Gear the makeup to the face, attitude, and clothing. High-fashion makeup on a sweet, unglamorous face tends to look unrealistic and cheap. Sweet faces work best with simple makeup jobs. Sexy faces work well with all types of makeup as do high-fashion faces. Young girlish faces look as if they're playing dress-up in high-fashion makeup. Preteens look like young punks with too much makeup; a natural look is required on younger mannequins. Check *Seventeen* for makeup styles for teenagers and nontrendy juniors.

The best sources for learning are *Vogue, Seventeen,* and the local dance clubs—rock, disco, and punk—where the latest trends will be seen fresh on the faces of potential customers.

Figure 6–5
An Adele Rootstein junior active (but not sporty) mannequin. A subtle, sexy look for the junior customer.

Figure 6–6
D. G. Williams children's mannequins. They make some of the best children's mannequins in the business.

Figure 6–7
These interacting mannequins are made to work together. They are by Greneker.

Figure 6–8
A seated adult woman by Adele Rootstein. An elegant bored look—somewhat petulant.

Figure 6–9
A terrific example of a mannequin house display. These are active male runners interacting with stiff, priest like figures. The see-saws are actually moving up and down.
Credit: Toshihisa Hagawa. Director, Poil Kyoya, Tokyo, Japan, 1982.

Figure 6–10
Large-size woman's figure by Greneker. She looks a little mean.
The coat was draped over one shoulder to the other side of her figure
where her hand is on her hip.

BUYING MANNEQUINS

Buying a mannequin is probably more fun than any other single display purchase. It's a little like buying a big doll—and a lot more expensive. An average adult mannequin retails anywhere from $300 to $900 in 1983 depending on quality, style, country of manufacture, and quantity. Some manufacturers will have a lower price for a larger order while others refuse to give a discount to anyone, ever.

The variety of poses is extensive and ranges from high-fashion poses to diving, running, or handstanding acrobatics.

The first thing to judge when determining what pose fits an area is if that pose will allow for certain clothing restrictions. A large space between the legs on a female mannequin may work for full skirts, but makes dressing in straight skirts and most lingerie impossible. Check the pose carefully and determine what future problems may occur before choosing that particular pose (Figure 6–11).

Different poses suggest different attitudes and, as was discussed earlier in the chapter, the attitude must suit the department image and merchandise. A mannequin must be bought to fit a specific need. In a smaller store it must also be versatile enough to use in other areas as needed.

For example, abstract fashionable feminine mannequins are perfect for lingerie. An abstract mannequin doesn't have a painted face. It may or may not even have sculpted features. The hair may be suggested by a sculpted look or the head may be totally bald. Usually the neck and hands are elongated to give a more ethereal and fashionable image. Because the form is abstract, it can get away with

Figure 6–11
*This is a junior mannequin that has a shy demeanor and widespread legs.
Because of these legs, this mannequin cannot easily wear a straight skirt.*

sheer illusion, whereas realistic mannequins are required to look "real." The abstract forms are efficient in lingerie because they can be changed frequently by the sales manager without their hair or makeup being ruined. Lingerie is also the easiest apparel to change because it slips on and off easily. It should be changed often as lingerie is often an impulse item.

Male mannequins should be bought carefully. Many look effeminate and the image they project may subconsciously turn off prospective customers. Men are as conscious of fashion and image as women. Don't ever underestimate the impact of a good fashion presentation on a male form. Men look to mannequins for dress styles in the same way women do—just less often.

Male mannequins, like female, can be conservative, junior, sexy, fun, serious, fashionable, and dumb looking. Naturally, stay away from the dummies (Figure 6–12).

If you're having a difficult time reading the attitude and image of a mannequin, try to bring it to life. What kind of person does this form resemble? What kind of clothes would this person wear? Where would he or she be most likely to wear them?

Summary of Mannequin Buying

1. Determine the pose and personality appropriate for the area for which it is being bought.

2. Check the pose to make sure many different styles of clothing will fit on the figure.

Figure 6–12
Male and female adult mannequins.

3. Pick a skin tone that compliments the merchandise and the skin tone of the other mannequins in the store.

4. Choose a subtle makeup. More can always be added later.

5. Specify whether you want a metal or glass base plate and if you want the rod to slip into the rear or through the foot.

6. Order the mannequins at least six to eight weeks in advance of the deadline for their use on the floor.

7. Mannequins are ordered by:

    a. Style number for body pose

    b. Style number for face

    c. Style number for makeup

    d. Style number for skin tone

    e. Painted or unpainted nails

    f. Eyelashes (yes or no)

    g. Painted or glass eyes

    h. Horsehair wig (yes or no)

    i. Extra set of arms and/or hands (breakage is high on these parts), and

    j. Touch-up paint (if offered by manufacturer)

CARE AND STORAGE OF MANNEQUINS

Mannequins are very fragile. Even though they are made of plaster-coated fiberglass, they can crack, scratch, and break easily. Extreme care must be taken in their handling and storage.

Following are some tips:

1. Always keep the rod and base plate with the mannequin.

2. Store the mannequin upright in an untrafficked area.

3. Put a plastic dry cleaners bag over the head and tie it around the neck.

4. If arms or legs need to be separated from the torso, make sure they are marked with the mannequin's number and placed in a safe area where they can't fall down and chip.

5. Fantastic (or a similar cleanser) will remove fingerprints from the skin surface.

Mannequins are expensive and fragile. Proper care can keep a mannequin looking fresh for several years.

A last point to remember is something fashion designers and Madison Avenue advertisers have understood and successfully used for years: sex sells.

Sex doesn't mean cheap or sleazy, but seductive and alluring. A projection of elegant sensuality combined with a self-assured attitude makes any clothing look terrific. It's an attitude many people want to project or emulate.

A perfect example is an Adel Rootstein mannequin (a popular English manufacturer) that was located in the better sportswear department of an elegant women's department store. The mannequin had on a silk blouse that was left unbuttoned to the waist, with just a belt to hold it closed. Although practically nothing that shouldn't show showed, the illusion was that of unselfconscious sexuality.

The outfit sold out within three days. The customers were women who averaged in age from 45 to 65 and who would never wear a silk blouse without a brassiere or unbuttoned to the waist. But the image projected by the mannequin was how they wanted to look, and every time they put that blouse on they felt as sexy as the mannequin.

Mannequins are all about selling an image. Getting all the pieces together in such a way that there are no false notes and creating an illusion at the same time is the job—and sometimes the joy—of a visual merchant.

SUMMARY CHECKLIST

Key Concepts

1. Mannequins, more than any prop or fixture, contribute to the image of the store.
2. Today's mannequins are lightweight, durable, fiberglass forms, sprayed with a thin plaster coating.
3. Attitude is the single most important aspect of a mannequin's look.
4. The future of mannequins will be influenced by computers.
5. Basic principles work for every style of mannequin.
6. It is important to understand how to set up a mannequin.
7. The proper procedures for dressing and undressing a mannequin should always be followed.
8. Mannequins may be purchased with just their features painted on, so that makeup may be applied later.
9. Pose is an important consideration when purchasing mannequins.
10. Mannequins are used to sell an image.

KEY TERMS

1. Abstract forms
2. Mechanized mannequins
3. Pneumatic valves
4. Fulcrum
5. Kanelkalon
6. Half-figures

DISCUSSION QUESTIONS

1. What is meant by the statement, "attitude is the single most important aspect of a mannequin's look?"
2. List the various types of mannequins that can be purchased.
3. Why are mechanized mannequins and figures known as animations?
4. Why is it important for a mannequin to convey the message of a particular department?
5. Explain the proper procedure for setting up a mannequin.
6. Discuss what tools are necessary for changing a mannequin.
7. Explain the proper procedure for undressing an adult mannequin.
8. Discuss the proper procedure for dressing an adult mannequin.
9. Explain the proper procedures for applying and removing makeup from mannequins.
10. Discuss the relationship between mannequin pose and clothing restrictions.

STUDENT EXERCISES

Number 1

Obtain a full-adult mannequin—male or female—and place it in a convenient location in your classroom. Obtain clothing from a community business and dress the mannequin using the proper techniques for setup, dressing, makeup, and undressing. Upon completion, evaluate your work by responding to the following questions:

A. Is the mannequin "look" appropriate for your display? (explain)
B. Is your mannequin balanced properly? (defend your answer)
C. Did you use the proper techniques when dressing and undressing the mannequin? (explain)
D. Was makeup applied and removed properly? (explain)

Number 2

Utilizing two community businesses with which you are familiar, analyze the mannequins that are available for display construction by answering the questions indicated below:

A. When were the majority of the mannequins purchased?
B. What various types of mannequins are available?
C. Are full, realistic, and abstract forms available?
D. In what manner are mechanized mannequins or animations being utilized?
E. Are the mannequins properly dressed? (explain your answer)

CASE PROBLEM 1

The New Store

During November, the board of directors of the Case Clothing Company was in the process of purchasing a single-floor building for the purpose of establishing a full-price store operation.

The Case Clothing Company operates four full-line discount department stores in medium-sized cities in the Midwest. All stores operate as a single unit.

The board of directors recognized the fact that their store managers had no experience in the operation of a full-price store. Due to this fact, the Reibel Consulting Company was hired to determine what departments should be included in the new discount store, and whether or not the full-price store concept is feasible.

In April, the Reibel Company presented a comprehensive report to the board of directors. A brief summary of the report follows:

1. The total sales volume increase would be approximately 25 percent.
2. There would be no loss to the other four stores because the new store is attempting to reach a different type of customer.

3. The addition of the full-price store would allow the company to increase their markdown percentage while still increasing total sales volume.
4. Case Clothing Company is presently losing sales volume at the low end of the price scale.
5. The initial departments to be opened should be:
    a. Men's clothing and furnishings
    b. Coats (men's and women's)
    c. Women's clothing and furnishings
    d. Boys' clothing
    e. Girls' clothing.

Activities for Completion

1. Prepare a list of needed mannequins for each department.
2. Prepare a list of necessary accessories needed to dress mannequins by department.
3. Develop a rationale for each of the above purchases by department.
4. What special tools/equipment/supplies would need to be purchased?

CASE PROBLEM 2

The Proper Display

The Best Dressed Shop is a clothing shop that caters to male and female college students. The store is located in a college community with a population of 48,000 and the store has been in business for 10 years. Four years ago, the store moved to the new mall with no apparent reduction in gross sales volume.

In the past two years, several other clothing stores have located in the mall and the competition has caused the owner of the Best Dressed Shop, Mr. Jim Alton, to rely on window displays and advertising to attract customers into the store.

Jim and Linda Peterson (the store manager) recently spent considerable time planning the back-to-school promotion that will be a central theme throughout the store, especially where the window displays are concerned. Jim has left the planning of the main window display entirely up to Linda.

The size and shape of the window is shown in the diagram below. The ceiling height is 12′ with various types of lighting available. The only stipulations that Jim gave Linda are (1) the window must emphasize back-to-school and (2) both male and female mannequins must be used. Linda can utilize any of the clothing and accessories in the store.

(Front of store)

20′

10′   10′

17′

Activities for Completion

1. Complete a sketch of the window display.
2. Indicate what mannequins will be utilized in the window:
   a. What clothes and accessories will be utilized with each mannequin?
   b. What pose will the mannequins be assuming?
3. Are there any special considerations? If so, what are they?

CHAPTER 7

Props

LEARNING OBJECTIVES

At the completion of this chapter, you will be able to:

1. List the reasons for utilizing props in visual merchandising.

2. Discuss the pros and cons associated with buying props from a commercial vendor.

3. Describe the importance of a proper relationship between the merchandise, the space surrounding it, and the props.

4. Justify the value of using in-store merchandise as a prop for a display.

5. Discuss the value of making props in-house.

6. List the basic props that are generally utilized in all stores.

7. Describe the importance of having a positive relationship with salespeople who represent display manufacturers.

Since the beginning of theater 3,000 years ago, props have been used to help tell the on-stage story. As in the theater, props are being used today in visual merchandising to tell a story about the product, the department, or the merchandise concept. A prop is anything that is used with the merchandise to define or describe its function or style.

A prop may be merchandise from one department used to highlight and describe merchandise in another department, such as tennis racquets used in conjunction with tennis wear. Merchandise from other departments used to highlight other salable items will lead to multiple sales. One item can inspire the purchase of several others. An attractive briefcase used with a suit suggests that the two belong together. The suggestion prompts the buyer to think about buying a new briefcase to go with the new suit. Although the briefcase is used as a prop to describe the function of the suit, it is also a salable item which adds dimension to the customer's perception of the merchandise selection of the store.

Prop ideas originate in the imagination. Within a store is a treasure of potential props that are not necessarily other merchandise. Chairs, desks, paper, pencils, shopping bags, garment racks, wastepaper baskets, tools, hangers—anything used correctly—can work with the merchandise to help tell a story. The props that come from everyday use are sometimes called "found objects." Found object art developed when artists literally found objects on the street and incorporated them into works of art. The found objects to be used as props don't have to be beat up or dirty to show character (as they were originally used in the art world) but should act as descriptive devices for the salable merchandise. An example of this type of prop would be in a briefcase display. A professional briefcase open, with an apple, ruler, and lined notebook will give a touch of humor; childish props in a business person's case. These props are easily found and don't require production time or buying trips.

Other props can be either produced within the store's display shop area (in-store) or bought from display houses (vendors).

In-store production requires a design and a professional execution of that design to make it a finished-looking prop. Often props can be made quickly with little time or expense (Figure 7–1). An in-house prop has the advantage of timeliness. If an area needs a quick definition and there's not enough time or money to buy the needed prop, or that prop doesn't exist in the marketplace, then designing and producing the prop in-house becomes a necessity. Using the briefcase again as an example, a ladder motif can be used on a valance to suggest the "ladder to success." The ladders can be built quickly of wood and dowels and either stained (takes longer) or spray painted to give a finished look. With the proper signage, a shop feeling is described by the simple ladder image and the cliché it brings to mind.

Buying from a vendor can be the easiest and riskiest way to acquire props. Catalogs, visual merchandising shows, showroom visits, and vendor calls all serve to acquaint the visual merchant with the millions of different props available in the market today. Why risky? What you see initially isn't always what you get! Showroom samples are usually prototypes and the actual prop may not measure up to

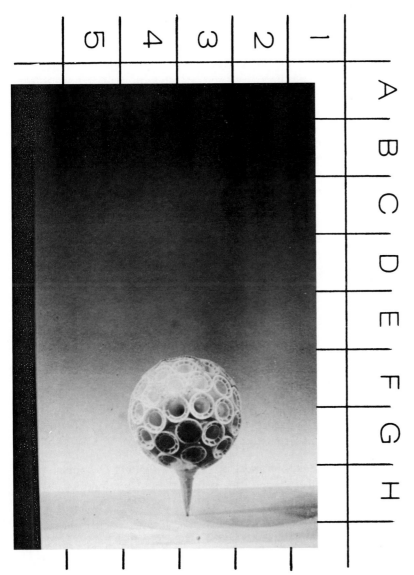

Figure 7–1

A simple but elegant prop was created by Gene Moore out of ice cream cones
and glue. The piece of jewelry is in front of the prop (H-3).
Credit: Gene Moore, Display Director, Tiffany and Co., N.Y., N.Y., 1978.

the high standards displayed in the showroom. This problem is not encountered
often but the buyer should research the reputation of vendors before buying from
them. Another risk is that the vendor will ship the beautiful prop you ordered but
not pack it well. It will arrive scratched, broken, in pieces—and can develop into a
mess of red tape before you either get a new prop or return the ruined one. If you

were in a hurry to receive the prop in the first place, you're behind schedule as soon as the prop arrives damaged. Naturally, if either a vendor ships incorrectly so that the merchandise arrives in a battered state, or if the shipped prop is not of the expected quality, the vendor should be contacted immediately and allowed to right the wrong. If this does not happen to your satisfaction, ordering props from that vendor again should be considered a risk and fairly foolish.

In-store merchandise used as props, found objects, in-store produced props, and vendor-bought props are all available to the visual merchant daily. Using these props correctly can be the factor that determines whether a display will sell merchandise as well as retain the image of the store.

The most important question to ask is if the display prop is appropriate for the merchandise. This question is the basis for all selection of props.

Refer back to the chapter on design. One of the basic rules of display design is to develop a relationship between the merchandise and the space around it. First, look at the merchandise to be displayed. What kind of merchandise is it? Is it old-fashioned? Contemporary? Futuristic? Conservative? Classic? What does it suggest? If confronted with the job of displaying solid white china in an appealing, fresh manner, where do you start?

1. The china is white—white suggests eggs, sugar, salt, snow, white grapes, white vinegar, black as a contrast.

2. China is fragile, e.g., the eggs, or the contrast of a solid object, e.g., a hammer.

3. China is for food, e.g., the white vinegar, grapes, salt, sugar, or any other food.

4. China is for eating off of—the actual process of eating—forks, knives, napkins, table, tablecloth.

5. China indicates a more formal meal, e.g., subdued lighting, elegant accessories, or just the opposite for contrast to play up the obvious fragility and stark whiteness of the china.

Not all of these ideas should be used at the same time. Their purpose is to develop an understanding of the thought process that is involved before selecting a prop to define the merchandise. Decide on the direction you want the display to take and think of all the possibilities before going with the final design. Trying to think of different concepts will spur new ideas and help develop creative thinking.

Two of the pleasures involved in visual merchandising are the chance to make an artistic statement as well as a comment on contemporary events.

The reason visual merchandising is such an exciting art field is its ability to react quickly in an artistic and public manner to events that affect the lives of the shoppers.

During the gasoline shortage, numerous displays poked fun at or commented angrily about the problem we all shared. They related the gasoline crisis to merchandise in ingenious ways. It was a case of making the merchandise fit the statement. As it was a common problem that almost everyone could relate to, it made sense to use it as a basis for a display. An example was a window filled with bicyclists. The copy was "leg power" and all the mannequins wore appropriate sports clothing. Unless there's a current event so universal that 90 percent of the customers will relate to it, you're better off allowing the merchandise to determine the message rather than the other way around.

Look again at the merchandise and decide what item or prop will convey your message. Now it's time to consider where to get the prop and how to use it.

IN STORE MERCHANDISE

Before using in-store merchandise as a prop for a display two factors must be considered. Is the merchandise/prop appropriate, and is there enough of the merchandise/prop to sell in its parent department if the demand arises from the display? The relative appropriateness of prop selection was just discussed. What happens to the merchandise is the next question. Using merchandise as a prop gives it free advertising in a different area of the store. To take advantage of the potential sales of this item, it should be on view and well stocked in its parent department.

A sign-out procedure is necessary in most stores to take merchandise from one department to another. If the selected prop is one-of-a-kind merchandise, or the only item left in stock of its kind (the others having been sold), it may be a good idea to buy the item for the display department's permanent use. The buyer may be willing to give the visual merchant a better price on the item to get it off his or her books. When buying an in-store prop, make sure its usefulness can be extended beyond the immediate project. A tennis racquet for a sporting goods display can be used in different ways for different areas. Buying the racquet from the department can save a lot time in sign-out procedures in the future.

The use of in-store merchandise as a prop can work as long as the prop is integrated into the total design of the display. Remember proportion and the balance between positive and negative spaces. Don't let the availability of an in-store prop cloud your artistic judgement. It either works as design/art or it doesn't. If it doesn't, you can choose to use it anyway and try to fake it—or go with another prop. If you can't find what you need among the merchandise available to you within the environs of the store, your next step may be to find what you need among the non-merchandise.

FOUND OBJECT PROPS

Simplicity of design works well with found object props. Usually a found object isn't beautiful on its own but serves well as a definition of the merchandise.

The found objects must relate in some way, either as a reaffirmation or as a contrast statement. A reaffirmation would be in Figure 7–2. The newspapers suggest news and business and the way they're stacked indicates a city street early in the morning before delivery. The mannequin dressed in a business suit looks like

Figure 7–2
This window is a very good example of props reaffirming the statement made
by the merchandise.
Credit: Richard Cartlige, V.M.D., Bonwit Teller, N.Y., N.Y., 1978.

an executive standing on a corner waiting for a taxi. The papers have nothing to do with her life directly, yet they are an integral part of her environment. She looks like the type of person normally associated with reading the *New York Times* (the newspaper on the floor).

As Bonwit Teller is a large advertiser in the *New York Times,* the display is dually identifying its customer and its newspaper.

A contrast statement would be in Figure 7–3 where the humorous athletic figure has fallen through one chair and has its feet tangled in two others. This excellent window by Gene Moore of Tiffany & Co. is a studied contrast between the acrobatic natural wood figure, the wooden chairs, and the precise metallic watches. An expensive wristwatch is associated with command of time. The clumsy wooden mannequin humorously contrasts with the time pieces.

Newspapers are an example of a found object prop. If you're unable to find the look you desire, you can make the desired prop in-house (in the shop). Some very simple props can be made in the shop. Using a roll of seamless paper and some sisal rope, the John Anthony (designer) window (Figure 7–4) comments on color as opposed to merchandise definition. The color of the paper matches the suit and makes a strong color statement from the street. The rolls of seamless paper are hung at different heights throughout the bank of windows to create a continuous

Figure 7–3

This is a contrast statement. The clumsy and humorous attitude of the wooden acrobat compared with the precise time keeping of the displayed watches is amusing and eye catching.

Credit: Gene Moore, Display Director, Tiffany & Co., N.Y., N.Y. September, 1976. Photo by: Malan Studio Inc., N.Y.C.

Figure 7–4

Seamless paper rolls are used as large-scale color props in this long bank of windows.
Credit: Richard Cartlige, V.M.D., Bonwit Teller, N.Y., N.Y., 1978.

band of color. The straight lines of the rolls and the soft curl of the paper edge compare with the lines of the suits.

Another way to identify the merchandise is seen in Figure 7–5. In this case the pattern of the fabric has been picked up on the back panel of the window. The pattern was cut out of shiny colored contact paper and applied to the vinyl panel. Not only does the pattern create a harmonic tension between the mannequin and the back wall, but also adds a splash of color that compliments the dress. This is very inexpensive and relatively easy. The example isn't given to be copied but to be understood for its successful simplicity and ease of execution.

Making props in-house can be simple or difficult depending on the amount of thought put into the project before it's started. Plan out the project before actually tackling it physically. Figure out what materials will work best. Best often means the easiest to cut, paint, install, and remove. Often you have a choice of painting

Figure 7–5
A simple prop, designed to highlight the pattern on the dress, is cutout and attached to the back wall.
Credit: Maggie Spring, V.M.D., Bonwit Teller, N.Y., N.Y., 1978.

directly on a surface (which will have to be repainted after the display is removed) or painting fomecore or upson board and applying it to the surface with brads, hot glue, or tape. Obviously, if the display is painted on a removable surface it can be preserved for possibly another use and the original surface will be relatively free of scars (Figure 7–6).

Making in-house props can be accomplished with any or all of the materials listed in the tools of the trade chapter. You're limited only by imagination and budget. If the prop is to be used only once in a window or out of the reach of customers for a short period of time, it doesn't have to be built of wood or steel. In Figure 7–7 is a perfect example of an easily built prop intended for limited use. A see-saw built for a bunny can be made of gatorboard, fomecore, or plywood. As long as the surface can be painted successfully, the prop will from a distance appear to be any material desired.

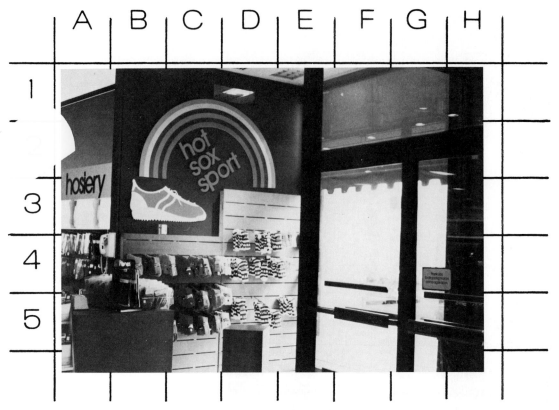

Figure 7–6

This display makes excellent use of a small area. All the pieces were cut and painted individually and then attached to the wall. The rainbow was bought from a vendor. The sneaker was cut out of gatorfoam and painted with latex. The letters are also made out of gatorfoam and were ordered from a vendor. Hot glue was used to attach the pieces to the painted wall. Note the rainbow coloration of the merchandise featured below (4–5-B-D). The socks are lined up in the same sequence as the rainbow.

Props don't always have to be three-dimensional. Changing the background of a display can act in the same manner as a 360° prop. Figure 7–8 shows how lighting used creatively can create a "prop" out of shadow. The lighting picks up the mannequin from the side of the window. The negative space is lively due to the pattern created by the figure.

If a person on a visual merchandising staff has artistic skills, use that person to create props. If the person is given enough time to do a professional job, the prop will be better than anything that could be vendor-bought because of its originality and its custom design that works in a specific area for a definite purpose.

VENDOR-BOUGHT PROPS

The industry that creates and sells display props is large and fascinating. The selection can be overwhelming or disappointing depending on your needs. There

Figure 7—7
This prop, made in-house, is simple and effective.
Credit: Colin Birch, V.M.D., Bonwit Teller, N.Y., N.Y., 1978.
Photo by: Jerry P. Melmed.

Figure 7—8
The shadow created by the mannequin highlights the stark figure centered in the window.
Credit: Colin Birch, V.M.D., Bonwit Teller, N.Y., N.Y., 1978. Photo by: Jerry P. Melmed.

are certain basic props that are bought for each store because they work in a variety of ways. The basics are:

- Bamboo poles, 6–12′ high
- Assortments of ribbon, felt, solid-color fabric
- Buildups out of wood or Plexiglas to add height to table displays
- Birch poles, from 6–12′ high
- Sand, wood chips, scatter
- Fans that can be painted
- Bricks
- Dried flowers
- A selection of silk flowers and greens
- Urns
- Screens (to create different wall effects, small areas on short notice, e.g., cosmetics facial area within the department)
- Thick rope, hemp and white

This list could be endless. There are many basics that a visual merchandiser counts on for quick and inventive solutions to problems that arise. In Figure 7–9, a window was created out of basic bamboo poles used in an interesting way. These poles have been used to solve numerous problems. In this photograph they suggest a field of bamboo and their angled stance suggests movement. The dramatic lighting gives the entire picture a surrealistic feeling. The bamboo poles almost seem to be people talking and interacting. The cleanness and sterility of the floor and walls keep the eyes on the mannequin and bamboo poles.

Vendors who design and manufacture display props have designers on their staff who try to interpret what will be the future needs of the industry based on the direction fashion is taking at that time. Trying to be responsive to the needs of the visual merchants is difficult and a gamble. At times the designer will ignore the merchandising trends and go off in his or her own stylistic fashion. The results can be visually stimulating but the visual merchant must understand that the merchandise may have to fit the prop as opposed to buying a prop to define the goods. In the budget chapter we discussed meeting with the store manager to get a firm commitment on the budget as well as from the buyers before any display buying to get an understanding of the types of merchandise that the store will be carrying. Once prepared with a direction to look in, the visual merchant can approach the market with financial awareness and be prepared to buy necessary props for the incoming merchandise before succumbing to the interesting and decorative items that are alluring but not immediately useful.

Relationships develop between the visual merchant (as a buyer) and the

Figure 7–9A
Bamboo poles are suspended upright on angles to indicate movement.
Credit: Maggie Spring, V.M.D., Bonwit Teller, N.Y., N.Y., 1978.

Figure 7–9B
This photograph is a forerunner of Figure 7–9A. The difference is not in the props as much as in the attitude of the mannequin. The props (bamboo poles and leaves) were set up realistically in 1954 and surrealistically in 1978.
Credit: Bonwit Teller, June, 1954.

salesperson who represents one or several display manufacturers. A visual merchant will come to count on certain people for different things. Some vendors can ship their goods quicker than others. Some specialize in custom-made props and their quality can be relied on. Other salespersons forget the likes and dislikes of the visual merchandiser from visit to visit and continue to show unwanted or inappropriate merchandise. If the salesperson is personable and charming, the visual merchant may be tempted to buy an item that's wrong for the store. Salespeople generally prefer the visual merchants to buy only what will work for them. If they buy unnecessary props, they may come to resent their own weakness and also the salesperson for an unfortunate buy. Rather than create any negative feelings, the best way to do business is to buy what is needed and be honest at all times. Honesty need not be rude or abrupt. Saying "I hate your line, it's all junk" is really unnecessary. If the visual merchant says nicely that the line is inappropriate for the particular store, or the items offered are not what is needed for the current budget period, the refusal becomes strictly a business matter and doesn't relate to either party personally.

Common courtesy requires that the visual merchant keep any appointments with salespersons that are made in advance unless circumstances arise that are completely out of the visual merchant's control. A salesperson coordinates several trips in one day and pays for them out of his or her own pocket. Take a salesperson's phone number when you make your appointment. Call and cancel the visit in advance if there is any doubt of attending the meeting at the scheduled time due to business pressures.

Salespeople are human beings and deserve the same thoughtfulness that you would give any visitor. Remember, this person can be in 100 different stores in any year. For the sake of your personal reputation as well as the basic rules of human kindness and consideration, give this person a chance to show the line and approach both with an open mind. If you feel pressured to buy things you really don't want or need and can't seem to be able to say no, realize this problem and try to solve it. Why can't you say no? Are you afraid of hurting that particular person? Are you unsure of your needs? Do you feel insecure about your taste level—what's "in" or "out." If the salesperson says, "Everyone is buying this item, it's really hot," ask, "Who is everyone?" Are the stores that are mentioned in the same image as yours—or are they higher or lower priced? Do you want to look the same as the next store? What other prop in the line creates a similar impression but is different from the hot one?

Being a good buyer of display props requires an understanding not only of the budget and store needs, but also of the market and what's available. NADI (National Association of Display Industries) and WAVM (Western Association of Visual Merchandising) are two organizations for manufacturers. NADI is generally the eastern half of the country (with quite a few west coast firms as members) and WAVM concentrates on the west coast. There are several trade shows every year for the visual merchandising field. Two are in New York City—in December (for spring items) and June (known as the Christmas show). These are sponsored by NADI and are very comprehensive. There's a large show in San Francisco (WAVM) in May (Christmas) that has some unique vendors that don't show on the east coast. A new show has just started in Los Angeles in September.

There are Canadian and European exhibits at all of these shows as well as major trade shows in the individual countries. Some of the most innovative ideas come from Canada.

Attendance at each trade show may be virtually impossible because of time and budget limitations. But if you're near either coast during show time, either on business or for a vacation, attend at the *very least* one show a year to understand the trends in the industry and to acquaint yourself with all that's available in the marketplace.

Other than manufacturers catering strictly to the display field, interior design studios, giftware houses, and industrial suppliers can all be useful resources. Use the yellow pages. A more inspiring book will be hard to find!

How to use a prop after you've found it, made it, or bought it? Think of safety, design, lighting, and signage—then incorporate all these elements in one well-defined, exciting display (Figure 7–10). Remember, the prop is there to define the merchandise and add visual excitement to the surrounding area. It is not there to distract the customers from their main goals: shopping and buying.

Figure 7–10
Forks are used as a "bed of nails" in this classic, dramatic window by Gene Moore. The forks are merchandise used as props in a unique way.
Credit: Gene Moore, Display Director, Tiffany and Co., N.Y., N.Y. September, 1961.

SUMMARY CHECKLIST

Key Concepts

1. Props are used in visual merchandising to tell a story about a product.
2. A prop is anything that is used with the merchandise that defines or describes its function or style.
3. In-store prop production requires a professional execution of the design to make it a finished-looking prop.
4. Buying from a commerical vendor can be risky or an excellent investment.
5. The question, "Is the display prop appropriate for the merchandise?" should always be asked before selecting a prop.
6. Visual merchandising managers react quickly to events that affect the lives of the shoppers.
7. Simplicity of design works well with found object props.
8. There are basic props that can be utilized in a variety of different situations.
9. A professional relationship should always exist between the buyer (visual merchant) and the salespeople who represent a display manufacturer.

KEY TERMS

1. Prop
2. Found object
3. Parent department

DISCUSSION QUESTIONS

1. Discuss the importance of using merchandise from one department to highlight and describe merchandise in another department.
2. What are the advantages/disadvantages of using found objects when constructing a display?
3. What are the advantages of using props made in-house?
4. What are the risks associated with purchasing props from a commercial vendor?
5. What is meant by the statement, "The display prop should be appropriate for the merchandise?"
6. Before using in-store merchandise as a prop for a display, what two factors must be considered?
7. Why is it important to plan a project before making in-house props?
8. Name the basic props that should be purchased for a store.
9. What should the relationship be between the buyer and the manufacturer's sales representative?

STUDENT EXERCISES

Number 1

Assume the role of visual merchandising manager in a large hardware store. You are in the process of planning a spring display which will feature lawnmowers. What props could you utilize in constructing this display? Include in-store, vendor-purchased, and found objects.

Number 2

Obtain a copy of the yellow pages from your local telephone directory. Analyze the businesses listed and determine which ones could provide you with needed props that could be used in a variety of situations. List the name of the business and the props they could provide.

CASE PROBLEM 1

The Forgotten Order

The Atheses Company is a small, exclusive, general merchandising store that is located in Petersonville, a small, wealthy community. The population of the community is approximately 25,000 with the majority of the workers commuting to the city of Ralston approximately 50 miles away.

During the spring, the manager of the store, Ms. Larson, met with Jane and Linda (the store buyers) regarding the annual pre-Thanksgiving sale. The sale runs for three weeks and features new fall merchandise that the buyers were able to obtain at a discount from manufacturers. The discount given on the merchandise ranges from 10 to 25 percent.

The sale serves three purposes:

1. To provide the customers with quality merchandise at reduced prices
2. To obtain larger discounts from manufacturers due to quantity of merchandise sold
3. To utilize the sale merchandise as a leader to more expensive items which will be available for customer purchase

It is store policy that enough sale merchandise be purchased to satisfy the customer needs. The event has always been highly successful, and approximately 90 percent of the customers return to the sale on an annual basis.

Due to the smallness of the store, Jane and Linda are also responsible for planning and building all interior displays and the one window display available. It is Sunday, the day before the sale is to begin, and Jane and Linda have completed all of the interior displays and are ready to begin working on the window display, which will feature an antique wood-burning stove and will be the major display attraction.

All of a sudden Jane had a worried look on her face. "What is the matter?" Linda asked. "The props we ordered for this display haven't arrived," Jane replied. "What do we do now? Ms. Larson will be furious when she finds out!"

Questions To Discuss

1. What could Jane and Linda have done to prevent this situation from happening?
2. Should they tell Ms. Larson?
3. What display props did they probably order from the commercial vendor?
4. What in-store or found object props could be utilized?

CASE PROBLEM 2

The Anniversary

The Apple of Your Eye, located in the city of Longston, is an exclusive furniture store whose gross volume last year was $350,000. Mr. Bitel, the store manager and owner, has a philosophy that "displays sell merchandise."

Due to this philosophy, Mr. Bitel employs a VMM and two assistants. Mr. Al Christensen, the VMM, has worked for the store for 25 years. Each of the VM assistants has 10 years experience in the visual merchandising industry. Part of Al's responsibilities include the ordering of materials and props necessary for constructing displays. Al has a reputation of being one of the top VMMs in the region.

On Monday morning, Mr. Bitel called Al into his office and informed him that the store's 25th anniversary sale would begin in approximately six months on June 1. Mr. Bitel explained that he wanted this to be the biggest sale ever sponsored by the Apple of Your Eye.

All furniture will be on sale for one month. Mr. Bitel suggested to Al that the store should resemble its appearance of 25 years ago. He felt that this visual merchandising approach would bring back memories for the older customers and be exciting for the newer customers. Both customer reactions should increase sales of furniture. All store promotions, displays, and advertising will be based around the memories theme.

Questions To Discuss

1. What props should Al utilize in this total-store promotion?
2. What specific props should Al purchase from a commercial vendor?
3. What props should Al design and produce in-house?

CHAPTER 8

Lighting and Signing

LEARNING OBJECTIVES

At the completion of this chapter, you will be able to:

1. Explain the importance of lighting as it relates to the visual merchandising industry.

2. Define the three major types of lighting and the advantages/disadvantages of each.

3. Describe how lighting can be used to help the visual merchant.

4. Identify the type of lighting to be used in special situations.

5. Describe the importance of signing in today's visual merchandising schemes.

6. List the appropriate materials for making signs.

7. Describe the procedures for placing signs on valances, walls, and columns.

8. List the appropriate times for using floor-standing signs.

9. Name the reasons for using cardboard or temporary signs.

10. Describe the importance of electrical signs in visual merchandising.

11.   **Identify the materials from which letters can be made and the advantages and disadvantages of each.**

12.   **Demonstrate the proper procedure for positioning letters on various surfaces.**

LIGHTING

There is a wide variety of lighting available for both general and specific use in retail stores today. It's very important to understand the uses and abuses of lighting not just for display, but for its total effect on a store. Visual merchandising in a store is directly affected by the type of lighting used in each department, on each display, and in the showcases. Understanding how different types of lighting can be used to enhance the visual presentation of merchandise is essential to creating more exciting and profitable displays.

Lighting was originally left to the architects of a building. Now, the operations staff (or, in a small store, the owner) considers carefully the lighting patterns as well as the type of light source for energy reasons. The energy costs go up every year at rates that cut drastically into the profits. One way to make a profit is to keep the operating costs down and a large portion of these costs are for lighting. The large companies that manufacture lighting—General Electric, GTE-Sylvania, and Westinghouse—as well as many smaller firms—have all developed low-cost, energy-saving bulbs. All three companies have different systems and there are pluses and minuses to each. Every year there are innovations in the lighting industry to improve the color and cost efficiency of the bulbs and total systems.

When professionally entering the visual merchandising field, it's useful to find out the type of lighting being used at your store and who manufactures it, and to attend any local seminars to learn about the newest lighting inventions and techniques. These seminars are given by the large companies and are extremely informative and interesting. Even if you are not in a position to buy the large bulk of the light bulbs used by your store, learning about them can help you gain an understanding of how to use them more effectively. Also, in visual merchandising, the spotlight costs for display use are often placed into the visual merchandising budget, and understanding the differences in wattage, effectiveness, and cost can help to trim or augment the budget when necessary.

Spotlights are just one type of light used in a store. Fluorescents, incandescents, and HIDs—high-intensity discharge—are the general categories for bulbs and light systems.

Fluorescents

Fluorescents are used for general lighting. They are very energy-efficient and are getting more so every year as they're improved. The bulbs or tubes are long,

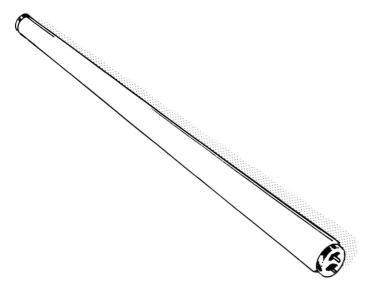

Figure 8–1
Fluorescent tube.

narrow, and fragile (Figure 8–1) and are used most often in showcases, valances, and in ceilings as general lighting. They cannot be focused or directed toward a specific object as the light they throw is always diffuse. They "wash" an area with light, thereby creating no sharp shadows or accents. The color of fluorescents has the property of green light but has improved over the years so that natural, "cool" lighting can be achieved if wanted, warm (yellowish) lighting is available, and an ultralume (prime color) fluorescent has been developed that strengthens the colors in skin tone and merchandise in a way that is complimentary to both. Fluorescents can create an ambiance in an area by their color tone. In a fur department, a cool white bulb gives a "bluer" feeling, which is the color of snow (and cold) on a wintry day. Warm, sunny bulbs will create the opposite effect. If a department is done totally in cool and is located next to a department with warm lights, the contrast is going to be too strong and will look disjointed and unpleasant to the eye.

In a situation where two departments are adjacent and require different color light bulbs, the use of incandescents will temper the harsh feeling of the cool lights and add highlights to the warm bulbs.

Incandescents

Incandescent bulbs are probably the type you have at home. Incandescents give a warm, red light that appears yellow and are used in stores mainly for highlighting. In the past they were used as general lighting. As costs have risen, the energy used to power an incandescent is much greater than that needed for a fluorescent and they have become very expensive for general use. They also throw off a lot of heat (try touching a lightbulb that's been on for several hours, and imagine a bulb five times as large producing five times the heat). This heat generated by the light bulbs in the warm seasons dramatically increases air-conditioning costs.

The advantage of incandescents is their ability to spotlight and focus in on an area or object. The bulbs for incandescents are heavier and less fragile than those for fluorescents (Figure 8–2). Their life span is increasing every year with new developments in the lighting industry. In 1981, the cost for one spotlight or flood light ranged from $8 to $13 retail (the costs rise steadily with inflation). Multiply this cost by the large number used in a store and assume that a bulb will last an average of three to four weeks, which explains why these are used mainly for accents and not for general lighting. Flood lights are shaped so that a wide circle of light hits the merchandise. Like fluorescents, flood lights wash an area with light. With the advances made in bulb color for fluorescents today, it's somewhat impractical to use the energy-inefficient incandescent flood for wash effect lighting. One good use for incandescent floods is to light a lettered wall that identifies a department. Often the lettering stretches in length beyond the light circle created by a spotlight so a flood will encompass the entire name and act as a highlight in comparison with the general wash lighting of the fluorescents. Spotlights, on the other hand, are absolutely necessary to highlight merchandise and displays. Light as a design element works only when there are shadows for contrast. A light and dark pattern can be achieved through the use of highlighting the important parts of the merchandise and letting the shadows create depth and pattern (Plate 10). On a larger scale, spotlights on merchandise racks make the entire department look more exciting if the area around it is bathed in a wash of fluorescent lighting. Often, a store will turn off the lighting in the aisles so that the departments on either side will stand out and appear brighter. This method also cuts down on the electrical costs.

Spots are used to highlight fixtures, displays, mannequins, and for window lighting, and are installed either in the ceiling (recessed) or on a track (Figures 8–3 through 8–5). They are surrounded either way by a can. The can is then either

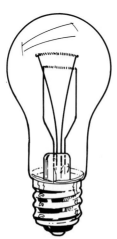

Figure 8–2
Incandescent light bulb.

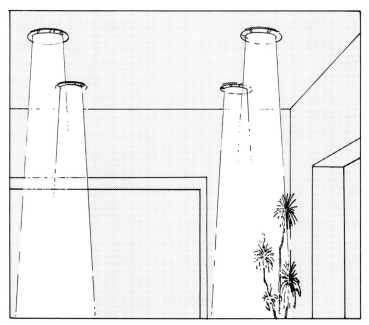

Figure 8–3
Recessed ceiling lights aka: spots or cans.

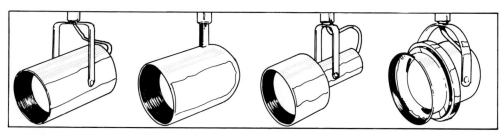

Figure 8–4
Track spotlights for interiors.

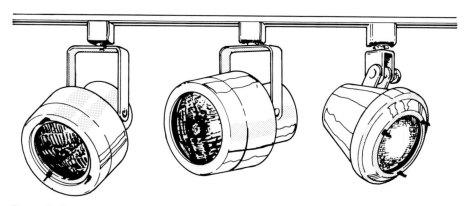

Figure 8–5
Track spotlights for windows.

recessed into the ceiling or attached to a track by a special clip that allows the electrical current to flow to the bulb. When a spotlight is toward the back of the can (Figure 8–6), the light that is emitted is more concentrated because the edges of the cannister don't permit the light to escape in a wide circle. More light can be achieved by bringing the bulb closer to the opening of the can. There are bulbs created now that will emit light in a cross-pattern (Figure 8–7) to allow the bulk of the light rays to hit the floor—and not stay in the can.

The angle at which a spot is directed from the ceiling to the floor is very important. It's not enough to just hit the desired object with light; it's equally important not to blind a passerby. Any angle sharper than 45° will catch the eye, and the customer or salesperson will see "spots." The lighting fixture should be unobtrusive and not catch the eye in any way other than by the light thrown onto merchandise or an escalator entrance. An escalator entrance must always be clearly lighted for safety.

There are many colored filters that can be applied to the face of a spotlight to change the color of the light. Filters are round, colored glass with a light metal trim. These filters block much of the light while changing the color, and a higher wattage bulb may have to be used to achieve the same amount of light. The filters used most often are pink for the faces of mannequins, amber for dramatic effects, straw to intensify warm colors, and daylight blue for icy feelings. Many other colors are used on occasion to create special effects, but not as often as the ones mentioned. Always make sure that the filter doesn't change the color of the merchandise. Filters should be used to highlight backgrounds, props, faces, and walls—not to distort colors of salable goods. Too much confusion arises when a customer calls and asks for the purple dress in the window—and there is no purple dress, just a red dress with blue filters over the spotlights that are trained to light it up.

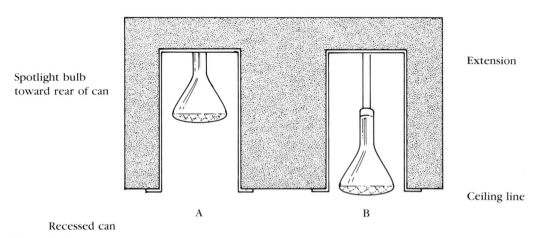

Spotlight bulb
toward rear of can

Extension

Ceiling line

Recessed can

A   B

Figure 8–6

(A) Recessed spotlight bulb. (B) Bulb with an extension. A wider beam of light is emitted when not trapped inside the cylinder of the can.

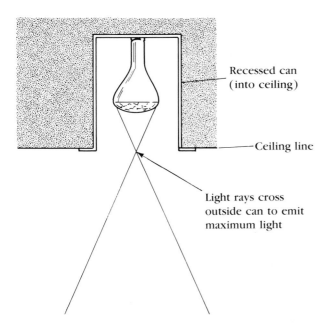

Recessed can (into ceiling)

Ceiling line

Light rays cross outside can to emit maximum light

Figure 8–7
Certain bulbs are designed to emit a cross-pattern of light so that the maximum amount of light reaches the selling floor.

Gels are colored acetate that are placed over bulbs. They work similarly to filters by changing the light color and are much less expensive because they come on acetate rolls and are either cut by hand into a circle to fit the aperture of the spotlight or used full length over a fluorescent tube. Filters are about $8 each while gels may be as little as 50 cents. The problem with gels is that they only last a week, before the intensity of the bulbs burns through the gel and the color effect is destroyed. Gels are perfect for one-week windows or for very short-term displays.

HIDs

The new high-intensity discharge lamps are the most efficient bulbs available today because they provide more light per watt than either fluorescents or incandescents. The light from these smaller bulbs is more concentrated than that of a fluorescent, so that shadows can be achieved as opposed to a total wash. All the major companies have produced HID bulbs that emit excellent light color so that both merchandise and customers are flattered. These bulbs are new and therefore more expensive than the traditional bulbs, but they save so much in energy costs that they may be the future in the lighting industry.

The major problem with the wide selection of color in fluorescent tubing is how merchandise and skin tone look under each color. A tan pair of socks can look pink, grey, cream, tan, or brown depending on the type of light source and the color of the bulb. Cross-reference lighting when coordinating colors by holding the same object under ceiling fluorescents, case fluorescents, incandescent spots, and natural sunlight. You will get a much better idea of the real color of the garment and how each type of light and color bulb will affect color perception.

Being aware of the different types of lighting available in the market is the first step to using light to your advantage. With light there are two main design elements to work with: light and shadow. Working with light to make displays and merchandise more dramatic is essential, but it's important to watch out for too much shadow which can hide merchandise and important detail. If, by the use of spots alone, you design the lighting for a window or display presentation, the intense "spots" of light will leave the rest of the display in the shadows. Look at the light sources available in the area. Possibly a few floods would brighten up the area and then by the addition of several spots (which will highlight the display even further), the entire display will vibrate with energy, color, and light.

Pin spots can be used to accent small areas (Figure 8–8). These are small spotlights with a very small aperture for the light to come out, thereby intensifying the beam on a single spot. An important point to remember is that the heat these spots give off can be enough to fade or burn merchandise and props if it's directed at one spot for a long time. The use of mirrored surfaces can also cause a fire if light is reflected onto a flammable object for a long time. Considering the sun the ultimate light source is also an important consideration when planning the use of mirrors or mirrored surfaces in a window.

Surprisingly, the same amount of lighting is needed in a window whether the surroundings are dark or light. Because of natural light from the sun during the day, the windows need to be lit up with a large number of spots (and possibly floods) to compete with the outside. At night the windows become brilliant with light and should be rechecked again to see that the light is properly placed and that the shadows fall in the right places.

It's important to remember to unplug the lights in a window well before you're ready to change them to give them time to cool off. A pair of asbestos gloves would be a good addition to the tool chest and for the work space (if any) behind a window. Check each spot light plug to make sure it's not frayed or damaged, then reconnect each light as you direct it onto the display. Be aware of floor lights (lights that are directed up from the floor) which could cast unnatural shadows on mannequins. By holding a flashlight under your own face you can understand in an exaggerated way how light and shadows can distort regular features.

A store was designed recently in San Francisco to resemble the owner's idea of heaven. It's a fantastic place with pearlized walls, marble floors, graceful columns, arches, and curving surfaces. The architect placed $2' \times 2'$ tiles of translucent marble on the regular (lower level) floor and trained spotlights on each tile which left the area around the tiles slightly shadowed. The tiles glow with light and look as if they float in air. The bulb cannisters are on a track system that is painted the color of the ceiling. The customers' eyes are drawn to the translucent tiles instead of to the ceiling. It is a light trick that works well without looking overplanned and labored. The merchandise, very feminine apparel, looked as ethereal as its setting.

Painting the light fixtures is a good way to minimize the distraction of the

Figure 8–8
This window by Jim Crilley is an excellent example of the use
of pin spots. The porcelain heads are as fragile and fine as the china on display.
Credit: Jim Crilley V.M.D. David Orgill, Inc., Beverly Hills, CA.

actual fixture. When ordering light fixtures try to match ceiling colors as close as possible to reduce the fixtures attracting the eye upward.

LIGHTING FOR SPECIAL EFFECTS, OCCASIONS, AND SPECIAL DEPARTMENTS

Special Effects

Movement combined with light is a powerful visual attraction. Chase or sequential lights are often used to create a sense of excitement in a department or window. Chase lights are small "cosmetic type" bulbs—10–20 watts—that are screwed into sockets in a flexible covered wire. One end of the wire is attached to a box that controls the light movement which can be either made faster or slower. The chase light set can be bought with a plastic U-shaped long rod that, once screwed into a flat surface, will hold the lights in place. The lights flash in a progressive pattern that suggests that the light is traveling in a path. Chase light bulbs come in several colors and the system is very effective in attracting attention. Lighting that is *too* effective can be distracting to the customer. For instance, if there are a lot of mirrors or shiny surfaces around the bulbs, the image will be repeated many times and could become an irritant instead of a good prop.

A new light device on the market is a skinny vinyl/plastic tube containing small light bulbs. The tube is usually 3/4" thick and comes in several colors, including red, blue, green, yellow, and clear. The lights are white (or clear) bulbs and take on different colors depending on the color of the tube. These have a machine similar to the sequential lights such that the small lights can be made to run up or down the tube at varying speeds. These can create fantastic effects when used with imagination.

Occasions

Christmas lights in many sizes, styles, and colors are bought by the millions every year by visual merchants to illuminate the holiday season trim. The most popular kind is the Italian light or miniature light. The available styles change yearly, but the basics are either a green or white cord (it's important to match the cord to the decor), a small pointy bulb, a variety of colors or just one, and the choice of flashing, twinkle, nonflashing, or sequence lights. The flashing and twinkle lights are very effective in trees, and their excitement can be had by buying the lights already twinkling or flashing. There is a big difference between twinkles and flashes. Twinkles have an intermittent electric charge for each bulb so that not all the lights go off and on at the same time. With the twinkle, some lights will stay on while others twinkle off, and then go off themselves. There is never a "dark" look to the twinkle style. The flasher lights and the flasher attachment from the hardware store (to add to regular light sets to make them flash) will make all the lights go on and off at the same time. This will make the tree or decoration look dark every other flash. By using several sets of flashing lights in each tree, they can be plugged in so that they flash at different times, thereby creating a twinkle effect. The sequence lights are more difficult to find, but also create the twinkle effect when combined with other lights that are flashing in a different sequence. The sequence lights run in a continuous pattern from the beginning of the strand to the end.

The Italian lights come UL-approved and non-UL approved. UL stands for Underwriters Laboratories. It is a company that's supported by the manufacturers of electrical products that checks all products according to a strict set of standards. *Always* buy the UL-approved for reasons of safety and practicality. The local fire marshall who inspects around Christmas time will possibly close down the store or at least your displays until the lights are replaced with UL-approved wires and bulbs. Another fire law is that all light wires must be attached to nonflammable surfaces with insulated staples (Figure 8–9). These staples are more difficult to use

Figure 8–9
An insulated staple.

than a staple gun but are an important safety law. A lot of time and effort will be wasted when the lights have to be installed twice as the first time was with regular metal staples. As for the flammable surface, using your head helps.

Attaching lights to a tree of dry branches can be asking for trouble if a short occurs in the electrical system. But attaching them to solid wood beams is relatively safe if the bulbs don't touch the surface.

When buying Christmas lights, look for the ones that will stay lit when one bulb burns out. Otherwise, you'll be replacing the lights every few days. These light sets will not go on if a bulb is loose or missing as a safety feature so that no exposed wires can cause shock or fire. If you are hammering insulated tacks into a wall to hold up the light set, keep the set plugged in so that if the force of the hammer dislodges a bulb, you can find it quickly without having to test every bulb in the set. Be *very* careful not to penetrate the wire as it may cause an electric shock.

Special Departments

Lighting for a furniture floor, lamp department, or domestics area is a special situation that requires different uses of lights.

A furniture floor or area is usually less bright than the rest of the merchandise areas. This is to provide a relaxed atmosphere for the furniture and to sell the lamps in the department. A lamp can rarely sell until it's turned on. Spotlights and regular lamps are used most often in this department to create a natural (lamps) yet dramatic (spots) look. The bulbs in the lamps need not be more than 40 watts to achieve the wanted effect of a natural, homey feeling.

In the brighter domestics department, lamps used next to beds displaying sheets and blankets will soften the harsh ceiling lights and give a more intimate feeling to each area they illuminate.

The lamp department must have every lamp that is displayed lit so that the area glows with their combined light. The ceiling lights can be dimmed or completely turned off if the walls of the department are colored in light tones which will reflect the light cast by the lamps. A turned-off lamp looks dead as if no one is home. There's a lonely, sad feeling to an unlit lamp and the last thing a customer needs to feel is lonely and sad.

Lighting can make or break a display, a department, or an entire store. Remember to use the shadows as well as the light. The shadows give depth and draw attention to the more visually stimulating areas. A shadowed area in a department, if too dark, can swallow the surrounding light, creating a dark feeling for the entire area. The shadows and spots should be evenly spaced in a department and creatively spaced in a display.

With all visual merchandising it's the merchandise that is to be highlighted and sold. Lighting is a means to this end.

SIGNING

Signing is gaining in importance every year. Signing and lettering mean the same thing: identification. Originally, signing was used primarily to identify the store on the outside of the building, occasionally to name different departments and to announce sales and sale merchandise. Today, signing does all that and much more. Vendors are often identified within each department by three-dimensional letters applied to the walls or valances. Individual shops require identification as do outposts and some merchandise statements. Paper or posterboard signs are no longer used just for sales, but are now used to advertise new vendors, colors, or act as an explanation for the merchandise. For example, one frequently sees cardboard signs placed on fixtures to translate French sizes into English for Izod or Sasson merchandise.

A good sign gives the most information in the fewest possible words. Few customers pay attention to more than the top line and the price. For shop identification, usually one to three words works best, e.g., Serendipity, Hot Kamali, Plastics Plus, and For Kids Only. "Love in the Afternoon" (a shop conceived for tee-shirts and nightwear for soap opera buffs) is too long, and a customer glancing at this lengthy sign might turn away before scanning it completely and understanding its meaning. If a four-or-more-word name is necessary, the accompanying graphics should tell the viewer the same story as the words.

Generic signing throughout a store should be uniform in style and color. This includes the general store name, large departments, fitting room and cashier signs, as well as sale signs and merchandise identification cards. Special shops and boutiques can use different styles if they don't clash with the surroundings in an unpleasant or confusing way.

Signing can be accomplished in several ways: Hanging signs, valance or wall signs, column signs, floor-standing signs, cardboard signs that fit into sign-holding fixtures, and electrical signs for either interior or exterior use.

Materials

Innovations in materials have made heavy wood signs rare. Today, the most popular material used for hanging signs is Lucite or Plexiglas. Advantages of Lucite are its range of colors; excellent shape and color retention; the choices of transparent, translucent, and opaque; and its ability to be cut to any shape. Disadvantages are its dust attractiveness and brittleness when dropped. It scratches easily and is fairly heavy. Painting on Lucite is easy and effective. If the sign is to be viewed from both sides, one must decide whether to use transparent Lucite, where the name will appear on both sides of the sign, or translucent Lucite, which is more visible and therefore heavier looking. If clear Lucite is used throughout, its use should be continued. Only if a small shop or merchandise statement requires a special look and color should different colors be used. For example, a Valentine's Day shop might use red plexi with white lettering for its valances while the rest of the store has clear plexi with black letters.

Canvas or fabric banners silkscreened with the name of the shop on both sides have become very popular due to low cost and easy installation. Usually two pockets (wide hems) are sewn on the ends of the fabric (Figure 8–10) so that metal or wood rods can be inserted to give a rigidity to the fabric and pull down the material to keep to a minimum the sway from the blowers and open doors. Fabric banners are so lightweight that they can also be made into box-shaped valances by using stretcher strips (normally used for canvasses) (Figure 8–11). Several valance and structural signs that can be created from fabric are illustrated by Figures 8–12 and 8–13. Fabric is popular because of its relatively low cost, easy maintenance,

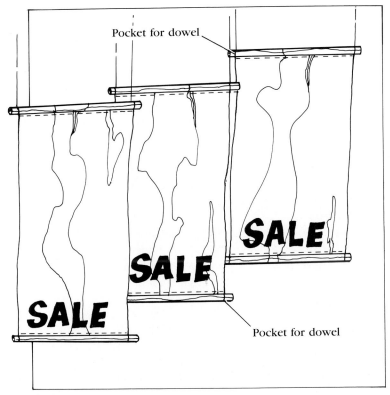

Figure 8–10
Banners are made of pieces of cloth with pockets sewn on both ends.
Dowels fit into these pockets to give shape and weight to the hanging banners.

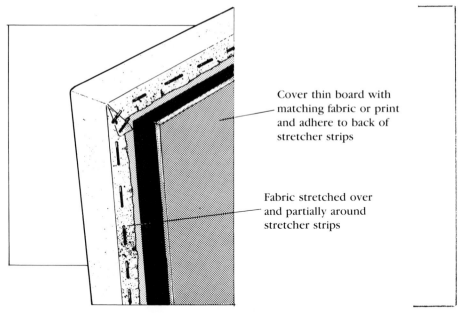

Cover thin board with
matching fabric or print
and adhere to back of
stretcher strips

Fabric stretched over
and partially around
stretcher strips

Figure 8–11

To make a hanging fabric sign or valance, cover stretcher strips totally with fabric and staple it on the back of the strips. Cover a board with the same fabric and adhere it to the back of the stretcher strips to cover the staples and to finish off the back.

Figure 8–12

A fabric and stretcher strip suspended sign in a bath shop outpost.
Credit: Linda Cahan Schneider, 1981.

Figure 8–13
Horizontal banners used as temporary valances. These identify a department through a logo, color, and direction of placement.

adaptability, simple installation, and—with care—long life span. Some drawbacks of fabric are the fading tendency of many colors and dyes, wrinkles that are especially difficult to remove from heavy canvas, and the need to either silkscreen or paint identification on the fabric because letters stick poorly in many cases.

Wood signs give a masculine, outdoors atmosphere when the wood is stained or left natural. A beachy/summery mood is achieved by rubbing watered down white paint or stain into natural wood, then adding several coats of polyurethane. Wood can also be successfully painted and easily hung. Homosote, Masonite, and baraboard will accomplish the same things as painted wood for less cost. The edges of homosote and baraboard have to be framed as they flake and look unprofessional. Masonite has the best painting surface but is usually very thin. However, it can be framed out (Figure 8–14) to create the illusion of depth.

Hanging Signs

Signs that drop from the ceiling can be hung in several ways depending on the weight of the sign. Lucite rods with clear Lucite S-hooks give a suspended feeling to heavier signs while fishing tackle (monofilament) works in a similar way for lightweight signs (see chapter on safety, section on things that hang). Chain, metal rods with hooks on their ends, and threaded rod all work for hanging signs. Check the traffic flow before deciding where to hang the sign. Try to hang it where the greatest number of people will see it.

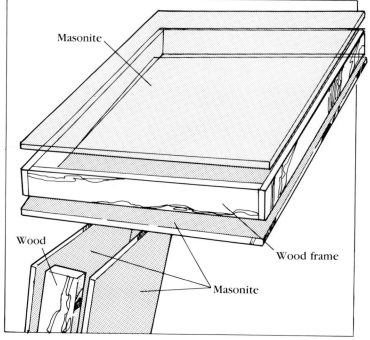

Figure 8–14
Masonite given depth by lumber. Two sheets of Masonite are nailed over a wood frame to make a lightweight sign or valance appear very solid.

Valances and Wall Signs

Signing on valances is simply a matter of deciding the best location for the letters and applying them in the best way for the surface of the valance and the back surface of the letter. Placement of letters on a valance is very important: the identification creates a focal point and the tendency of the eye is to look straight down from the valance to the wall and the merchandise below it. When the identification signs in the store start on the left-hand side of the valance and are positioned 1-1/2″ up from the bottom (and are all upper case), stick to that signing theme to create consistency throughout the store. If the store is set up in such a way that placement consistency is not important (such as not being able to view two departments at the same time), stand on the aisle to determine the most visible area for the sign. It's possible that two or more signs may be necessary to identify the department from all angles.

Wall signs require similar thought. An important consideration is how high the letters are placed above the merchandise and below the ceiling. The higher the letters, the further up the eye has to travel to see the identification, and with each foot the chance increases that the eye will drift away from the department altogether (Figure 8–15). If a department identity will be changed often (once a

Figure 8–15
An example of a sign placed too high on the wall within a department. No light shines on the wall or sign at this height. Also, it is not a good idea to draw the customer's attention this far away from the merchandise.

year or more), it might be a good idea not to adhere the identifying letters directly to the wall's surface. Walls in most buildings today are made from sheetrock. The sheetrock is then primed and painted. Almost all the adhesives that would effectively hold the letters to the wall will also rip the paint and the surface of the sheetrock when removed from the wall.

Vendor directories (Figure 8–16) work best when mounted on clear plexi or on a removable surface to facilitate changing the vendor names as the buyers change their minds about which vendor to stress and select different lines. Constant repainting of the wall will be avoided by this precaution. For a stucco wall, instead of plexi one could stucco a piece of upson board or Masonite in the same way to match the wall, and mount this false surface on the wall with the signage on the upson/removable panel. Though still requiring maintenance, this will allow for an uninterrupted textured wall flow without the glare from Plexiglas. This method works equally well with wallpaper (preferably a pattern that doesn't require a match), paint, and fabric (Figure 8–17).

Columns and Signing

The big question with column signing is whether to run the letters up or down? Side to side will only work with a 3–4″ letter because most columns are between 15 and 24″ wide. Up or down (Figure 8–18) is decided by current taste and manage-

Figure 8–16

An example of a vendor directory hot-glued or doublestick taped onto a slotwall end panel.

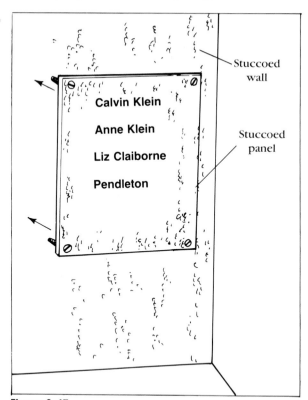

Stuccoed wall

Stuccoed panel

Calvin Klein

Anne Klein

Liz Claiborne

Pendleton

Figure 8–17

By placing a panel of the same material/background over a like wall surface, the repainting and resurfacing can be eliminated when vendor names are changed within the directory.

222

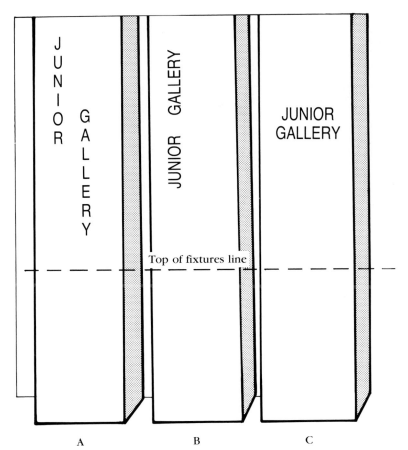

Top of fixtures line

A   B   C

Figure 8–18
*Three popular types of signing for columns. (A) Placing the letters upright, as they are
read, and working top to bottom. (B) Lettering on the side, reading from top to bottom.
(C) Left to right signing with smaller letters.*

ment. The major points to remember are (1) make sure you start your letters above
the fixture level so they can be seen and (2) test a plaster column at its bottom to
see if the adhesive used on the letters pulls out chunks of plaster when being
removed. One way around the up or down controversy is a column enclosure that
can be built out of anything from flimsy, lightweight fomecore to plywood (Figure
8–19). A column enclosure can be compared with a sleeve over a column that is
often much wider than the column itself. The column enclosure will give the
needed length on a horizontal plane to use larger letters. The only disadvantage to
this plan is that the rest of the columns on the line (and columns are almost always
in a straight line) will look naked and will need the same structure around them to
blend in with the signed one. This can help to identify a department that is lost in a
sea of merchandise fixtures.

Figure 8–19
A wood column enclosure suspended from the ceiling by threaded rods.

Floor Standing Signs

Floor-standing signs can serve a function similar to that of a column but not extend to the ceiling. Floor signs can be made to resemble arches, oblisques, large squares, and the like (Figure 8–20). The same problems of up/down or side to side are present with sign construction. When there are no columns, walls, valances, or hanging space available, floor-standing signs are a solution to the signing problem.

Cardboard or Temporary Signs

Cardboard and temporary signs are usually designed to fit into freestanding fixtures so that they can be moved from area to area when necessary. The normal generic signs are "Sale," "Clearance," "Special Purchase," and "As Advertised." Continuity in signing is important and using the same style print and the same color for these signs will add to the cohesive appearance of a store. On the other hand, special sale days are normal in retailing so either toppers or completely new signs can be used to identify these special days. Toppers are printed cardboard sheets cut to fit the existing sign holder, with the top slightly larger to stick up over the top of the holder and printed with the name of the special sale, e.g., After Christmas Sale. Usually, the new price and item will be identified below by two signs (with the topper slipped in between) in the fixture (Figure 8–21). The advantage of toppers

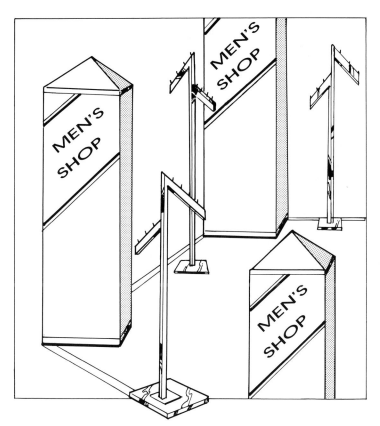

Figure 8–20
Large floor-standing signs can be used to identify and define a department.

Figure 8–21
The anniversary sign is a topper. The sign below is a merchandise identification sign.

is their ease of installation and change. The disadvantage is that if the sale's name is very long the toppers may hang over the frame and look sloppy.

Cardboard signs can be made in any size. If a signing program needs to be developed for a new or existing store, it's important to understand the uses and abuses of the sizes of signs. 5–1/2" × 7" is the most common size frame. This is an adequate size to catch the eye without being overly large and annoying. It is not possible to print a lot of information in this small size: it gets crowded and confusing. If necessary, the 7" × 11" size can be used. In ready-to-wear departments the 5-1/2" × 7" size is fine. In hard-goods areas where more information is needed (such as sheet, cookware, or mattress prices) the 7" × 11" size provides space for more information. Once sign holders are purchased for an area, the buyers should be made aware of what size signs they should order for each department and limit their wording to the specific size sign. If the dress department has 5-1/2" × 7" signs, all the cardboard signs including sales should be that size to ensure continuity. The only exceptions are freestanding floor signs that are poster size and usually announce major promotions with graphics or strong lettering. In larger stores the floor signs may also contain directories. It is almost always the responsibility of the visual merchandising department to distribute, collect, and maintain the special sale signs. Check daily to make sure the signs are current and not left over from previous events. Also check to make sure that there is information on both sides of a sign holder so that it tells it's story to customers approaching from different areas.

Sign holders are made in wood, Plexiglas, and metals, including chrome, wrought iron, and brass. The two most common materials are chrome and plexi. The cost and durability are similar. Plexi cracks sooner, but metal bends easily. Scratches and chips are typical of sign holders that are stashed in stockrooms by sales managers anxious not to lose one precious holder to another department. Stashing is a way of department store life that could be a chapter on its own. Occasional early morning "raids" on the stockrooms will allow you to find extra sign holders and display tools that may have been missing for weeks. Territorial imperative is a nicer term for stashing, but it's all the same thing in any store when signs, holders, and tools are involved.

Electric Signs

Neon is the most popular electric sign and has enjoyed immense popularity since its inception. It is available in a large variety of colors and unlimited shapes. Neon requires nearby installation of a converter box for the hookup of electrical current.

If ordering a neon sign, find in advance a suitable location for installation of the box (12" × 15") by an electrician. If there's no hiding place for the box, it will have to be somehow built into the design and can change the entire concept. Usually a wall-mounted or hanging sign can allow the box to be placed in the ceiling or behind a valance.

Fluorescent signs are usually Plexiglas painted in such a way that the lighter or translucent plexi forms the letters permitting the light to shine through, making the letters glow. Exit signs are a primary example of this. A new technique uses fluorescents placed below etched-out plexi. The light travels through the plexi and concentrates where the plastic is gouged out, making those lines glow like neon.

Electric signs are very bright and attract much attention. They should be carefully planned into the exterior and interior decor so they don't compete with one another or fight the environment.

Lettering

Aside from the use of paint, signs can be created in any type style from vinyl stick-on flexible letters, such as Chartpak and Letraset, to wood, plaster, plastic, Plexiglas, glass, Gatorfoam, fomecore, Styrofoam, metal, and Masonite, or any combination of these materials. Such infinite choices can be confusing. If the store you're working in has a definite style of lettering, e.g., Avant Garde or Helvetica (Figure 8–22), your choice of style is limited as continuity is a major concern.

Choosing Lettering

1. Flexible vinyl letters have no depth and are good for one application only. They adhere well to hard surfaces but are difficult to remove once their adhesive has aged or been exposed to strong heat or cold. If they are applied to a bumpy surface, every bump will show up on their surface. It is easiest to apply these by

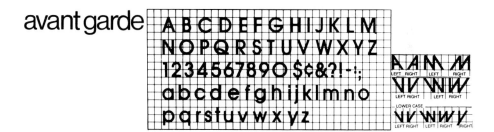

Figure 8–22
Two samples of popular signing/lettering styles that are currently in use in many stores throughout the country.
Credit: Ad Mart, Inc., Brooklyn, N.Y.

peeling off only one part of their protective back covering and positioning the letter perfectly before pressing down. They can be painted with spray paint in an emergency. Their letter edges should be cleaned off with an Exacto knife as the paint will pull up from the surface they've been sprayed on and give a ragged, uneven look. They come in very limited styles and are not expensive.

2. Wood letters are relatively lightweight and last a long time if handled with care. They can be stained, left natural, polyurethaned for a glossy finish, or painted. They can be as flat or thick as needed because wood comes in all thicknesses for a price. The cost is slightly higher than that of plastic letters, but the versatility of depth can compensate for the extra cost. They can be obtained in any style.

3. Plaster letters are beautiful and fragile. They have a range of depths, and can be applied with glue for a permanent sign or made with metal pins coming out of the back to stick into a porous surface. The pins will not go into Masonite, plexi, glass, or baraboard. Plaster letters may be made slanted for cases (Figure 8–23) and also made to stand on their own. Very few vendors make these; the most famous is Mitten. They arrive white and can be painted easily. If breakage is high, these are an expensive investment.

4. Plastic letters are molded in white and come in a large variety of sizes and shapes (Figure 8–24). They are lightweight, sturdy (unless dropped from a height on a hard surface), paintable, and easy to put up with either double-stick foam tape or hot glue. Plastic letters have very little depth—approximately 1/8"—and will crack if not removed carefully with a paint scraper or other long, flat, firm tool. These are readily available from many sources and are helpful for emergencies and rush orders because the larger companies keep them in stock at all times. Plastic letters are reasonably priced considering their life span and durability.

5. Plexiglas or Lucite letters are cut from sheets of these materials and are available in all colors and surfaces. These custom-made letters require more ordering time. More expense is involved in custom design, so naturally they cost more. Depth can be added to these by applying them to any material with depth, e.g., wood, foam, gatorboard, etc. These can be made in-house (with difficulty unless the proper tools and templates are available) or by any reputable sign maker or letter house.

6. Glass letters are rare and expensive. They can shatter easily and are heavy and slippery. They look great, but are recommended for areas that are protected from the public, and only for exclusive merchandise in stores with generous budgets and visual merchants with steady hands. Mirror letters are visually exciting

Figure 8–23
Slanted letters are manufactured in both plaster and plastic. They are most often used in cases and window floors.

Plastics

Interior or exterior use.
Sizes from ½" to 10"
Plain and adhesive backs

HELVETICA MEDIUM

Helvetica—Caps and L.C.** No. L.C. in ½"
Sizes: ½" ¾" 1" 1½" 2" 3" 4" 5" 6" 8" 10"
No Blue in 8" or 10"

ABCDEFGHIJKLMNOP
QRSTUVWXYZ
abcdefghijklmnopqrst
uvwxyz 1234567890
&()/$¢?¿¡!

Other styles not shown:
Script, Barnum, Style 5 (Roman),
Style 3 (Gothic), Old English and Helvetica Italic.

Modified Block: Caps only**
Sizes: ¾" 1" 1½" 2" 3" 4" 6" 8" 10"

ABCDEFGHIJKLMNOPQ
RSTUVWXYZ 12345678
90 $¢&

Jubilee: Caps only
Sizes: 1½" 2" 3" 4" 6"
Use Caslon Numerals

ABCDEFGHIJKLM
NOPQRSTUVWXYZ

Olympia: Caps and L.C.*
Sizes: ½" ¾" 1" 1½" 2" 3" 4" 6" 8" 10"
No. L.C. in ½" ¾" 8" 10"

ABCDEFGHIJKLMNOPQ
RSTUVWXYZ123456789
0abcdefghijklmnopqrst
uvwxyz-&,.?$

Bauhaus: Caps and L.C. No. L.C. in ½" or ¾"
Sizes: ½" ¾" 1" 1½" 2" 3" 4" 6" 8" 10"

ABCDEFGHIJKLMNOPQ
RSTUVWXYZ12345678
90abcdefghijklmnopq
rstuvwxyz&.``?%

Script: Caps and L.C.
Sizes: 3" 4" 6"

ABCDEFGHIJKLMNOPQ
RSTUVWXYZ&?!-$¢
abcdefghijklmnopqrstuvwxyz
1234567890

Condensed Gothic: Caps only**
Sizes: ¾" 1" 1½" 2" 3" 4" 6" 8" 10"

ABCDEFGHIJKLMNOPQRS
TUVWXYZ&?! 1234567
890

Microgramma: Caps and L.C.
Sizes: ½" ¾" 1" 1½" 2" 3" 4" 6" 8"
No. L.C. in ½" or ¾"

ABCDEFGHIJKLMNOPQR
STUVWXYZ1234567890
abcdefghijklmnopqrstuvw
xyz !?&$-"%

Peignot: Caps and L.C.
Sizes: 1" 1½" 2" 3" 4" 6"

ABCDEFGHIJKLMNOPQR
STUVWXYZ &$¢!? 12345678
90abcdefghijklmnopqrstuvw
xyz ¥

Caslon: Caps and L.C.**
Sizes: ⅜" ¾" 1" 1½" 2" 3" 4" 5" 7" 10"
No. L.C. in ½" or ¾"

ABCDEFGHIJKLMNOPQRSTU
VWXYZ$¢. 1234567890abcdefgh
ijklmnopqrstuvwxyz

Helvetica Bolder: Caps and L.C.
Sizes: ½" ¾" 1" 1½" 2" 3" 4" 5" 6" 8" 10"
No. L.C. in ½" or ¾"

ABCDEFGHIJKLMNOPQR
STUVWXYZ abcdefghijkl
mnopqrstuvwxyz 1234567
890 &?!£$()`"%

Clarendon: Caps and L.C.
Sizes: ½" ¾" 1" 1½" 2" 3" 4" 6"

ABCDEFGHIJKLM
NOPQRSTUVWXYZ
abcdefghijklmnopqrstu
vwxyz1234567890&$!;

Condensed Caslon: Caps only
Sizes: 1" 1½" 2" 3" 4" 5" 7"
Use Caslon Numerals

ABCDEFGHIJKLMNOPQR
STUVWXYZ&

Price Chart 1982

SIZE		½"	⅝"	¾"	1"	1½"	2"	3"	4"	5"	6"	7"	8"	10"
SOLID COLORS	PLAIN	.14	.16	.17	.24	.28	.39	.58	.82	1.42	1.54	2.46	2.78	4.13
	STICKY	.21	.24	.26	.36	.42.	59	.87	1.23	2.13	2.31	3.69	4.17	6.20
PAINTED COLORS	PLAIN	.23	.26	.28	.40	.46	.64	.96	1.35	2.34	2.54	4.06	4.59	6.81
	STICKY	.30	.34	.37	.52	.60	.84	1.25	1.76	3.05	3.31	5.28	5.98	8.88
TWO-TONE COLORS	PLAIN	.23	.26	.28	.40	.46	.64	.96	1.35	2.34	2.54	NOT AVAILABLE		
	STICKY	.30	.34	.37	.52.	.60	.84	1.25	1.76	3.05	3.31			

7

Figure 8—24

A sample page from a lettering/sign firm. The prices go up every year

as they sparkle and reflect light. They are more durable than glass because the mirror surface is usually attached to Masonite or gatorboard. To achieve depth, the mirror letter may be attached to deep Gatorfoam. Hang mirrored letters so that they don't reflect the merchandise, but reflect a solid area. Otherwise they will blend in and lose their definition.

7. Gatorfoam is Styrofoam laminated between two hard surfaces. This material can be cut with a sabre or regular saw. Letters in this material are ready-made by several manufacturers. Their depth varies from 1/2" to 3" deep and they come natural (unattractive off-white) unless painting is requested. Because their sides are Styrofoam, enamel spray paint cannot be applied to them until the sides are filled in very heavily with latex paint. If an enamel-based paint is sprayed onto a Styrofoam surface, the foam will dissolve. The result is terrible so extra care must be taken in the beginning to prevent this from happening. The advantages of light weight, good depth, durability, and ease of application outweigh the disadvantage of higher cost.

8. Fomecore letters are cut like gatorboard, but the surface is paper, much less brittle, and can be cut with a knife if needed. These letters are inexpensive but very fragile and must be painted with the same care as the Gatorfoam. These letters also tend to warp when painted with a watered down latex. Again, they can be cut in-house with an Exacto knife or cutawl. To look professional, the lines have to be clean and straight. A variety of depths are available in this material.

9. Styrofoam letters are the least expensive of the foam depth letters but have a rough texture due to the nature of Styrofoam. They go up well but are not durable and can come down in pieces. These are also available in many sizes and styles. All surfaces of these letters have to be painted with latex so they will adhere to a wall. Double-stick tape won't stick to them (unless there's a painted surface) and hot glue will melt right through.

10. Metal letters are very elegant for better departments. They are usually made of brass, aluminum, copper, or regular sheet metal lacquered with paint. These are custom-made, expensive, and look like they're worth the expense. They are extremely durable but scratch easily. Solid metal letters can be extremely heavy. Extra care should be taken to adhere these to the sign area in a safe manner (refer back to the safety chapter). For lighter letters a veneer of metal can be added to an existing dimensional letter. A Gatorfoam "A" with a brass veneer weighs very little more and gains a good effect from the metal front. The total effect of brass is lost, however, on the sides of veneered letters. The question of total metal versus metal facia with painted sides depends on the store or department image. Solid metal (with a depth of 1/2" or more) is much more expensive than veneered metal.

11. Masonite is easy to cut with a saw: the sides can be sanded and it has the best surface for painting (other than Gatorfoam). It is generally 1/8" to 1/4" thick, but can be bought in deeper thicknesses if more depth is desired. The letters can get *very* heavy when the board is thick. Masonite is not a lightweight material and, as it is a highly compressed wood cardboard, it can crack and tear if extreme pressure is exerted on it in one direction. It will bend in the 1/8" and 1/4" thicknesses and is very good for nailing over frames to achieve curved surfaces

(Figure 8–25). Masonite letters are useful because of their paintable surface and the flexibility of the thinner widths. They are usually not stocked by letter houses and must be made to order. For logos and for long, cutout vendor signatures that need a certain amount of rigidity combined with flex, they are ideal.

Chart 1 gives the adhesives and surfaces that work best with each letter material.

Choosing a letter material is a choice often made with the budget in mind. Two basic rules are (1) the less the letter costs, more time is probably required to paint it and the less depth it will have, and (2) more expensive materials require more care so that they can be used again and again.

Smaller letters cost less. The cost rises in direct proportion to the height and thickness of the letter. When ordering letters, the size of the letter is determined by the height of the L, not the O or S. So if you're interested in spelling "Pet Shop", you would order as follows: "I would like "Pet Shop" in 6″ Helvetica, 1/2″ Gatorfoam painted A12 orange on the chart, upper and lower case, please." Upper case are capital letters while lower case are the small letters.

Included is

Height of letters, 6″ on the L

Style of letters, Helvetica

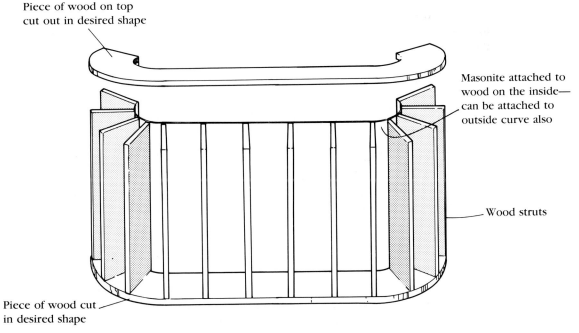

Piece of wood on top cut out in desired shape

Masonite attached to wood on the inside— can be attached to outside curve also

Wood struts

Piece of wood cut in desired shape

Figure 8–25

Masonite curved and attached to wood frames will make object appear solid.

CHART 1

LETTER MATERIAL	BARABOARD	HOMASOTE	MIRROR GLASS	METAL	FABRIC	PLASTER	PLASTER BOARD	
self adhesive vinyl (can rip or tear)	WW, HTGO, POS	WW, POS	WW, HTGO	WW, HTGO	vinyl-WW others- can peel off with temp changes	can peel off with temp, changes.	WW, HTGO POS	WW—works well on this surface
foam core (can bend)	WW, HTGO, HG, DST	WW, HTGO, HG, DST best	WW, HTGO, HG best	WW, HTGO, HG best	HG or SIL will mar fabric	WW, HTGO, HG & DOS	WW, HTGO HG or DOS	HTGO—hard to get off
painted styrofoam (can crack)	WW, HTGO, HG, DST	WW, HTGO POS, HG & DST	WW, HTGO, HG best	WW, HTGO, HG best	HG or SIL will mar fabric	WW, HTGO, HG, DST	WW, HTGO HG or DST	HG—hot glue
plaster (can shatter)	WW, HTGO EX or SIL	WW, HTGO, EX, SIL, or nails	WW, HTGO SIL	WW, HTGO, SIL	no way safely	WW, HTGO, SIL or EX	WW, HTGO SIL or EX	DST—double stick tape
¼″ masonite-lightweight	WW, HG	WW, HG	WW, HG	WW, HG	no way safely	WW, HG	WW, HG	EX—epoxy
glass/mirror (can crack)	WW, HTGO, HG, EX, SIL	WW, HTGO HG, EX, SIL	WW, HTGO, HG,DOS	WW, HTGO, HG, EX	no way safely	WW, HG, HG, EX, SIL	WW, HG HG, DST, SIL, EX	SIL—silicone
plexiglass/lucite (can crack)	WW, HTGO HG, SIL	WW, DST, DST, HG, SIL	WW, HG	WW, HG	no way safely	WW, HG, DST	WW, HG, DST	POS—pulls off surface
plastic (can crack)	WW, HTGO, HG, DST	WW, HG, DST	WW, HG DST	WW, HG	so-so, SIL, EX	WW, HG, DST	WW, HG, DST	1. DST will leave a film on any surface
wood (can chip or crack)	WW, HTGO, nails-drilled HG, DST	WW, nails, HG, DST	WW, HG + DST for safety	WW, HG + DST for safety	no way safely	WW, DST, HG	WW, DST, HG	2. Remove DST with a long knife
metal fascia (can bend)	WW, HTGO, HG, DST	WW, HG, DST	WW, HG + DST for safety	WW, HG + DST for safety	no way safely	WW, DST, HG	WW, DST, HG	3. HG peels off metal, glass, plex and baraboard best
gatorfoam (can crack or chip)	WW, HTGO, HG, DST	WW, HG, DST	WW, HG	WW, HG	so-so, SIL, EX	WW, HG, DST	WW, HG, DST	4. Painted baraboard is the best sticking surface for all adhesives. It doesn't get ruined when letter is removed
solid metal (over ¼″ thick can be exceptionally heavy)	WW, drill into both surfaces	not great	EX and prayer	drill into both surfaces	no way at all	drill into both surfaces	drill & EX & prayer	

Material to be used, 1/2" Gatorfoam

Paint or not, yes, A12 orange

Upper, lower, mixed—upper and lower case

All the information that is needed to ship your letters is given in this exchange. Remember to ask when the company will ship your order and if there is a question on the cost. Ask it directly in your first conversation. Don't wait until you've received the goods. Shipping back is a lot more complicated than receiving. For an exceptionally large order (over $1,000) you may be able to negotiate a discount based on quick payment of the bill. When ordering a sans serif face (clean-shaped letters with no short cross-lines), certain lower case letters can be interchanged.

d ——— p

b ——— q

n ——— u

Applying Lettering

After deciding what type of letter to use and the method of application, the next question is how to actually position the letter onto a surface. Several methods work, but developing an eye for signing will come only with practice. Certain rules apply to all letter types:

1. Set up your letters on a flat surface before permanently adhering them. Measure the space that the letters take so that you'll be able to position them accurately on the display surface.

2. Determine the spacing between the individual letters. You can use a ruler, your fingers, or your eyes, but remember to use less space for i's and lower case j, t, and l.

3. Establish a straight visual horizontal line from which to work. The customer will see the eye level lines (use valances, hang bars, or ceiling) before ceiling lines, so working with lower horizontal lines as a basis for measuring will work better than using the ceiling line. This line gives you something to measure up from to create a straight base line.

4. Use your eyes! The most important rule to remember when signing is that if it doesn't look straight to the eye, it isn't right. No one cares what the ruler says because in the case of proper lettering, appearances count most!

To apply letters straight you can go by the eye or, more accurately, by a ruler. For upper case letters (capitals), a ruler lightly taped to the wall works well. To get the letters perfectly vertical to the ruler's horizontal, use a 90° triangle or a T-square (Figure 8–26).

If the letters are lower case (small), the ruler will get in the way of the g, j, p, q,

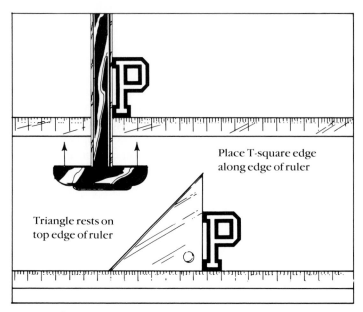

Figure 8–26

To use a T-square, place the inside T-edge against the straight edge of a ruler or valance/sign. A triangle may be used to check the squareness of a letter.

and y. If the words contain those letters, a chalk line will work better than the ruler. A triangle with a chalk line works better than a T-square.

Place each letter carefully, remembering to check for horizontal and vertical accuracy. As rounded letters (such as o's) are often larger than the straight letters, they look better when the extreme round part of the letter is placed slightly below the horizontal line (Figure 8–27).

Be careful not to make the common mistake of placing lower case g, j, p, and y above the horizontal. This can happen when a ruler gets in the way of proper placement. Another frequent mistake is attaching a letter upside down. Often the letters S, X, Z, and N are placed incorrectly. If in doubt, look up the letter in the vendor catalog.

The procedure for centering a word on a surface can be listed as follows:

1. Lay out the letters (no adhesives) on a flat surface, exactly as they will appear on the wall or permanent surface.

2. Measure the letters lengthwise from tip to tip. If the letters are also to be centered by height, measure again from the top to bottom, including the bottom of lower case letters. Always measure the longest letters: l's, g's, and so on.

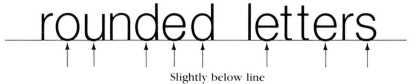

Slightly below line

Figure 8–27
Place rounded letters slightly below the straight line used for letter placement.

3. Measure the area in which the letters will be centered.

4. Divide the letters in half measurement wise and then the surface in half measurement wise.

5. The half point for both the letters and the wall is where to start to place your letters (Figure 8–28).

Signing is instant visual identification. If the signing looks sloppy or wrong, an identity is created that may not project the image you desired.

Give a lot of thought to signing because it is becoming more and more important in visual merchandising. Good signing is a graphic skill that can be acquired by looking at the best stores in your region as well as advertising copy and billboards. The placement, size, shape, and color of letters help to determine a successful image and presentation.

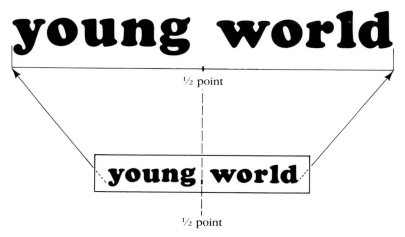

Figure 8–28
How to measure one or more words so that they can be centered on a valance, wall, or other surface.

SUMMARY CHECKLIST

Key Concepts

1. The lighting field is very diverse with a wide variety of different types of lighting available for general and specialized uses.
2. Lighting directly affects the visual merchandising in a store.
3. Light and shadow are the two main design elements to utilize when working with lights.
4. Movement combined with light is a powerful visual attraction.
5. A display can either be a success or a failure based on the lighting pattern used.
6. Signing is another major component of visual merchandising.
7. Temporary signs are usually designed to fit into freestanding fixtures to facilitate mobility.
8. Good signing requires good graphic skill.

KEY TERMS

1. Fluorescents
2. Chase lights
3. Lucite
4. Incandescents
5. Tube lights
6. Gatorfoam
7. High-intensity discharge
8. Generic signing

DISCUSSION QUESTIONS

1. Why is an understanding of lighting important to a visual merchant?
2. Discuss the advantages and disadvantages of fluorescent and incandescent lighting in visual merchandising activities.
3. Explain the purpose, advantages, and disadvantages of filters.
4. Is it necessary to have the same amount of lighting in a window whether the background is dark or light?
5. Why is the furniture display area less bright than other merchandise areas?
6. What is meant by "identification?"
7. Lucite is one of the most popular materials used for hanging signs. What are the advantages and disadvantages of using this material?
8. Why have fabric banners and canvas become popular sign materials?
9. What is the advantage of using plastic letters over wooden letters?
10. What are four rules to follow when positioning letters onto a surface?

STUDENT EXERCISES

Number 1

Develop an evaluation instrument to assess the proper use of lighting in all visual merchandising activities. When the instrument is compiled, field-test it utilizing two businesses in your community.

Number 2

Assume the role of a visual merchandising assistant in a local retail store. Your job is to prepare a general sign to promote sales for the Christmas season. Utilizing your classroom, complete this job using hanging, valance, walls, or column signing.

CASE PROBLEM 1

The New Career

Al Johnson, a local banker in town, has 15 years experience in the banking industry. Thanks to some good investments, he recently became independently wealthy at the age of 40. Al is married, has three children and a nice home, but is not happy with his present occupational status as a banker. After giving this issue serious thought and talking to friends who own their own businesses, Al made the decision to purchase his own retail business.

After surveying community needs, reading business publications, and reviewing research, Al decided to open a new furniture store. He had found the perfect location downtown. Last month a major retail department store moved to a new shopping center and the former store became vacant. The store has a main level and a basement. There is approximately 67,000 square feet of selling space on each level, with large display windows across the front of the building.

The ceilings are suspended and about 12′ high. There are large support columns located in the middle of the floor and running the length of the building. The floors are carpeted with a light brown industrial carpet and the walls are plasterboard. Fluorescent lights provide adquate general lighting but there is very little spot lighting available.

After purchasing the building, Al hired Ralph Leach, an experienced furniture salesman, to be the sales manager and buyer. He also hired Mary Oates as visual merchandising manager. Mary has four years experience as a visual merchandising assistant in a major clothing store.

The store will carry quality merchandise and will be geared toward middle-class customers. The store will be divided into areas displaying different types of furniture, such as dining room, bedroom, family room, etc. For the present, the store will not sell any appliances.

Mary and Al met for three hours this morning discussing Mary's responsibilities. The first major task assigned to her is to prepare a written report on the various types of lighting that should be utilized on the main floor. This floor will include a living area, family room area, bedroom area, and a special section for recliners.

Activities for Completion

1. Prepare the written report for Mary.
2. Be sure to include the following items in your report.

    a.   Types of lighting to be used
    b.   Rationale for using a particular type of lighting

    c.   Where lighting will be needed

    d.   Effect of lighting on departments and merchandise

    e.   Cost efficiency of each type of lighting

    f.   Availability within the community

CASE PROBLEM 2

The Rack Jobber

The Carpenter's Helper is a full-line hardware store located in a rural community. The store began operation 20 years ago and has always been a family operation. For the past 10 years, Mr. Gleason, the owner, has employed a rack jobber (the Davis Company) to merchandise various types of small electric hand tools, such as drills, saws, etc. Until recently, this had proven a very successful venture.

The rack jobber had the responsibility of ordering, delivering, and displaying all merchandise. The Davis Company furnishes all display fixtures, signing, and lighting needed to merchandise the products. During the past year, Mr. Gleason has become displeased with the performance of the Davis Company. He had noted that the merchandise was dirty, poorly displayed, and did not reflect the community needs. Mr. Gleason decided that the displays were no longer desirable.

In analyzing the situation, Mr. Gleason realized that he has three options available: (1) discontinue the product line, (2) take over the small tool area himself, or (3) find a new jobber. Mr. Gleason has always prided himself on the visual merchandise approach that he uses in the rest of the store. The customers always comment on how well the lighting and signs reflect the items that are being displayed.

Questions To Discuss

1. What decision should Mr. Gleason make concerning the Davis Company and why?
2. Should Mr. Gleason undertake a major visual merchandising renovation?

Activities For Completion

Assuming that Mr. Gleason elected to begin a complete visual merchandising renovation and to release the Davis Company, answer the following questions:

1. What generic signage would he need for the total store?
2. What signage should he utilize in the small electrical hand tool area that was previously the responsibility of the Davis Company?

CHAPTER 9

From Conception to Completion

LEARNING OBJECTIVES

At the completion of this chapter, you will be able to:

1. Explain the importance of visual merchandising.

2. Explain the job responsibilities of a visual merchant.

3. Describe the need for short- and long-term shop planning.

4. Analyze the importance of a shop-planning sequence.

5. Explain how a mannequin presentation can be the most theatrical area of a department.

6. List the proper retail merchandising setup procedures.

7. Outline a sequence in the utilization of mannequins as a visual merchandising tool.

8. Discuss the importance of windows as they relate to visual merchandising.

To do it is to learn it. That is the reality of visual merchandising. This chapter will discuss techniques for handling the three major elements encountered most often in department store display. These elements—shops, mannequin displays, and windows—are all designed by the visual merchandiser.

A visual merchant is first a merchant. As such, an understanding of selling your customer and the store's merchandise content is vital. Since the VMM often has the responsibility of aiding in the merchandising of an area, an intimate knowledge of selling is necessary.

Retailing is a rapidly changing business. In order for a store to be successful, it has to pick up on trends quickly. The VMM can successfully plan when buyers foresee large trends in advance and buy accordingly. On the other hand, planning is nonexistent when a fringe business takes off unexpectedly. A buyer may notice a trend in sales that is unrealistically high for one item. A smart buyer, sales manager, or store manager who notices this trend will supply the need by distorting the merchandise content for an area. Distortion means to overbuy an item to create the image of a major product statement. To really sell this merchandise, it must be housed in one area. For multiple sales, related items should be grouped in the shop with the major best seller.

An example of buyer awareness would be with leg warmers. A major New York City department store put a small number of leg warmers in the knee sock area. The movie "The Turning Point" was successful that year and leg warmers instantly became a desirable fashion accessory. Leg warmers sold out in the knee high department and the buyer immediately bought five times the original order. She then had the merchants and visual merchandising department create a separate area for the leg warmers and the sales were brisk. Leg warmers are now a basic fashion item in cold climates and are merchandised separately by all good merchants.

SHOP PLANNING: LONG TERM

In theory the visual merchant has several weeks to plan and execute an idea. Suppose a buyer, sales manager, or store manager wants to capitalize on an upcoming trend and requests visual merchandising to develop a shop in which to house the merchandise. With several weeks notice plans can be made in advance with the manager on the shop location and what merchandise will fill it. With this information you can develop a potential visual plan for the area. Stand back and look at the area. Discuss with the managers the merchandise content, fixturing needs, and the area concept. Discuss also how to reach the customers and identify who these customers are, what they need, to what they respond. How much business per square foot is desired and expected? If this is a small, low-key area, spending a lot of money on props may be a waste of a valuable budget unless the shop is in a prime visual location and a "big money" look will add visual excitement and theatricality to the entire section of the store.

Valances

A direct way to change an area into a shop is to recolor or redesign the valance (Figure 9–1). If there is no valance, one can be built and hung over the merchandised area, but beware that it is not out of step with the existing architecture. To redesign an existing valance one can either paint it, cover it with fabric, cut and cover boards to fit it, enlarge or stripe it, or add graphic elements to it. Props can also be added to the valance as long as they don't distract from the merchandise but instead add to the customers' understanding and pleasure of the shop.

Painting

Now for the practical aspects of shop design. Does the shop need to be painted? Make sure that the new color will work with the surrounding areas. The old color can be duplicated for eventual repainting if the shop is temporary and the paint you order is the correct type to use over the existing paint (latex over oil-based does not wear well; it scratches off easily). Make sure, too, that you order enough paint in advance so that the job can be completed quickly. If you are unsure about a paint

Figure 9–1
A valance was redesigned to look like a road with a traveling bicyclist. This was designed for an active wear area in a men's department.
Credit: Linda Cahan Schneider, 1981.

Plate 1

An opulent Christmas greets customers as they walk down an aisle in Bloomingdales' Broadway cosmetics area. The aisles are canopied by richly ornamented garlands held up by gilded fiberglass cupids.
Credit: Colin Birch, V.M.D., Bloomingdales, New York, New York, 1981

Plate 2

This Christmas window makes good use of both dried and metallic props. The centralized wreath and the metallic balls are rounded objects that are picked up by the circular plate in the center of the composition. Silver and brass gifts are combined among the glass items to solidify the composition. The metallic gifts are accented by the metallic balls.
Credit: Jim Crilley, Jr., V.M.D., David Orgill Co., Beverly Hills, California, 1982

Plate 3

This window is an excellent example of a traditional prop—an egg—used in an untraditional way. Gene Moore uses eggs every Easter in a different way. In this window, a hidden fan blows gently to give movement to the suspended "floating" eggs. The sapphire in the foreground (center) is highlighted by a pin-spot.
Credit: Gene Moore, Display Director, Tiffany & Co., New York, New York

Plate 4

Gene Moore uses this surrealistic painting to create an otherworldly atmosphere. He uses a sphere at the base of the composition in the foreground as a riser for the jewelry. The spherical shape relates to the large balloon in the painting.
Credit: Gene Moore, Display Director, Tiffany & Co., New York, New York, June 1978

Plate 5

This window works very well as a monochromatic statement that glows in both daylight and in the evening light. The belt on the mannequin may be difficult to read in the photograph but clearly says "Night and Day." The use of blue light hasn't hurt the color of the merchandise as it is a deep navy blue. The silhouette effect created by placing the mannequin in front of the lights heightens the lines of the dress at the expense of the detailing. As the lines (in this case) were a more important statement than the details, the whole concept works well as both a merchandise presentation and as an artistic statement.
Credit: Colin Birch, V.M.D., Bloomingdales, New York, New York, 1982, Photo by: Jerry P. Melmed

Plate 1

Plate 2

Plate 3

Plate 4

Plate 5

Plate 6

Plate 7

Plate 8

Plate 9

Plate 10

Plate 6

This interesting and beautiful window was designed in Japan. It creates a world of opulence in a surreal setting.

Credit: Robert Currie, V.M.D.

Plate 7

This surrealistic window technique was developed during the 1930's. Colin Birch has brought it back with a 1980's flair. Note the offset figure on the right. The shoe is positioned exactly as if the figure has legs. The hat is tilted on an invisible head. A mirror is used to reflect the strange figure. Note the color of the vase and how it picks up the suit fabric. The textures work together to give warmth to the slick background surface.

Credit: Colin Birch, V.M.D., Bloomingdales, New York, New York, 1982

Plate 8

The patterns that are created in this window make it a very successful merchandise presentation. The shadows that are created by the pieces of leather that are stretched and suspended in the window give a strong sense of movement. The mannequin in the foreground has an aggressive stance that is picked up in the shape and pull of the black leather piece. The pieces of leather create the horizontal lines that offset the vertical standing mannequins. The colors of the pieces of leather are the same as in the leather clothing that is being worn by the figures. Note how the red is carried through in leather and lighting.

Credit: Colin Birch, V.M.D., Bloomingdales, New York, New York, 1982, Photo by: Jerry P. Melmed

Plate 9

The seated mannequin has a defiant air and seems to be saying, "I'm holding my own umbrella (protection)"—while the three mannequins in the far corner are hiding behind theirs.

Credit: Robert Currie, V.M.D. Henri Bendel, New York, New York, 1979

Plate 10

Exciting negative space is created by the dramatic use of lighting in the window. The shadow created by the standing figure is dramatically different from the actual mannequin pose. The lights were placed to the far right of the figure (on the side of the window). The pattern on the dress of the standing figure is reflected in the diamond shapes on the floor. The colors of this dress are echoed in the outfits of the other mannequins. The attitude of the seated mannequins seems bored and resigned while the standing figure is haughty and removed. This suggests several stories without actually giving away a plot. This window was televised by N.B.C. on their "Real People" show in a segment on window art narrated by Sara Purcell.

Credit: Window by Anne Constantin, Bonwit Teller, V.M.D.: Frank Calise, New York, New York, 1981, Photo by: Willo Font

color, buy a quart and test a lighted area first to get an idea of how it will look finished. Dark colors will take a primer coat to repaint when the shop is removed and, with a small budget, paint can become expensive. List all colors used so that touchups are easy. Try to stay with the same paint company for consistency.

A VMM in a union store must work well in advance with the operations manager to ensure smooth installation of the shop. It is vital that you have the working understanding and agreement of the operations manager (or whoever directs the painters and carpenters) on a date to have the area painted. In a small store, you may have to do this basic work yourself. It pays over and over to keep a change of clothes in your work area for the days that you become a painter/ carpenter.

Fixtures

Consider fixture changes while developing the visual plan. What fixtures would be most appropriate for the new merchandise (Figure 9–2)? Do you have the fixtures

Figure 9–2
These fixtures are perfect for a store that utilizes the high-tech look. They are low cost and highly efficient. The entire store makes use of basic restaurant supply equipment that highlights the gourmet merchandise.
Credit: Greg Turpan—David Sanders, Turpan Sanders, N.Y.C., 1982. Photo by: Eileen Freidenreich.

in stock? Can they be switched from one department to the new one? Does anything require carpentry (such as cubes for folded merchandise) or front-ons for hanging goods? Again, all arrangements for carpenter time and fixture installation must be worked out with your operations manager. Needless to say, a good relationship with this person is essential.

Signage

Signage is usually used to define an area unless there are graphic elements so strong that lettering would be redundant. Order the signage well in advance. The VMM should discuss the name of the shop with the buyer, sales manager, and store manager. Generally the signage in a store should be uniform; otherwise the store starts to look confusing and the customer becomes distracted from the merchandise. If the new shop requires unusual lettering to get the message across, the signage in the surrounding areas should be considered. New, unusual signage can sometimes only add to the confusion. It may be better to order letters that fit in with the rest of the signage, and get the message across with a color change, a prop that works with the merchandise, or strong balance presentation. If the unusual signage does work, make sure it is legible from a distance (Figure 9–3). Order the

Figure 9–3
This valance was redesigned for a special merchandise presentation of costly infant apparel and accessories. The signage was different from the basic Helvetica that was used throughout the store yet was clear and easy to read.
Credit: Linda Cahan Schneider and Joan Wheeler, 1981.

letters in advance, making sure the size is appropriate for the area. Several vendors will ship stock letters within 24 hours if the shop name changes on short notice.

Props

Props are important for creating excitement and theatrics in a shop. However, the props should never overshadow the merchandise, and they should be appropriate (Figure 9–4). Abstract neon sculpture in a western wear shop is inappropriate, but if that neon is in the shape of a lasso, it becomes appropriate. Think your props out carefully and then consult the yellow pages. Quite often you can find many more interesting things by going through the telephone book instead of through lists of vendors.

If you know your shops in advance, you can buy knowledgeably and not waste your money on unusable possibilities. For those last minute shops, make sure you

Figure 9–4
This window of Ralph Lauren clothing uses stencils on the floor as appropriate props. Their simplicity of design and excellent execution make this a unique example of an appropriate use of props.
Credit: Colin Birch V.M.D. Bloomingdales, N.Y.C., 1982. Photo by: Jerry P. Melmed.

take notes on props available from various display houses. Do get information on shipping, since quite a few vendors require a two- to three-week delivery time. If you are under pressure to complete an area, this delay could ruin your best efforts.

Mannequins

If your new shop requires mannequins, prepare them in advance. Perhaps special makeup will be necessary for the shop concept: tans for beach wear, minimum makeup for unusual boutique items, outlandish makeup for punk fashion, and the like (Figure 9–5).

The platform for these mannequins may already exist or, if something unusual

Figure 9–5
This mannequin was painted to match the bathing suit and the surrounding decor. It makes a strong visual statement and is a very effective technique to tie in an entire area.
Credit: Ilene Rosenthal V.M.D., 1982.

is desired, it may have to be constructed. The carpenters and operations manager will need a detailed drawing of your idea so that it can be constructed to your specifications. If materials need to be ordered, order them well in advance. The day of setup should be relatively simple. Newly painted areas should be dry; the props and signage should be in; needed platforms should have been built; and fixtures should be ready for installation. All that is needed now is a person or two or three to make it happen.

SHOP PLANNING: SHORT TERM

We've discussed a plan of attack if you have several weeks to develop your shop concept, but in reality you may have three days, not three weeks, to develop and execute a shop. What do you do in three days? Now your working relationship with your operations manager, your notes on props, and your knowledge of sign vendors comes into play. In an old store, a supply of fabrics, letters, and old props have accrued over the years. Check existing supplies, and if what you have isn't perfect but will work, use them temporarily and order custom lettering and props in the meantime. With luck the vendors will come through and the temporary signage and props will be up for only a few days.

Don't panic. A freestanding valance can be constructed of stretcher strips or regular wood and fabric within a morning. Hanging it takes 15 minutes. Having a supply of gatorboard (see chapter on tools of the trade) handy is essential; with it you also have an instant valance that is sturdy and lightweight. If a valance is impractical due to ceiling height or tiles, a quick definition of an area can be made with floor covering, such as different colored tiles or carpet, and by raising the area with a large, low platform (if there is one in the back area of your store). T-stand fixtures on the perimeters of the shop define the area and show off particular styles. In a hard-goods area, cubes in various height combinations work well to highlight merchandise. To create an instant shop impression with cubes, cut pads to fit on top of each cube and cover them in the same fabric. Repeat this color in the signage and/or valance and floor covering (if a different one is used). With a minimum of construction, the shop should be complete within two days.

Ask the sales manager for the figures (sales) of the area from the last season. Keep a record of the sales in the new shop. This is the record of the success of your shop and the execution of your shop concept.

SHOP-PLANNING SEQUENCE

1. Discuss concept with merchandisers (store manager, buyers, sales managers, etc.).

2. Choose name for shop.

3. Select merchandise content.

4. Discuss fixturing needs with merchandisers.

5. Order signage

6. Order needed props and lighting needs.

7. Set up schedule with operations manager for fixture installation and any necessary painting, carpeting, and construction.

8. Make sure supplies are on hand for any operations work. Order with operations anything that is needed.

9. Test paint sample in advance, if possible, in the area to be painted.

10. Sequence for setup: paint, flooring (if a change is desired), fixturing, signage, mannequins, props, and lighting.

MANNEQUIN PRESENTATIONS

Few props will sell merchandise as well as a mannequin. An exciting mannequin presentation can be the most theatrical area of a department because mannequins are still-life people. If your mannequins are working properly, people will stop to look at them and be influenced by the look projected to buy what is on display or buy the "look." Never underestimate the power of a single mannequin to make a statement and the knockout power of a group of mannequins to tell a total story. If you only have a few mannequins for a department, group them to make a strong presentation.

There are two viewpoints as to where to place a grouping of mannequins within a department. One theory is to place them in the front of the department to introduce the concept of the shop to the customers before they enter. The other idea is to have the platform toward the middle of the department so that the customer has to walk into the department to get a better look at the merchandise. No matter where the platform is, two things must exist: spotlighting on the mannequins to highlight the group and T-stands around the platform to project the merchandise shown on the mannequins. By lighting the display well, attention will be drawn to the merchandise, and once that attention is gained, the T-stands nearby will provide easy access to the goods (Figure 9–6).

At one point visual merchants felt that all the mannequins on a platform should have the same face or be from the same manufacturer. The 1980s have begun with a more natural feeling in groups of mannequins. Different faces lend a more exciting feeling, but watch out for too many different heights or awkward positions. Too much going on within a small area that doesn't relate or make sense can detract from the merchandise. Grouped mannequins should seem natural. Have them doing something real, such as waiting on line, reading on a park bench (seated mannequins), playing ball, lassoing a horse, telling stories, etc. If possible, create conversational groups among the mannequins that seem realistic. If all the merchandise is for women, you don't necessarily have to have all female mannequins. Male mannequins can add some reality and impact to a group of female mannequins.

Figure 9–6
This mannequin presentation is flanked on either side by T-stands that house the displayed merchandise.

If there is only one mannequin per area, highlight that mannequin with a strong light, two T-stands (one on either side), and a simple prop to draw attention to the area. Some classic props are vases filled with silk flowers, columns, lighted objects, and plants. The prop should never be more important than the mannequin and merchandise. It should complement the merchandise rather than compete with it. Try to keep the colors in the same family so that the merchandise, makeup, hair, props, and platform all go together well. If the theme is bright colors, using white or a neutral tone as a background will tie all the discordant colors together. In developing a monochromatic color theme, brighter accessories will add a touch of excitement.

Being creative with fashion can be a lot of fun, and one purpose of display is to educate customers in the new fashion looks; but beware of alienating your customers with a look that is too far-out or freaky. Know your customers, and go a little bit further than they would in real life. Go too far, and you'll lose them to the fear of looking strange. In New York City you can get away with a lot more than in Erie, Pennsylvania or Petoskey, Michigan. Save your super way-out fashions for one or two select departments and then, using mannequins and props to their best advantage, go all out and really make a futuristic fashion statement. In a shop the customer will understand that the merchandise is for a certain customer—not necessarily for her—but nonetheless fun to enjoy. If the way-out look is projected all over in a conservative setting, the customer becomes confused and afraid of the new look.

Setup

To coordinate your setup, discuss with the sales manager the look to be projected. Pull the most recent merchandise and avoid items that are on sale or scheduled to go on sale within a week. Coordinate all the outfits at the same time and try to pick clothes that will work with specific mannequins. Figure out the setup in advance so that the clothes make a good color sequence. There should be a balance between darks and lights, and brights and muted shades. If the makeup on the existing mannequins will not work with the new clothing, use some Fantastic spray cleanser to get rid of the old blush and lipstick, and redo the makeup before putting the clothes on to avoid ruining the merchandise. Obviously care must be taken when dressing the mannequins to avoid ruining the makeup, but care should be taken at all times because mannequins are more fragile than they look.

If the mannequin platform is protected from customers, the mannequins can be wired as in a window display. If customers have access to the display, use the stands that come with the mannequins. The stands are much sturdier, and people have a tendency to pull on clothing and tip over unsteady figures. Children are naturally curious and can hurt themselves badly if the mannequins are unsteady. Tighten all the bolts and screws well so that the shoes are difficult to remove; shoe stealing is very popular in department stores today.

Once the merchandise is pulled, accessorized, signed out, and ready, wigs on hand, mannequins made up, platform set and cleaned, you are ready to put the display together. The best time of day is early in the morning before the store opens or at the dinner hour. If all preparations are completed the night before, the setting can be done easily before the store opens, with just the fine tuning left before customer inspection.

Turn on the lights, get the merchandise in place, and you have a theatrical area in your shop or department that will entertain and sell!

Mannequin Sequence: Day 1

1. Discuss with the sales manager what is wanted for display, keeping in mind major advertising and sales.

2. Pull coordinating merchandise. Remember to sign out everything according to your store security regulations. Take into account the poses of your mannequins and which clothes will look right for each type of pose.

3. Accessorize. Remember multiple sales, but don't overkill!

4. Touch up or redo makeup as necessary.

5. Get wigs together and style unusual ones in advance.

6. Make sure platform area is clean and fresh, not scratched or stained.

7. Ready all props (if necessary).

Mannequin Sequence: Day 2

1. Strip and redress mannequins before store opens.

2. Add accessories and props after everything else is finished.

WINDOWS

Three seconds is the time passersby give to a store window, if they notice it at all. Your job is to stop them for more than three seconds and sell the merchandise projected. In a large city store, windows are determined by the buyers, and the advertising department coordinates the schedule with visual merchandising. Windows are planned weeks in advance, and props can be built, bought, or scrounged in plenty of time to keep to the schedule. In a city store the windows are usually changed once a week, on the same evening. Wednesday is window changing day in many New York City stores.

A large city store will usually have a special staff just for the windows. This staff is composed of the director of windows, production manager, and staff. The staff usually will include a fashion coordinator, wig and makeup specialist and carpenter. The budget for a large store has a special window category that will pay for unusual props and exciting visual effects. A store in a suburb, smaller city, or mall is in a totally different situation from that of the large city store. Windows in the suburbs have been deemphasized because most stores have drive by, rather than walk by, traffic (Figure 9–7). In malls the windows are important, but most stores are designing see-through departments so that merchandise is seen from the outside. Budgets are dedicated to interiors in the suburban stores as most of the traffic is walk-through and the interiors have to catch the customer. Therefore the suburban store VMM who has windows really has to work his excitement into a small budget meant mainly for interiors. Props can be found objects—sheets of paper, feathers, fans, beach balls, old tires—anything in quantity that works with the merchandise and doesn't cost much. Local shopkeepers may loan merchandise for a window credit. Try a car dealer for automobile bodies (if you have an exceptionally large window) or boat manufacturers, etc. As in all your displays, make sure your props work well with the merchandise, enhancing the story.

In a large store, a merchandise schedule is followed so that props can be bought or built in advance. The merchandise can be pulled and accessorized, mannequins dressed, wigs styled, and copy arranged all days before the window is actually installed. A change of background is often desired to complement the new merchandise. To facilitate this change, large pads are usually cut to exactly fit the window walls. This is a tedious job and requires teams of several people to accomplish the task in the evening of a window change. If two sets of pads exist, one set can be changed in advance, saving a lot of time. Floors are often changed in

Figure 9–7
This window is located on the main street of a small town. There is a large combination of walk-by and drive-by traffic. Although the overall display is uninspired and flat, the mannequin's attitude lends a feeling of humor to the window.

a city store where the windows are raised above eye level so that the floor becomes very important and visible. A flooring company will often donate flooring for a credit. The window installation will take place at night so that the least amount of walk-by traffic will observe the change. Lighting at night will appear dramatic, but the same lighting during the day will compete against daylight. Professional photographers are usually on yearly retainer to record all the city windows.

In a smaller store the windows are generally changed during the day, occasionally with a sheet over the window so that passersby don't see the transition. The setup is usually done by one or two persons or a freelancer because the staff is much smaller or part time. Although management may not emphasize windows, customers do notice them and are affected by the style they project (Figure 9–8).

The mirror of the soul is said to be the eyes, and the mirror of a store is its windows. Light them well; keep them clean; project the best looks; accessorize for impact, style, and multiple sales; excite your audience—and your windows will be a success.

Figure 9–8
This window is a very innovative liquor store window done by freelancer Toshi. Each basket and its contents are painted a different color. White, red and brown with natural bottles in the last cart makes a strong graphic and visual statement.
Credit: Toshi, Wine Cart, New York City, N.Y., 1982.

Window Installation Sequence: Week Before

1. Discuss concept with merchandisers.

2. Prepare any props to be used.

Window Installation Sequence: Day 1

1. Re-makeup mannequins as necessary.

2. Pull clothing and accessories, using proper sign-out procedure.

3. If a furniture or hard-goods window is being installed, after pulling and signing out the merchandise, store it in a safe place and arrange for stock help if necessary to move it.

Window Installation Sequence: Day 2

1. Pull out mannequins and props carefully.

2. Vacuum floors.

3. Install new wall pads and flooring if needed.

4. Redress and/or exchange existing mannequins.

5. Wire mannequins in place.

6. Add props.

7. Adjust lighting.

8. Vacuum again and clean glass if necessary.

Organization and creativity are the keys to a successful presentation. A successful presentation means sales, and increased sales means more business and profit. If more business can be directly attributed to your efforts as a visual merchandiser, you will be a success and a credit to your store and profession.

SUMMARY CHECKLIST

Key Concepts

1. Shops, mannequin displays, and windows are the three major elements encountered most often in department store display.
2. Shop planning can be either short- or long-term.
3. The shop-planning sequence is an excellent checklist for the designing of a shop.
4. Signage is used to define an area and should be uniform.
5. Few props will sell merchandise as well as a mannequin.
6. The mirror of a store is its windows.
7. Organization and creativity are the keys to a successful presentation.
8. Props are important to create theatrics in a shop.

KEY TERMS

1. Distortion
2. Valance
3. Signage
4. T-stands

DISCUSSION QUESTIONS

1. Why is it necessary for a visual merchandising manager to have a knowledge of selling and basic sales techniques?
2. When could the concept of "distortion" be utilized in a small appliance store?
3. What information is necessary when preparing a long-term shop-planning sequence?
4. List and discuss five major items that may be included in a visual merchandising plan.
5. What specific types of information should be considered before beginning a fixture change?

6. New and unusual signage should be used whenever possible. Agree or disagree with this statement and indicate your reasons.
7. What is the relationship of mannequins to light, color, and merchandise?
8. Why would visual merchandise planning be different on a short-range basis than a long-range basis?
9. Why is it important to know your customers when setting up displays?
10. How would the planning, setup, and scheduling of department store windows in a large city differ from that of a small city?

STUDENT EXERCISES

Number 1

Utilizing a community business with which you are familiar, decide on an area to make into a shop. Develop the merchandise concept based on today's trends, the customers of that particular store, the store location, and the section of the country.

A. Complete a floor plan, fixture plan, and color plan.
B. Complete a prop and signage plan.
C. Draw the total shop concept as you see it.

Number 2

Design a display for a window that measures 12′ long, 6′ wide, and 12′ high. Your theme is either:

A. Easter (women's and/or men's apparel)
B. Back-to-school (children's)
C. New country style (furniture, lamps, hard goods)

Design the window from the floor up; draw the window as it would look from the street. Remember lighting and the shadows it creates.

CASE PROBLEM 1

What Toys to Select

M. C. Johnsons is a major department store in a community of approximately 185,000. The store features various types of merchandise such as clothing, appliances, hardware, furniture, toys, sporting goods, and more. The store carries a range of medium- to high-priced lines. M. C. Johnsons has been in business for approximately 30 years in the same location.

During the past three years, the downtown area has undergone a complete renovation which is hoped will entice retail shoppers to once again shop in the downtown area. If all construction is completed as planned, the new downtown pedestrian mall will be opened by November 15. One of the major attractions of the mall will be the window displays that will be found in the various stores. M. C. Johnsons will have six windows facing the pedestrian mall.

On July 1, Mr. Bain, the store manager, called a meeting of all department managers to discuss the November 15 "Welcome Back" grand opening. After considerable discussion, it was decided that four of the six windows would be designed to display various children's toys utilizing the Christmas theme. Mrs. Witzler, the toy department manager, was instructed that at least two of the four windows will feature electronic items, of which M. C. Johnsons has one of the largest selections in the community.

Mrs. Witzler was asked by Mr. Bain to prepare a visual merchandising plan for the two windows featuring electronic items, even though it is approximately four months until the displays will be constructed. Mrs. Witzler knows she will have to prepare the justification/response for the following areas:

1. Rationale
2. Merchandise content needed
3. Reaching customers
4. Needed fixtures and props
5. Necessary rebuilding
6. Signage to be developed

Activities to Be Completed

1. Prepare a visual merchandising plan that will include all items discussed in the case problem.
2. Have another student analyze your visual merchandising plan. Discuss any improvements or changes that could be made.

CASE PROBLEM 2

Windows Are Important

Billies Fashions is a highly specialized womens apparel store that is located in a major shopping center. Billies customers are very wealthy and expect to be waited on at all times. The store is small and has two windows that face the mall area.

For the past nine years, Billies has introduced fall fashions on the first Monday in September with a special sale for preferred customers. The store is opened to the general public the next day. It is August 15, and Mrs. Ann "Billie" Baxter, the store owner, has called a meeting of all sales personnel to begin planning the September promotion.

Mrs. Baxter has announced to the sales staff that the fall promotion will include such sales tactics as radio spots, newspaper advertisements, and flyers. The theme for the store will be fall, utilizing several interior displays and many mannequins. As in the past, the two windows will be covered with paper advertising the sale. No window displays will be utilized.

Ann Telton, a student in the local community college fashion merchandising program, has been working part time at Billies Fashions for the past year. During the meeting she questioned Mrs. Baxter's decision about the store windows. She told Mrs. Baxter that she felt it was a serious mistake not to utilize the store windows for display. Mrs. Baxter became very irate and told Ann that "no student would tell her how to run her business." She then gave Ann an ultimatum. Ann was to justify using the windows and submit the justification with a display plan by 8 A.M. the following day. If Ann failed, she could begin looking for a new job.

Questions For Discussion

1. How would you justify the use of the windows during the promotion?
2. In what ways would the window displays increase sales?
3. What theme would you utilize in building the window displays? What types of merchandise would you include?

CHAPTER 10

Freelancing and Special Situations

LEARNING OBJECTIVES

At the completion of this chapter, you will be able to:

1. Explain the value of working and learning under a qualified visual merchandising manager.

2. Discuss the importance of the visual merchant seeking alternative employment other than a retail visual merchandising position.

3. Write a position paper on the free-lance visual merchant as a small-business owner.

4. List and explain the pros and cons of becoming a free-lance visual merchant.

5. Outline the steps necessary in starting a new free-lance visual merchandising business.

6. Summarize the importance, difficulties, and financial arrangements related to using props in free-lance visual merchandising.

7. State the importance of trade shows as an employment opportunity.

8. **Describe the training and experience required for a career in prop design and sales.**

9. **Discuss the relationship of hotel promotions and the visual merchandising field.**

This chapter is separated into two sections: freelancing and special situations. This book has so far been dedicated to teaching visual merchandising skills based on retail store experience. The skills that are learned during a career can be applied to many different situations. The alternatives to working for a large store are unlimited. Freelancing, trade shows, fashion events, and business conferences all depend on the skills learned in the early years of a career. The confidence gained by working and learning under good teachers will help a person throughout his or her career.

FREELANCING

The word *freelancer* has several definitions. The traditional one is "a person who works in a creative field but not on a regular salary basis for any one employer." Not all stores or businesses have in-house display departments. Many stores find it advantageous to hire visual merchandisers to work on a part-time basis.

The origin of *free-lance* may be its early application to the mercenary soldier or military adventurer of the Middle Ages, often of knightly rank, who offered his services to any state, party, or cause.

Freelancing, not by strict definition, can be separated into its two roots. *Free* means freedom of choice in terms of jobs, when to work, what kinds of work to do, and how to do it. It's also the freedom to make or not make a lot of money depending on luck, talent, negotiating skills, and the ability to "hustle" (be assertive/aggressive). *Lancing* is a sport that requires a strong thrust. The effort required in freelancing necessitates a definite thrust for each job. In a regular full-time job the work can be planned for and spread out fairly evenly. If a job can't be finished in one day, it can be fine-tuned and finished the next. Freelancers usually plan to try and finish a job in units of a day rather than partial days because travel to and from individual jobs is considered a business expense. The "lance" in free-lance sums up the life-style of the freelancing visual merchant. Several days or weeks can go by when there are no jobs and then one big one or several may come in at once requiring a major thrust of effort and concentrated time.

The Market

Freelancers can be found in all types of retail situations. Major department stores often hire free-lance makeup specialists, wig designers, and help for Christmas display or special promotions, e.g., theme promotions. Smaller, visually oriented stores usually hire freelancers for all their visual merchandising needs. The stores to approach are not just ready-to-wear but also shoe, jewelry, hardware, furniture, accessory, housewares, and cosmetic stores, to name a few. Art supply stores, plumbing shops, electrical suppliers, and banks also require the services of visual merchants.

A walk around New York City from 34th Street and Herald Square to 60th Street and Third Avenue shows numerous examples of free-lance designers at work. At Macy's on 34th Street, freelancers are occasionally hired to create special wig or makeup designs for the window mannequins. Christmas can necessitate the assistance of many more freelancers. On 36th Street, D. G. Williams, an established manufacturer of high-quality mannequins, once hired a free-lance person every six months to redecorate the showroom for the NADI market week but now has a person on staff full time to maintain an exciting showroom. The people whom display houses hire are experienced and innovative. Many display houses that open their showrooms hire freelancers for the same period.

Another interesting stop used to be Takashimaya, a Japanese department store that tended to put a lot of merchandise in each window. Trendy display was rarely seen here yet an image and style were imparted by the windows. Many different styles and images are imparted along the streets of New York City and Main Street, USA. A free-lance visual merchandiser must first learn about the image a store wants to project before starting a job. The initial interview must both sell the store to the freelancer and the freelancer to the store and its image. If a person is uncomfortable working with an alien style or with undesirable merchandise, his or her ambivalence will show in the final product. Jobs should be accepted when they make sense to both the visual merchandiser and the employer.

Uptown on Fifth Avenue, in the 40s, are the international airlines offices. Air Mexico and Air France are two storefronts that sell vacations. All the airlines change their displays monthly to excite the imaginations of a constant stream of strollers. They often employ free-lance visual people to create this excitement. A small town may not have major airlines represented, but the leading travel agency in town could conceivably be sold on the idea of travel-oriented displays to attract attention and customers.

Gucci is also on the Avenue. There are several Gucci stores, each specializing in different fashion classifications. A main store was opened that encompasses all fashion, yet the smaller stores only blocks away continue to do a strong business. Gucci, like the many other high-priced and quality stores along Fifth and Madison Avenues not mentioned here, depends on the support of a wealthy clientele. The displays and merchandising are conservative and elegant. New-wave and trendy displays rarely appeal to the Gucci- or classic-oriented customer. When applying for a free-lance job, the portfolio sells best when geared to the type of display that the store's image requires. Included can be other styles and ideas, but the versatility of presentation concepts should be apparent to an interviewer.

Roberta di Camerino, Bottega Veneta, Mark Cross, Saks Fifth Avenue, Steuben Glass, Tiffany's, and Bergdorf Goodman are all stores within blocks of each other that use freelancers. Hallmark Cards is another huge retail outlet that requires visual merchandising personnel. Usually a full-time person is on hand but occasionally part-time freelancers are employed. Large book stores often require displays on a part-time basis and could provide excellent free-lance jobs for visual merchants with less experience.

Fifty-Seventh Street not only has clothing-oriented stores such as Henri Bendel, Bergdorf Goodman, Bonwit Teller, Ann Taylor, Burburrys, and Courreges, but also Sherle Wagner (elegant bathroom fixtures), Tiffany's, and many other fine specialty shops and art galleries that provide unique opportunities for the freelancer. Other than retail outlets, industry showrooms offer good job opportunities for freelancers. Decorator fabric houses often do elaborate showroom windows to promote the most current fabrics. Companies such as Spring Mills (Springmaid) have entire floors of model rooms to show buyers their products lines. Cosmetic firms, hosiery firms, and shoe manufacturers all have showrooms that need to be decorated.

Art galleries may occasionally require free-lance help but usually do all their work in-house. Drug stores will sometimes want interesting window displays, but usually this concept has to be sold by the VM freelancer to the store owner. Men's specialty stores, such as Brooks Brothers and Paul Stuart, are on Madison Avenue and have full-time display staffs, but free-lance help is required at Christmas. Cartier, Buccellati, and other exclusive jewelers use freelancers for their small windows and seasonal trims. Jewelry stores all over the country spend time and money on their scaled down elegant windows. Classic windows have been done for Tiffany's by Gene Moore. Using a select variety of everyday objects, Gene Moore (a great display artist) has created legendary windows that continue to have an immeasurable influence on jewelry displays and visual merchandisers.

New York City has more elegant shops and showrooms per square mile than any other city in the world. Surprisingly, Paris and London actually have fewer high-priced shops concentrated in the same small area. Although not every visual merchant can live in New York City, Paris, or London, much can be learned from their examples. Every city has shops, bookstores, fixture houses, and the like. Hustle, imagination, and a good portfolio are all that are needed to get a free-lance job.

Freelancing is a business and a freelancer is a small-scale businessperson. Courses are available at most colleges or high school adult education programs dealing with starting a small business. It is a good idea to take a course to fill in your practical education. Although the direct monetary outlay may only be the cost of business cards, the pros and cons of a free-lance career must be understood. The financial, tax, and legal ramifications are important considerations.

Pros And Cons of Freelancing

1. You can make your own hours—but these hours may be very long in order to get certain jobs done on time. The freelancer has to organize the work load so that everything can be accomplished within the deadline. There is no supervisor to oversee the progress of a project and self-motivation is the key to successful job completion.

2. You can choose your jobs—and/or they can choose you. It can work both ways. Sometimes the jobs come easily. One store owner or manager can

generously spread your name to other stores so that the business grows quickly. A falling out with that person may cause the loss of the same jobs. There are no constants or contracts in most visual merchandising freelance work. It is most often done on a handshake. Sometimes work is admired and the artist is sought by passing merchants. Other times word-of-mouth is the best advertisement. Without self-promotion you may go unnoticed for months. A pleasant personality is a strong plus in freelancing. You're selling yourself as well as your services.

3. You can do exceptional work and be very proud of your accomplishment. The store owner may then give you the ultimate compliment: "We love your window and want to leave it in a week longer." How nice. On the one hand, your talent has been recognized. On the other, you and/or your family don't eat for a week. When you begin to count on weekly pay checks, freelancing is a frightening business. Advance financial planning, budgeting, and careful savings are an integral part of a freelancer's life.

4. You can use any props you desire within a given budget. If you pay for them out of your personal account and the store decides not to pay you back, you're the proud but poor owner of a prop. Usually this problem doesn't occur in reputable business relationships but caution should be taken when entering into any business transaction. Get all the finances ironed out in the beginning. Some people feel uncomfortable discussing money—and others take advantage of this. A freelancer is in business and must approach each job professionally. The question of who pays for and subsequently owns the props is a major point of negotiation. The freelancer is always responsible for designing the windows and buying the props. The budget for props should be determined by the store and the freelancer when the job is first transacted.

Often a freelancer will borrow or make props for the store. The advantage of this approach is the lesser cost and more individualized look. The disadvantage is the construction time that cuts into the overall profits. The best and most common arrangement is when the freelancer gets a flat fee for each display and the merchant pays for the props. In many situations the props will travel with the freelancer—as a favor from the merchant. Merchants realize they may end up getting more props for their money by allowing the freelancer to use their props for other stores. The freelancer will often rotate props from store to store if they are in uncompetitive areas, e.g., different cities or towns spaced far apart.

Summary of Pros and Cons

1. Hours are flexible; may be more or less than wanted

2. Choice of for whom and where to work; may not get the jobs wanted

3. Management may like the work so much that they keep it up longer; tighten belt—you only get paid for new work, not old work twice

4. Get to buy or make a lot of interesting props; may end up owning the props if the store doesn't pay for them.

Given the pros and cons, freelancing may be one of the last frontiers in the job market. The challenge of starting a freelancing business requires much energy, money, time, talent, and guts. It can definitely be worth the effort once the jobs build up and the income becomes steadier. The pros can eventually outweigh the cons as business sense grows through experience.

STARTING A NEW BUSINESS

Essential Steps

1. Put together a portfolio to show at interviews for both your freelance display business and other potential jobs. Make sure the portfolio reflects *professional* abilities.

    A. The portfolio should show a wide range of displays including windows, interiors, and promotions.

    B. The pages of the portfolio work best graphically when they are uniform in background color and clean and simple. The photos should be attached by back mounts, e.g., rolled tape or rubber cement.

    C. Any explanatory writing should be either printed in an architectural style or printed with Letraset, Chart Pac, or Transfer Type (Figure 10–1)

    D. Included in the portfolio are a resume, business card, and written references if they are available.

    E. The portfolio itself should be of a high quality material, e.g., canvas, vinyl, metal, or leather. The surface should be clean with no stains or rips.

    F. Don't get too cute. Classic or clean graphic styling and lettering are best when presenting an image.

2. Scout the market before quitting a full-time job. Try to line up several accounts on a moonlighting (evening or weekend jobs) basis so that there will be immediate income after leaving the 9–5 work world. If this is impossible, you may be in the wrong place at the wrong time to try freelancing. Your success at this point will act as a barometer for your success in the future.

3. Figure out your overhead costs by the month. Add your fixed costs first—rent or mortgage, car payment (?), telephone service charge, loans, insurance (health—a necessity when on your own), and the base heating/electrical/water costs. The following cost estimates are very approximate!

Estimate:

Rent/mortgage	$550	a month
Telephone	46	a month
Insurance	80	a month
Base heat/light/water	100	a month
Total	$776	

Next, add up the overhead costs that are variable:
Very approximate:

Food	$300	a month
Laundry/cleaning	35	a month
Entertainment (movies, etc.)	100	a month
Gasoline for car	100	a month
Clothing/extras	150	a month
Approximate Total	**$685**	

Total approximate monthly expenses is $1,461

A freelancer can easily make over $1,461 in one month with drive and an excellent portfolio. Understand the fixed and variable expenses and develop a plan to deal with them before starting out as a freelancer.

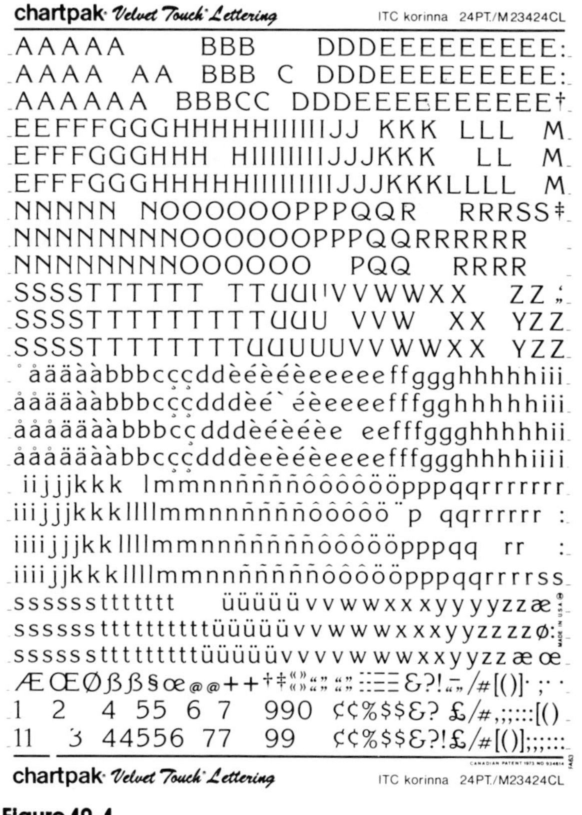

Figure 10–1

A used sheet of Chartpak rub-off letters. The actual size of the sheet is 8½ × 11". These letters can be applied to a clean, smooth surface by rubbing the sheet with a hard, blunt object. The letter will then be transferred to the new surface from the Chartpak sheet.

4. Have business cards made that reflect your style and professionalism. There is no need to spend a lot of money on cards. A good graphic design will speak more effectively than a flashy metallic card. The cards should have a name, phone number, and an idea of your profession. What you do for a living need not be totally spelled out but the concept should be immediately apparent (Figure 10–2). The cards should be left at each free-lance job in case some other merchant is interested in your work and wants to get in touch with you. A card placed discretely in a window is also excellent advertising but permission to do this must be granted by the store's owner or manager. Five hundred cards may cost from $30 on up, depending on the stock (type of paper), the color print, how many colors are used, and if any parts have to be typeset. As with all printing jobs, the cost rises with each additional color printed. A plate has to be made for each color plus the presses have to be completely cleaned to remove the old color so that the new one will be pure. Black is the color traditionally used on printing presses. Having work printed in another color will sometimes double the cost of the regular printing charge. Some printers have a "color of the day" where one press prints a different color daily and there's no extra charge for the ink. Let your fingers do the walking . . . !

5. For another (approximately) $50, stationery can be printed using the same logo or type style as your business card (for continuity). The stationery can be used for invoices (bills to your employers) and/or letters. When terms are agreed on with a prospective employer, they should be written out and duplicated so there are no questions left unanswered. A sample would consist of:

Letterhead

Store's Name   Date

Address

Dear M. Store Owner:

    As per our meeting on February 10, 1984, the working terms of our agreement are as follows:

1. Storeia will provide an electric outlet, a ladder, and three spotlights plus bulbs for the front window space.

2. L. Cahan will provide all props and display materials that will be used and needed for the window.

3. The fee for the window will be $400 per change.

4. The window will be changed twice a month on the second and last Monday of each month.

5. Storeia will notify L. Cahan no less than one week before a new window installation as to the type/color/style of merchandise to be featured in the window. This is so appropriate props may be bought or made.

Thank you for your enthusiasm and cooperation.

Sincerely,

L. Cahan

(Your name typed)

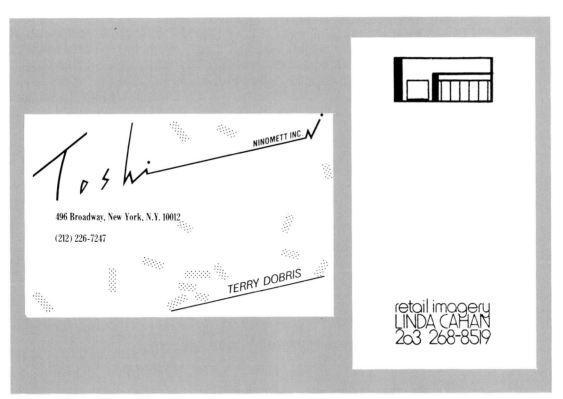

Figure 10–2
Two well-designed business cards.

6. You may want a listing in the yellow pages under "Display Designers and Producers" or under "Display Fixtures and Materials." The yellow pages representative will direct you to the appropriate section. A listing may cost from $10 and up per month for a regular typed listing, on upward depending on the size of the advertisement.

   All throughout this text the Yellow Pages have been recommended as a source guide. The phone listing doesn't have to be among the first things done to start a business but it will help you to develop more business in the future.

7. The phone will be a link to the rest of the working world and to potential jobs. An answering service or a phone answering machine may become vital if there is no one at home to answer the phone. Potential customers don't want to keep calling back. If rushed, they may try another name rather than attempting to track you down. Phone machines cost between $100 and $700. A personal answering service can be far more expensive than a machine as real people are paid to answer your (and many other people's) calls. The service is much more individual than the machine and the higher cost reflects this positive feature.

8. One good job can start off a successful free-lance career. In any city or town there is a group of stores that are the most avant garde, prestigious, or expensive. Go first toward the best. If you can say, "I'm doing the windows for Brooks" (the best small store in town), you have a good name to use on future interviews. Status names always impress people. Merchant A may think if Brooks or Maud Frizon has enough confidence in your skills to hire you, then you're definitely good enough for Merchant A's store.

Summary of Essential Steps

Following are points to remember when starting a new business:

1. Have a professional portfolio.

2. Line up jobs before quitting a full-time job.

3. Figure out cost of living expenses and what will be needed to survive.

4. Have business cards made.

5. Have stationery made and use it for all bills and written agreements.

6. List your services in the yellow pages.

7. Get a phone machine or answering service if needed.

8. Your first few accounts are the most important as they are visual advertisements for your services. Use the names and reputations of these accounts to help secure others.

Props

Props are the responsibility of the visual merchant. It is the duty of the freelancer to communicate with the store to discuss what kind of merchandise will be displayed in the next window change. The freelancer must then determine what kind of props and/or background would be most appropriate for the merchandise. The visual merchandiser's job is to showcase the merchandise rather than just decorate the window.

Props for freelancers should be mobile. The freelancer has to be able to carry the props from the car (or public transportation) to the store. Some small stores have space in which to construct and paint props. Many free-lance jobs are planned to be finished within one day. There is rarely time to build and/or paint props on the job. They should be prepared beforehand and carefully packed so they arrive undamaged at the store. Props are also bought by freelancers for jobs. The cost of the props is usually assumed by the merchants. Cost guidelines should be discussed in the initial meeting between the freelancer and the store.

Renting or borrowing props is a solution that many freelancers elect. Props, as discussed in Chapter 7, can be anything that is made, found, or bought to highlight merchandise. Often, the store where the freelancer works is surrounded by other stores that have different merchandise that can be used as props. Possibly the freelancer is next to an antique store. A credit in the window thanking the antique store for the loan of their merchandise may be the only payment required as it displays and advertises the loaning store's merchandise as well as highlighting the original goods. A credit may read:

> "Chinese vase circa 1700
> loaned by Highbee's Antiques
> 270 Main Street"

This can be either typeset or typed and enlarged at a printer on a 5″ × 7″ card. Hand printing rarely looks professional but transfer type is a good do-it-yourself alternative. The card can be placed in a corner of the window so that it is visible but doesn't interfere with the design of the display.

If renting or borrowing props isn't the appropriate solution to a window design, the next step is to buy or make props.

If the props are to be built into the store's bill, this should be discussed and arranged for in the beginning of the working contract. The store owner/manager may insist on keeping the props as they feel they're paying for them with each window change invoice. When a freelancer makes $100 per window change, the fee is supposed to include props. If the store owner/manager requests that they be more exotic or expensive, the extra cost will have to come out of the $100. A freelancer may end up owning a lot of expensive props but not eating or paying the rent. To avoid this situation, many freelancers will make their own props because the cost of raw materials is much less than that of the finished prop. Again, borrowing or renting props works best under this arrangement. If forced into buying an expensive prop, the visual merchant should carefully choose a prop that is versatile and that will work for several other jobs. The prop's cost will be justified if it can be reused in other situations. If the store insists on keeping the expensive props, let experience be the best teacher. Explain the financial situation and ask for money to cover the extra cost of the requested props. Otherwise, insist that the props be available to the freelancer for other jobs when not in use in the original store.

If the freelancer agrees to pay for the props outright and not build them into the bill, the displayer owns them. Again, the VM should be practical when buying props and consider their multiple uses for other jobs.

The answer to these problems is also the summary. The freelancer will usually charge the cost of the props to the merchants. Renting, borrowing, or building props is the customary solution to the stated problems presented by some store owner/managers. The good VM will often be able to create a strong design without the use of expensive props. If the designs work well with the store's image and merchandise, the owner will be pleased with whatever is bought.

Conclusions

Freelancing is an occupation of the brave entrepreneur. A daily effort must be made to work on existing stores and to develop new jobs. Experience and professionalism are needed to get and keep free-lance positions. Freelancing should be planned for by careful research into job possibilities in the surrounding business community, the financial environment and climate, and careful personal budget analysis. Contracts and agreements are a major part of business and communication skills. Getting as much as possible in writing and agreed on in advance will help keep a working relationship pleasant and profitable.

Finding and getting free-lance jobs involves a certain amount of creative searching ability. Every community offers potential but this potential should be investigated before striking out on one's own.

A good way to build accounts is to do some weekend freelancing in smaller neighborhood shops while employed somewhere else full time.

Saying that freelancing is a frontier in the job market may be overstating its appeal but its potential cannot be overemphasized. Successful freelancers can earn more on their own in a week then in a month of regular pay checks from a department store.

SPECIAL SITUATIONS

Other avenues to explore with visual merchandising experience include trade shows, prop design and sales, hotel promotions, and party decor.

Visual merchandising develops creative generalists. Skills that develop during years of display work involve a good sense of design, marketing and merchandising techniques, budget consciousness, working within a deadline, and coordinating many different jobs and people to complete projects. The construction, design, fashion, and art skills gained are icing on the cake. These skills can be applied to other fields.

Trade Shows

Every industry has a trade show. There are shows for robotics, visual merchandising, men's and women's fashions, accessories, tennis, general sporting goods, plumbing supplies, interior design, home repair and improvement, medical equipment, weapons, military supplies, office systems . . . the list is endless. Each show generally is held in a large, open building with few, if any, partitions built into the interior. Generally the only permanent structures are the restroom facilities, the building offices, the heating/cooling electrical equipment areas, and the elevator/escalator walls. The interior is rented to exhibiting companies by the square foot. Therefore, if a space is 100 square feet and the charge is $12.50 per square foot for the run of the show, the total rental charge would be $1,250. Added to that are the costs of the exhibit design and construction, setup costs, shipping, electricity, travel expenses, entertainment of clients, handout literature, taxes, and breakdown costs. The exhibit itself must display the merchandise in an appealing and stimulating manner. Each exhibit has to create an immediate and strong identity in a given space. Because usually no walls are provided, the elements needed in a trade show are as follows: walls, valances or something to lower the usually high ceilings, floor treatment, and interior and exterior environments.

A typical trade show that is gaining in importance yearly is the robotics show. This show is for companies that produce robots to do mechanical tasks that are difficult, dangerous, or boring for humans. Many companies have invested large amounts of money in robotics and the trade show booths reflect their desire to do business (see Figure 10–3 for GE's robotics exhibit).

Each of these elements must be designed to define the exhibitor and merchandise. High ceilings can encourage the use of long banners, enormous suspended signs, or identifying props. Valances can either be suspended from the ceiling or built up from the floor to identify the area. The materials used in trade shows encompass a vast variety of inexpensive display boards as well as more expensive stock. Some staples used in the construction of trade show exhibits are Masonite, hardwood, Plexiglas, gatorboard, flakeboard, extruded polyvinylchloride (PVC) sheets, Kydex (plastic sheets), aluminum composites such as Alucabond and planium, plastic laminates, combination plastic and metal laminates, polished aluminum (Colkac) and metal structure systems, e.g., Allied, Trend, Syma, and Abstracta. Velcro is used 30 percent of the time to hold signage to the walls. The other 70 percent is made up of epoxys, wood glue, hot glue, and other adhesives, or nails and screws. Strong graphics are vitally important for instant identification of vendors and products. The use and repetition of company logos helps to reinforce the desired image. Some nonindustrial shows are very low key in their approach to signing by requiring each vendor to display one or two preprinted identifying signs. An example would be an 11″ × 14″ cardboard sign saying "Clockwork

Figure 10–3
One small area of General Electrics' extensive trade show booth at the National Robotics Show in Detroit, Wisconsin. The railing is painted in primary colors to define each separate area. The red plastic curtains are necessary for safety when the machines are operating. They also serve as visual backdrops for the robots. The red is part of the primary red, blue, yellow and white color scheme. Note how the signing "ARC WELDING ROBOT AW7" is on a slant. This attracts attention because it conflicts with the strict verticals of the pipe fixturing.

Images, San Francisco, Booth 118." The job of further developing the image of Clockwork Images then falls to the owners and/or display people. The name and cardboard sign are meaningless product identification as they relate no necessary descriptive information to passersby. In shops that have this subtle signing, the vendors create identification through banners, interior signed suspended valances, and occasionally handouts, e.g., shopping bags with the printed logo on both sides.

Lighting is frequently used for graphic purposes. Backlit photo transparencies are often employed to highlight messages, products, and/or services. These are huge photographs that are printed on translucent plastic and inserted into a light box. The light source behind the photo illuminates it so that it appears bright and colorful. A box is constructed of a hard material, e.g., wood, chipboard, or the like, and is either stained, painted, or covered in a formica or metal finish. These boxes are occasionally constructed in unusual shapes to lend an interesting design feeling to the exhibit.

Exterior lights, such as chase lights (lights that move in sequence), or colored lights create other special effects that catch the eyes of potential customers.

Walls can be created from a vast variety of materials. The prerequisites are most often flexibility, lightness in weight (to keep down shipping costs), ease of setup and take-down, and general attractiveness. The walls are often printed with messages to the viewer and may have to be strong enough to hold shelving for merchandise.

There are many knock-down exhibit systems on the market and they are sold as put-together panels with printed material either attached or slotted into shaped framework. These systems require graphic designers to work out the creative design and salespeople with an understanding of graphics and customer needs to sell the systems. The systems are portable so they may be shipped easily and installed by one or two persons. An advertisement for a portable system is shown in Figure 10–4.

Figure 10–4

An advertisement for a portable trade show booth. The company is Outline by Extraversion, Inc.

Getting a job designing trade shows is difficult even for one with visual merchandising experience. Often a person must start in an entry level position (beginners) at a low salary to learn the field from the outset. If an interest in visual merchandising is geared mainly to industrial trade show design, production, and installation, department or specialty store experience is almost unimportant. It makes more sense to try to get a job as an apprentice with an industrial trade show design firm in the very beginning of a career. Experience and/or education for this kind of job should consist of a degree in industrial design, some woodworking knowledge, and a good grasp of graphic techniques such as photography, silk-screening, layout specifications, type styles and typesetting, color separation, and color processing. This is a well-paid field that offers tremendous opportunity for the design- and production-oriented individual. An ability to work with details is an important aspect to success in this field. (See Figure 10–5 for a visual merchandising trade show display presentation.)

Figure 10–5
An exhibit of Poil Kyoya mannequins done by Toshihisa Hagawa for Euro-Shop 1981—a visual merchandising trade show.

Prop Design and Sales

Both a degree in art/design and experience in visual merchandising are invaluable assets for a career in prop design and sales. An understanding of the varied needs and uses of props in the retail environment will give a designer or salesperson workable, concrete information. A designer actually creates the props from initial sketches. A display salesperson will travel to different stores (and in some cases interior design firms) selling the line. The line is a group of items, for sale during a particular season. Canthus's (a fairly new display and interior design firm) current line for fall includes all the new designs that are created for this period. Some firms carry the same line from year to year but add new items instead. An item is another piece of merchandise for sale. This merchandise can range from an animated Santa Claus to a Plexiglas towel displayer for countertops. Each is considered an item by its manufacturer.

The designer of display props has several choices of what type of line to design. As mentioned in the props chapter, designers will either design props that are needed for the upcoming merchandise season or will go off on a tangent, making their own artistic statement. If a display prop designer is aware of the upcoming fashion trends, the designs will reflect and meet the needs of visual merchandisers. The trends in the architectural design and home-furnishing industries occasionally influence the fashion industry. Magazines such as *Domus, Interior Design,* and *Abitare* give good insight into new design trends. *Women's Wear Daily* is the best newspaper for fashion merchandising direction and *Communication Arts* determines and follows current graphic art styles. A display designer may choose to follow the trends in fashion or direct energies toward futuristic or historical design. Vendor and manufacturers have styles for which they are known. A designer is hired either to design within the existing style, to upgrade the line, or to make the line more commercial and inexpensive. The type of material used and the amount of work that is put into building the prop determine its final cost.

An example of an expensive prop would be a fiberglass horse's head that has a special *faux* (trompe l'oeil, see glossary) painted surface. A mold to hold the fiberglass must be made first from an original sculpture. Then the fiberglass is poured into the mold. There are several chemical processes before the mold and head are removed. The fiberglass is then sanded and custom-painted. Even a small fiberglass form takes many steps to complete. The amount of time, energy, and skill needed to create a complicated fiberglass prop makes it necessary to charge extra to cover expenses (Figure 10–6).

A simple prop would be a plexi U-bin used as a riser (Figure 10–7). This is an easy cut-and-shape operation. The sheet plexi ($4' \times 8'$) is cut down its length in straight lines to the width and length of the riser. The sides are then polished and/or beveled by experienced plexi workers. Plexi is bent with heat. Two heat rods are set up for the riser so that the cut sheet only has to be placed on the rods for a specified period of time until it's bendable. Once it cools, the shape is set into the plexi forever—unless it's heated again. The plexi operation may require several experienced people but takes far less time than the fiberglass process. The horse's

Figure 10—6
Relatively expensive high quality fiberglass props. Made by Davila Studios,
4717 S. Citrus Drive, Pico Rivera,   CA 90660.

head may retail (sell to the public) for $350, while the plexi U-bin riser may retail for $5. Both may be made on an assembly line but the customized painting and sanding of the horse along with the original sculpture and expense of the fiberglass adds a great deal of cost to the finished product.

A design must be cost-effective, i.e., not cost more to make than the market is willing to pay. A designer must follow fashion, design, and art trends while creating designs that meet the needs of buyers.

A job in the design field requires the previously mentioned experience as well as a period of apprenticeship at a prop house to learn the material production skills and techniques. It can be a challenging and lucrative field, especially when a percentage of the profits is part of the financial payoff.

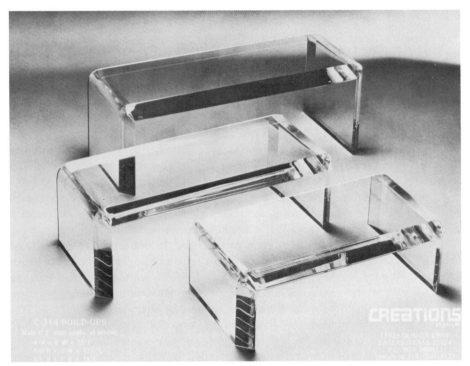

Figure 10–7
A basic but well-made U-bin molded out of a curved and beveled piece of Plexiglas.

Sales are usually based on commission. A salesperson will receive between 10 and 20 percent of each gross sale, not including shipping or taxes. Commission is paid on the base amount the buyer purchases. If commissions are paid on net (rarely), the salesperson is paid for the cost of the item before it's marked up for sale, e.g., a $5 gross plexi riser is actually $2.50 net. The markup is double the net. The first $2.50 will cover the costs of manufacturing the riser and the second $2.50 is profit.

A salesperson relies on the line and personal relationships to make sales. Some personalities are suited to selling and can live with the uncertainty of a commission pay check. Others may feel the need for an unchanging work environment and a steady pay check. A salesperson rarely remains in one place for any length of time. Travel is a way of life and can become tiring after a few years for some people. Personal relationships may suffer if there is too much time spent away from home. For younger adults, travel and sales are an ideal way to learn about business, people, and the country.

Two years in visual merchandising with a good VMM as a teacher is adequate preparation for a career in sales. It's enough time to learn the basics about props, presentation techniques, requirements for and uses of display materials.

Hotel Promotions

Each large hotel or resort makes a substantial amount of money from business meetings, conventions, weddings, and special dinners. Often these events need decoration and coordination. Hotels hire and retain people on staff to take care of these functions. Retail visual merchandising experience isn't required for a hotel job but a knowledge of props and vendors is invaluable to creatively decorate a special party.

Floral decoration and design is often learned as a visual merchandising skill when creating urn arrangements. Weddings require floral skills and really creative floral designers are rare in the field. The sense of large proportion and scale that is learned in display also makes a strong impact for special events.

Large corporations often hold meetings that include the employees' spouses at resorts and hotels. The evenings are sometimes planned around themes. One business within General Electric has a special coordinator of all meetings, trips, promotions, and parties. This person hires party decorators to display theme events, e.g., Gold Rush Days in Colorado. There are a limited number of party decor firms and they are often comprised of only two or three individuals. After learning style, technique, and resources in retail visual merchandising, opening a business in party design could be a lucrative and challenging business.

The special situations listed—trade shows, prop design/sales, and promotions involving parties, conventions, and hotels—are all fields related to visual merchandising. Each area is unique and requires specialized skills. Visual merchandising develops generalized abilities, e.g., to handle several jobs at once, problem-solving skills, successful handling of budgets and deadlines, and a design sensibility that can relate to a myriad of challenges. Although these skills are applicable to the special situations named, most of these jobs require that the applicant start in an entry level position.

One or two years in visual merchandising will give an overview and experience in the mentioned skills. If working in visual merchandising on the retail level isn't as appealing as it once seemed, the potential candidate for a trade show or special-situation job should apply as soon as this lack of enjoyment is apparent so that the entry level salary won't come as a financial setback.

There are many interesting ways to channel creative abilities. Free-lance display work can be marketed to much more than retail clothing stores. The creative and organizational skills developed as a visual merchandiser are applicable to many other artistic fields.

SUMMARY CHECKLIST

Key Concepts

1. Visual merchants have the opportunity to work in areas other than retail display positions.
2. Freelancers can be found in all types of retail situations.

3. A free-lance visual merchant must know how to manage and operate a small business.

4. The steps in starting a new business include: creating a portfolio, making contacts in advance, preplanning a budget, creating business cards, creating business stationery, placing a service ad in the yellow pages, getting an answering service, and doing excellent work on first accounts.

5. Props are the responsibility of the visual merchant. The purchase, building, rental, or borrowing of props is done at the discretion of the visual merchant.

6. Other employment opportunities to the visual merchant include trade shows, prop design and sales, hotel promotions, and party decor.

7. Visual merchandising develops generalized abilities and a design knowledge that can relate to a myriad of challenges.

8. Most specialized visual merchandising work requires that the applicant start in an entry level position.

KEY TERMS

1. Freelancing
2. Fixed costs
3. Avant garde

4. Kydex
5. Colkac
6. Chase lights

DISCUSSION QUESTIONS

1. In which retail positions would freelancers be able to work?
2. Why is it important that a freelancing visual merchant be competent in the management of a small business?
3. List and explain the pros and cons of a career as a free-lance visual merchant.
4. Describe what should be included in a quality portfolio that will be utilized to obtain employment.
5. What information should be included on a complete business card?
6. Analyze the relationship that exists between the free-lance visual merchant and business owner in regard to the purchase and use of props.
7. Summarize the elements necessary to assure that a trade show exhibit displays the merchandise in an appealing and stimulating manner.
8. What skills are necessary to obtain a job designing trade show exhibits?
9. Discuss the job responsibilities of a visual merchant who is employed in the field of prop design and sales.
10. Name the design activities that a free-lance visual merchant would be involved in if working in the area of hotel promotions.

STUDENT EXERCISES

Number 1

Utilize two community businesses with which you are familiar. Conduct an interview with the store owner or manager and determine what fee you could receive if you designed and decorated the store windows. Based on this information, estimate how much money you could make in a month if you had five more clients.

Figure out your monthly expenses. Fill out a ledger for expenses indicating each expense, the amount, and the total amount. Compare the expenses with your estimated monthly income.

   A. Would you have an income or loss? In what amount?

   B. Would it be feasible for you to be employed as a free-lance visual merchant in your community? Explain and defend your answer.

Number 2

Assume that you have decided to become a free-lance visual merchant specializing in hotel promotions. You have completed all necessary activities except development of a business card and placing the listing in the yellow pages.

   A. Develop a business card. Utilize a 5″ × 7″ card to accomplish this task.

   B. Develop the listing that will appear in the yellow pages. You will purchase a 3″ × 4″ ad.

   C. What is the cost of each of these items?

CASE PROBLEM 1

The Lost Job

Leonard Gennenger has been employed by R and R Clothing Store for the past 10 years as visual merchandising manager. R and R Clothing is a large women's and men's clothing store in Logston, a major metropolitan city in the eastern United States.

During the past three years, Leonard has received outside consulting work from various businesses. The majority of his work has been designing displays for functions that are held at the major hotels. Logston is a major recreation and hotel convention center.

Mr. Fredrick, the owner of R and R Clothing, has been concerned about the amount of time that Leonard has been spending on outside consulting work. Mr. Fredrick feels that Leonard is not giving his full attention to the needs of R and R Clothing. Mr. Fredrick has indicated to Leonard that he must not spend more than 10 hours per week on outside consulting or he will be released from his position at R and R Clothing.

Leonard went home that evening and analyzed his situation:

Age: 49

Marital status: Married, Two children, ages 17 and 15

Salary: $32,000 per year. Given a 5% raise last year

Outside consulting fees: $10,000 income last year

Relationship with R and R Clothing: Good

Small-business experience: None

Reputation in the field: Excellent

Miscellaneous: Portfolio and business cards are developed

Questions to Discuss

1. Do you feel Mr. Fredrick was fair in his analysis of this situation?
2. Should Leonard quit his job to become a free-lance visual merchant?
3. Are there any other options available to either Leonard or Mr. Fredrick?

CASE PROBLEM 2

The Proper Design

Ralph Laddel is a qualified visual merchant with 12 years experience in the industry. During the past year, Ralph decided to start his own company called Visual Images, Inc.

Ralph started the business on his own but recently he hired two other visual merchants to help him in the business. Each employee has two years experience. Ralph lives in Landerson, a large southern city with a major convention center and excellent hotel/motel facilities.

During the past three months, the majority of work completed by Visual Images, Inc. has involved designing booths for various trade shows holding their conferences in Landerson. The city draws nearly 40 major trade shows per year to the community.

Educational Consultants recently hired Mr. Laddel's firm to design and build a display booth for the upcoming educational trade show that is going to be held next month. Educational Consultants is a firm that specializes in

1. Student leadership conferences
2. Motivational speakers
3. Multimedia presentations
4. Test scoring
5. Student organization officer training
6. Banquet programs

The educational trade show is scheduled to begin in three weeks. They have reserved a 10' deep × 15' wide space. All that will be provided by the convention center is rails and valances separating the booths on both sides and the back. The side rails are 3' tall and the back rail 8' tall. Electrical outlets will be provided.

Activities for Completion

Design a booth for Educational Consultants.

1. Prepare a sketch of what the booth design will look like.
2. Prepare a materials list of all items that will be needed, such as carpet, valances, walls, signs, lights, and so on.

CHAPTER 11

The Four Seasons

LEARNING OBJECTIVES

At the completion of this chapter, you will be able to:

1. Explain the influence of the individual seasons on the total look of a store.

2. Describe the different themes possible for each season and their relationship to various regions of the country.

3. Outline the major points to remember when developing an overall trim theme for a store.

4. Recite the importance of utilizing special themes in store promotions.

5. Outline the promotional activities necessary during various times of the year.

6. List the important holidays and special dates that have an affect on store promotions.

7. Describe the special shops that are found within stores during the Christmas season.

8. Explain why each store has its own merchandising strategy based on seasons, location, and the calendar year.

Whether it be Florida or Maine, San Diego or Seattle, the selling year is broken up the same way in each climate. The four seasons—spring, summer, fall, and winter—determine the total look of a store in any three-month period while holidays determine the selling promotions. The major themes of store displays revolve exclusively around the seasons except for Christmas. Christmas, the largest selling holiday of the year, has six weeks and millions of visual merchandising dollars devoted to the promotion of the "holiday spirit."

Understanding the promotional and seasonal thematic retailing year will help improve skills for planning budgets, buying props, planning manpower needs, and handling general work loads.

Monetary budget planning will be discussed in the budget chapter. This chapter will discuss the individual seasons and the general display patterns that are seen throughout the country. Then these seasons will be broken down by the retail calendar into promotions, and ideas for each special promotion will be discussed. Within each section, special attention will be given to displays that are universally employed to create a special mood, e.g., plants for spring and poinsettias for Christmas.

THEME SEASONS

Because winter means different things in different locations, knowing the weather patterns helps you to determine the type of displays for the season. Rainy season in San Francisco is the beginning of spring in New York.

Regional differences must always be considered when planning a seasonal display theme. What does that time of year mean to the particular region?

Winter

As the fiscal or financial year starts at the end of January, winter is the first total theme. January and February are the months of sales, inventory, and bleak weather throughout a large portion of the country. Coming directly after the excitement of Christmas, winter themes, when used at all, are bland in comparison. After the Christmas trim is taken down, many stores opt to put up spring trim as quickly as possible for the uplifting impact that the bright colors create or reuse the fall displays for a short period until spring themes are ready for installation. Some stores may invest in a 1-½- to 2-month winter trim, but this is not a common practice. Quite often a Christmas trim can be revamped for winter by removing the red and green and leaving the white. Planning ahead for the January and February freeze in Christmas trim by allowing for the subtraction of ornaments will enable you to maintain an interesting look in the store for the month or two before the spring trim is installed. Budgets for theme periods are determined by the amount of money that particular season will generate. Winter and summer months generate the least amount of profit because they are mainly sale and clearance periods.

Therefore, very little is budgeted for these periods in comparison with spring, fall, and Christmas.

Winter in the northern snow belt areas means hat/scarf/glove displays, boots, fur coats, parkas, ski equipment, heaters, long underwear, electric blankets, flannels, insulated drapes, comforters, and leg warmers to name just a few of the special displays and merchandise that may not be found in the south. The southern states introduce lightweight flannels or corduroy for winter.

In summary, the winter months of January, February, and some of March are not the most visually stimulating months of the year. Some stores ignore them while smaller stores have the flexibility to introduce a winter theme. Budget stores may keep up sale banners for several months as the main form of display. Others introduce spring trim at the end of January while pushing sale items in the main section of each department until the new spring stock comes in to take prime selling space away from the now clearance merchandise.

Spring

Depending on the wishes of management, the spring trim begins in January, February, or the first of March. All over the country spring holds the same meaning: new growth, nature's rebirth, and flowers. Generally, spring trim is employed in every store. Unlike the winter trim, the decor for spring signals new merchandise and the arrival of warm weather.

Winter is energy conservation minded, while spring is nature, fantasy, and romance. Fewer visual merchandising dollars are spent for spring trim than fall because the spring sales generate less capital. Spring and summer clothing is generally less expensive than winter and fall because the materials are lighter. Most 100 percent cotton products are less expensive than 100 percent wool. 100 percent linens, a popular fabric often used by designers for a spring line, is less costly than 100 percent vicuna or suede. Polyester, a year-round fabric, is more expensive in the winter because it generally is combined with wool to create a blend. With less money budgeted for spring trim than fall, the decor has to be planned carefully to get the most impact for the least expense.

As with each seasonal display theme, the overall impression of spring has to be created on the first floor of a store. This feeling will encourage the customer to buy spring clothing even if the temperature is 0°. Spring is such an appealing alternative to winter that a good spring trim will subconsciously convince the customer that spring isn't far off and it's time to start buying new clothing and accessories while they're fresh.

The spring trim will sometimes reflect the fashion colors for that season. One year, large peach-colored urns of peach and apricot blossoms were used in many stores to echo the influence of that color on fashion. A color theme once introduced may be used throughout the store. To achieve a strong impact the color should appear not only in florals but also in the merchandise caseline, on pads, around the mannequin platforms, on pads on top of the core units, and even in the promotional signage. Huge floral arrangements in an assortment of bright colors often herald spring displays. Dogwood branches as well as forsythia and other early blossoming trees may be used to indicate spring in a store.

Besides floral arrangements, huge plants have been successfully employed to give a sense of nature and growth. Many stores rent plants from plant maintenance firms by the month. These firms maintain the plants every week and replace any plant that isn't doing well. Maintenance consists of watering, cleaning, or dusting the leaves, checking for bugs and exterminating them if they exist, repotting plants that need larger pots, trimming new and old growth, arranging the plants in a pleasing way, and rotating the plants for light and moisture when necessary. Before installing the plants, a good company will check the light levels in all the areas requiring plants in order to put the appropriate plant in each environment. Certain plants can survive only with a high light reading while others are called low-light plants and can be used throughout a store. Naturally, the more exotic plants require a lot of light and will die if kept in an improperly lit environment. Low-light plants often used in retail situations because of their hardiness and survival ability are the following:

Corn plant *(Dracaena massangeana)*

Chinese evergreen (*Aglaomema,* six commonly used varieties)

Bamboo pine (*Hamaedora erumpens* or *seifritzii*)

Cast iron plant (*Afpidistra*)

Philodendron—many different species

Rubber plants *(ficus elastica)*

Grape ivy (*cissus—rhombifiloa*), and

Kenthia palm

Medium-light plants that can survive if placed under "grow" spotlights or near a window are:

Peace lily *(Spathiphyllum)*—will grow under low light and flower under medium light

Snake plants *(Sansevieria),* and

Dumb cane *(Dieffenbachia)*

Plants requiring high light, i.e., full, direct sunlight or banks of fluorescents, grow lights, or spots, for survival as well as growth are:

Weeping fig *(Ficus benjamina)*

Ficus nitida (similar to weeping fig but heavier texture)

Cactus

Succulents

Areca palm, and

Schefflera arboricola (useful interior scape plant)

Plants that are going on top of core units in a store need to be placed in either galvanized steel or plastic containers to avoid leakage and damage from watering. To give the plants more humidity, a layer of rocks can be placed under the plants and a low level of water should be left in the container. As the water evaporates from the lights and heat, the moisture will be absorbed by the needy plants. The water should be replaced as needed during the plant's regular watering.

If a plant is moved from one location to another, the plant maintenance firm must be notified for two reasons. First, they must be able to find it in order to water and maintain it. Second, if a plant is put into a lighting situation that is bad for its health, the plant firm will either recommend a change of spotlight bulbs or suggest a different plant for that space.

Plants are used on the selling floor to impart a feeling of life, growth, and greenery. If a plant is brown and dying, it just depresses everyone who sees it. Stores will often try to save money by having the display staff maintain the greenery. Unfortunately, a professional is often needed to properly maintain the plants in the artificial and damaging atmosphere of a retail store. Spider mites, dry rot, root decay, dry atmosphere, and customer abuse are just a few things that often happen to neglected plants. Overwatering can also be a problem. If the plant sits in water, its roots will rot. Salespeople think they're doing the display staff and the plant a favor by watering it every day, but instead they kill it slowly. Having a display person untrained in plant care water the plants may shorten their life. If management insists on having the visual merchandising staff maintain the plants, one person should be permanently assigned the responsibility. That person should then spend a full day at the place from which the plants were purchased or rented to learn as much as possible from greenery professionals about the care and maintenance of each type of plant.

Fake greenery is quite often used in areas that are difficult to reach for watering. Fakes come in rubber/vinyl and silk/acetate. The fakes, like the real plants, get very dusty. But dusting is the only maintenance required by fake plants. Why aren't they used all the time instead of live plants? Because they're fake. Many people resent imitations and consider them relatively unappealing. There are some very good imitations on today's market that can be costly. Fakes are best on hard-to-reach ledges where real plants couldn't survive. Usually these areas are far removed from close scrutiny and the plants can appear real. Illusion, the name of the game for display, works best from a distance.

Plants are not limited to a spring trim—but spring is a prominent time of the year to use greenery. Massing a large amount of live growth creates the spring message quickly. Fresh, flowering plants add a fragrance (sometimes lost in the retail atmosphere) and freshness to spring. Flowering plants do not last long in a retail environment because there isn't enough light or moisture. They are really best for special, short-term promotions to create an overall atmosphere.

The R. H. Macy company traditionally has a spring flower show where the entire store is decorated with flowers and trees that are grown especially for Macy's and forced into blossoming for that period of time. The theme is carried from the street windows throughout the first floor decor and into selected areas all over the store. Special silkscreened sign posters advertise the show in all the Macy's branches. Macy's Herald Square and downtown San Francisco are the two most popular shows. A total spring feeling is achieved by planning, organization, money, and time. Macy's "kicks off" their season with this promotion and customers look forward to it every year.

Smaller stores can do the same on a less extensive basis. Certain visual promotions can be created that tie in to the seasons to start off a selling period and can be advertised as an exciting visual and shopping event. Doing this year after year (giving a few years to develop a following and response) will give a store a reputation for its visual and commercial events.

Spring can be summarized as a time of color, growth, and excitement. Clothing fads tend to emerge in the spring merchandise line because the fabrications are less expensive than winter fabrics. Visual merchandisers can have a lot of display fun with the colorful fashions in both soft and hard lines. Although less money is allotted for spring trim than fall, the color of the merchandise can inspire the visual merchandiser with even a small budget to great artistic achievement.

Summer

Summer, like winter, is a time of merchandise change, inventory, sales, and clearances. It is also a universal synonym for fun. Unlike the bitter chill of winter in many sections of the country where the only life seen is in the evergreens, summer, like spring, means growth and greenery. Swimming, surfing, sunning, and all outdoor sports are a strong part of summer's appeal. Summer promotions generally mean the same thing all over the country, no matter what the temperature reads.

Little business other than clearance sales is generated in the summer season, so the budget for a strictly summer trim is virtually nonexistent in many stores. Special shops may be created to add excitement and visibility to swimwear, straw or canvas accessories, patio shops, sporting goods, and barbecue areas in the beginning of the spring-summer merchandising season. These areas evolve around May and are continued throughout July (which is generally sales and clearance).

Shops for summer challenge the visual merchandiser. The budget is low but the need to create visual stimulation to promote image and buying is just as important in the summer as the rest of the year.

Summer shops, such as swimwear, are included in almost every ready-to-wear department. Another strong area is outdoor living. Barbecue shops are usually located in the housewares section, and props can be created from the merchandise within that classification.

Straw handbags and colorful canvas accessories are a summer staple. Bamboo and bright colors mixed with natural materials are often used. Canvas awnings also help create a summer accessory shop. Again, these are shops that are set up in mid-spring to take advantage of the imagined pleasures of summer.

Spring trim and shops will stay up through the summer months until the first of August when the fall decor is installed. Occasionally, summery props are added to the spring trim to slightly change the mood for summer. Adding natural-colored dried flowers or bamboo to existing urn arrangements can bring on summer at little expense. Some additions may look unprofessional with the existing arrangements and should be avoided.

Summer represents sales and clearances of spring and summer merchandise. Sales for this period are lower and therefore little money is budgeted for the months of May, June, and July. If the weather is exceptionally nice on weekends (the traditional shopping time), the sales may be even lower while the customers are outdoors enjoying the sunshine. Summer trims can be additions to the existing spring decor. Special summer shops relate to the annual purchases of swimsuits, sporting goods, lawn items, barbecue accessories, lightweight and colorful clothing accessories, sandals, straw hats, beach towels, beach chairs, and patio furniture. Summer represents a period of freedom that exists in reality for students and in the minds of working adults who remember the pleasures of a lazy summer day. Using the allure of summer as a selling tool within the spring trim is effective merchandising. Since reality often does not measure up to the creative imagination, summer pleasures are best imagined by the customer in spring buying rather than in the actual heat of July or August. That is one of the major reasons so little budget is allotted for the summer decor and total promotion.

Fall

Fall is harvest time. It is difficult to see orange, rust, and brown without thinking about the changing leaves and the fruits associated with that time of year. Gourds, pumpkins, apples, and nuts are symbolic of fall's harvest. Although the leaves change color in only select areas of the country, the illusion exists nationwide that colorful leaves represent the autumn season.

Fall is a big spending time. Back-to-school clothing, accessories, and supplies are promoted in the beginning of August. The fall merchandise ranges from transitional goods, such as blazers, sweaters, and corduroy items, to a full winter clothing selection. Hard-line merchandise gears itself to winterizing the home, canning the harvest, emphasizing hot beverage accessories, and furnishing the home to redecorate for the upcoming holiday season. The fall budget almost always includes the Christmas trim. Gearing the fall decor to allow for an easy installation and take-down of Christmas trim as well as a potential winter trim puts a lot of planning responsibility on the visual merchandisers. Christmas visual merchandising planning and buying may start in June and not end until mid-December. Christmas will be discussed separately in the promotions section of this chapter.

Fall trims are traditionally based on the back-to-school theme within the children's, junior, young men's, and individual department accessory areas of a department store. The main floor of a multifloor department store will reflect the total fall image. Darker silk flowers, natural dried arrangements, baskets and clay urns, tortoise shell bamboo, branches with colored leaves all are traditional elements used for fall trims. Apples for back-to-school is another basic display prop idea used repeatedly in different ways to suggest autumn. Pumpkins, gourds, and calico prints all suggest fall. Fall is usually associated with change in the colors of the leaves and that change is the most popular attraction of the New England and Pacific Northwest states. Whether a New England fall is used as a cliché in other parts of the country or the fall feeling is created through the use of the region's seasonal indicators, fall remains the major buying season of the year. A store has to make 80–85 percent of its yearly income within the months of August to December. Five months to create and sell the image of excitement and change is a major challenge. Fall exemplifies change: new classes, jobs, clothing to start off the year right. Even though the new year officially starts on January 1, it begins in the minds of children and some adults in September based on the beginning of the school year. Twelve to twenty years of schooling is hard to overcome, regardless of when the calendar year occurs.

Fall shops revolve around back-to-school for the younger set and career areas for the working consumer. The career areas are set up to complement the school displays. These areas try to recreate the need for new clothing in adults by subconsciously alluding to back-to-school thinking patterns. It's not as if the working adult took the summer off from the job and is just starting the office or shop routine in September. However, creating the opportunity for a new beginning in terms of work/career is the principal job of the visual merchandiser when dealing with adult soft-line goods.

Hard lines relate to the home and preparation for winter. As mentioned earlier, furniture has a good selling period in the early fall as people hope for delivery before Thanksgiving or Christmas. Windows devoted to furniture would take advantage of this desire and augment sales for the fall season. Energy consciousness is a strong selling point in domestics during this period.

In summary, fall is the period of highest sales volume and potential growth. The largest budget is allotted to this season to take advantage of the sales and to promote further growth. Because Christmas is included in this season, advance planning has to take into account the transition from fall to Christmas and then to the budget-deficient winter season.

Fall trim usually relies on the perception of a leaf-changing traditional decor. Regional differences can be added, ignored, or explored to develop a new fall concept within the store. These five months are the make-it-or-break-it period for small stores and the major determining factor of the profit outlook for large chains of stores. More than any other season, fall has the most promotions and must be planned and budgeted accordingly.

THEME TRIMS

Total visual merchandising trims help create, develop, and define a store's image. The trim in a department store is usually centered on the first floor on top of the caseline core units in the accessory, jewelry, and cosmetics areas. The columns are occasionally decorated, but are usually left clean until Christmas. As the areas mentioned are almost always the first departments that a customer encounters when entering a store, these caselines and core units require special display attention to create the proper initial impression on the incoming customer.

In a small store an overall trim is essential to avoid visual confusion.

A department store can vary its trim by departments. A men's area in a department store will invariably look different than the misses' area. The unifying visual feeling will have been created by the overall core unit trim as the customer enters the store.

Display decors or trims can be planned three ways. One is to take a theme and carry it throughout a store. The second concept involves using separate overall themes for each department. Last, a combination can be achieved by the core units creating an overall feeling and the individual merchandise shop areas having their own as well.

Total Themes

Total themes involve a combination of visual props. Usually a color or combination of colors is selected to best represent the fashion image the store wants to present at that time. These colors are then used throughout the store in graphic signs for merchandise, the floral arrangements or core unit displays, pads for cases and display areas including core unit tops and mannequin bases, wall pads, ceiling hung banners, sale signage, and merchandise presentations when possible. Try to imagine a store done in a total package of hot pink, cranberry, and white. The colors pop right out as the customer enters the store. Unfortunately, the colors pop so much that it takes a while for the customer's eyes to refocus on the less colorful merchandise. A small store packaged in that color combination can make it work visually by attracting customers with the exciting color projection and then backing it up with merchandise that reflects the displayed color. Naturally, the colors should be chosen after the bulk of the merchandise is bought so that the major merchandise color can be reflected in the visuals.

Choosing a color combination arbitrarily without considering the merchandise selection will do more visual and conceptual harm than good to a store's image. The major spring colors one year were mainly soft pastels. A major retailer in central Pennsylvania chose the hot pink, maroon, and white color combination for a total theme in all of its six stores. The stores in most cases were unrenovated and had no strong architectural visual impact. The areas were often uncarpeted and there were weak valance treatments. The concept of a total theme made sense in these large department stores but the colors chosen were so bright that they drew all attention away from the softer shaded merchandise. All that could be seen when entering the store were masses of pink, red, and white echoed in ceiling-hung banners, huge urns filled with large flowers, signs, and pads. The carry through of the visual merchandising team was excellent, but the colors drained all life out of the store's interior and merchandise. It was a case of too much color in too large a space. Each ready-to-wear department had the same concept: a flowered panel, a standing mannequin or two on a platform, and a large urn filled with matching flowers. After seeing this combination in every department, the concept lost its initial purpose, which was to create both visual excitement and unity. It had unity—but no excitement.

This overall theme concept works best in smaller stores because it can be changed more often to create a sense of vitality to the steady customer. In a smaller store the color theme can be changed with the addition or subtraction of certain colors to create a different impression. Planning for change when first buying and designing the trim can make the changes easier and more successful. Some points to remember are:

1. Overall trims should be selected after the bulk of the merchandise has been bought for the season.

2. Overall trims must relate to the merchandise in both color and concept.

3. Overall trims create an image instantaneously and it must be the correct image.

4. Smaller stores do better with an overall trim than larger stores. The customer won't be bored by a strong theme in a small area but will become uninterested in an extensive repetition of an overall theme in a large space.

5. Overall themes can be achieved by the use of hanging banners or signs; floor signs; matching case-wall-core top and mannequin base pads; flowers or props that relate to the signs and banners; matching urns; merchandise coordination; and valance colors.

Separate Overall Themes

Separate overall themes for each department create more visual stimulation in a large store and confusion in a smaller space. Henri Bendel in New York City is composed of many separate shop areas, each decorated and displayed differently to reflect their individual identities. They work as a cohesive unit because the taste level is universally high and carried throughout each shop as are common architectural details. The main floor of Henri Bendel is an arcade of different, exciting shops situated close together. On the upper floors, each shop is located apart from its neighbor and the shop facades, architectural details, and colors are all different. The empty space around each shop acts as the unifying factor to keep the customer's eye flowing from one area to the next. No one area stands out more than the next by the overuse of color or props. Each acts independently by looking as interesting as possible so that rather than being drawn into only one shop, the customer is enticed to go into all the shops on the floor. It's a perfect example of how separate total themes can work together to form a total image without destroying the viability of the individual merchandise shops.

Separate themes can work against the total store image if the themes compete with one another and confuse the customer. Junior departments may be broken up into many separate areas with individual themes. Similar architectural features or a coordinated valance color and structure will pull these themes together for a cohesive look.

Another large store in the New York area uses just one overall theme for its junior department. Management decided that the bulk of the new merchandise reflected the Victorian feminine lacy look. This theme was carried throughout the exceptionally large department and lost a lot of credibility when placed next to the new junior merchandising thrust—business and career wear.

Some points to remember are:

1. Separate overall themes work best where they are related by architecture, compatible coloration, or merchandise presentation techniques.

2. Separate overall themes can conflict if one is much stronger than the next-door shop. The visual merchandiser wants the customer to enter all the shops—not just one or two.

3. When selecting a department theme, make sure that it's compatible with all the merchandise and not just a selection of goods.

4. Developing resting areas for the eyes between theme areas will refresh the customer's desire to see another exciting area.

Combinations of Themes

An overall theme can be used in the core unit area (cosmetics, accessories, and jewelry) and then be carried out in a watered-down state throughout the store. Individual department themes that relate directly to the merchandise work side by side with the core unit theme hopefully creating a cohesive and interesting feeling. An example of this last theme concept would be a chain of department stores in Connecticut that used this concept to try and get the most visual impact per square foot for the budgeted money. Panels plus floral arrangements were hung and placed on every core unit top. These same panels and florals were on every exterior mannequin presentation. Individual themes were allocated to the junior area, sections of misses' sportswear, the men's department, and areas within housewares. The separate themes were created around specific merchandise presentations and reflected that concept. Juniors, for example, had hanging panels with a silkscreened horse head on each mannequin platform. Each platform within juniors had the same horse head screen, a 4' urn, and the same floral arrangement. This worked well for the western influence, which was the major merchandising thrust of the season, but failed next to the dressier or trendy fashions. The following season this same chain of stores opted for more specific merchandise display presentations so that the individual merchandising trends could be singled out and accorded visual highlighting.

Some points to remember are:

1. A mixture of total core concept and separate department trims is most effective if the separate trims relate to both the core decor and the unique merchandise classifications within the individual departments.

2. Overuse of the core trim can become dull even when worked in with the separate overall themes.

A good combination of trims occurs when a store achieves a strong opening presentation on its main floor and then carries out individual themes that relate to specific merchandise groups, e.g., geometrics, western, fringed Indian, etc., as opposed to trims based on size ranges, e.g., misses' or juniors, half-sizes and petites.

The upper management of a store is most often the factor that determines the trim concept. Starting out as an apprentice in visual merchandising gives a person an opportunity to experience all types of trims and merchandising concepts. Staying in the field for over a year, the VM will be exposed to special promotions that occur during the retail year—the next section of this chapter.

PROMOTIONS

Promotions evolve from national holidays, the calendar year cycle, religious holidays, and special theme concepts, e.g., Ireland, India, and other foreign promotions (Figure 11–1). *Special themes* are merchandise promotions that are invented by the buyers and management to create excitement and sales. Because their dates are arbitrary, they will not be included in this chapter. This section will be divided by months to explain related merchandise promotions important to the visual merchandiser.

January

White Sale Days all month, through February.

January 1—New Year's Day—national day off.

January 2—Start taking down Christmas trim.

January 10—All Christmas trim should be down and put away for the next year.

January 11—Get ready for inventory (depending on the store schedule).

January 16—(approx.)—Redisplay store after inventory.

January 25—Put up Valentines' Day shops, displays, and merchandise departments.

All Month: White Sale Days

Usually a large catalog will be released to acquaint the customers with all the bargains to be found during the white sales. Traditionally, white sheets and towels went on sale during this period, but within the last 12 years, patterns and other colors have become basic white sale items. New patterns are introduced by the manufacturers every six months requiring that older patterns go on sale. The visual merchandising staff will often be responsible for the display of all sale sheets and the distribution of signing to advertise the sale. Often a store will request that the

Figure 11–1
This window was part of a storewide "America" theme that showcased American goods and talent.
Credit: Colin Birch, V.M.D. Bloomingdales, N.Y., N.Y. 1982. Photo by: Jerry P. Melmed.

VM staff decorate the display beds to look like the pages in the catalog or create interesting bed arrangements for each sheet pattern. The inspired use of furniture and gift accessories combined with artificial window treatments and floor coverings can make these bed displays an exciting focal point within a domestics department.

Keep a file of *Architectural Digest* and other home-decorating magazines on hand for quick inspiration for bedroom decor.

January 2: Start Taking Down Christmas Trim

After the extensive amount of time and work put into installing the trim, taking it down will seem easy and quick. If pulled down carelessly, it will be twice as difficult to install the following year. Plan ahead!

If the trim is stored within the store in a stockroom or basement, consider the space and plan to refill it as logically as possible. Walls are needed to store the flat materials so leave at least one or more wall(s) free to place the pads and backdrops. Did you install the ornaments, garland, or column drops last? If so, they should go into the storage space first so they won't be in the way of the trees and other items that are needed for the first week of installation. Cover everything that doesn't already have a box with plastic bags or sheets. Keeping the dust off the trim will allow it to stay fresh years longer. All the trees should be placed carefully in boxes to avoid branches getting caught on other trees. Use a vacuum on reverse (blow) to blow excess dust off the garland, trees, and ornaments. There is far more time in January to work on refurbishing the trim than in November when the push to install Christmas decor on time is intense. Preparing trim for the following year makes for a much easier installation in November.

Most merchandise is removed during inventory. If management agrees, leave the red fabric on the wall and case pads until right before inventory. Then either change them back to the original pads or recover fresh for spring. This way the merchandise and caseline only have to be disturbed once instead of two or three times before and after inventory.

Arrange with operations before Christmas to have any Christmas red repainted so the store can return to its original colors. Stain-kill will have to be used on the red paint first, otherwise the color will bleed through the fresh paint.

If the trim will be shipped to another store for use the following Christmas, repack it carefully in the original boxes and mark the destination clearly on several sides of the cartons. VM department special identification stickers should be used liberally. Give the same attention to the condition of the trim for the next VM as you would for yourself. Don't jam the trim in boxes because you'll never see it again. You'll be remembered for your thoughtlessness when broken items need to be replaced.

Visual merchandising is not all glamor—and the take-down and packing of Christmas trim serves to remind the VM of that fact every year. The best that can be said for this period is that it only comes once a year.

January 14–17 (approx.): Inventory

Inventory is the counting of every piece of merchandise in a store. Although computer sales registers record the type and price of merchandise that is sold, nothing can record theft or loss. In order to get an accurate picture of the profit and losses in a six-month period, a manual count of each salable item must be taken. Inventory usually takes from 3 to 10 hours to complete depending on the size, organization, and merchandise of a store. Preparation for inventory often begins several weeks before the actual day. It's an excellent time for sales and department managers to "clean house."

Preparing for inventory means first getting your own display house in order. Everything that requires signing out from a department should be documented. The merchandise on the selling floor should have a tag or some form of identification to prove that it temporarily belongs to the VM department's account. Depending on the inventory procedures within a particular store, the sign-out procedure should be accurately followed to avoid a false "paper" loss to the store. A blouse from one department used in a display of another may not be counted in the inventory. Because no sale was recorded and the sales manager may possibly be unaware of the transfer, it will appear as a loss. This can continue to confuse the books for two inventories unless it is discovered quickly. In many stores, a visual merchandiser who fails to use the sign-out procedure correctly may be let go. His or her lack of concern directly affects the finances of the store and can look like a potential theft to the loss prevention staff.

After checking to make sure that all merchandise is signed out according to procedure, look within the individual departments to check if any merchandise that is used for display is within easy reach of the salespeople so it can also be counted. If it's out of reach, record it before inventory by using a ladder (or whatever is appropriate for the situation) and give all the necessary information to the sales manager of that department. Keep a copy of the information for yourself just in case it's lost or misplaced.

During inventory everything is usually placed by department number and classification. Usually the department is set up in a less rigid manner and the classifications are mixed to highlight (play off) one another. After inventory all the merchandise must be replaced in an interesting and visually appealing way. This is usually done by the sales managers and their staffs but the VMs should be involved to make sure the store regains a strong merchandise preparation.

Many displays may have been disturbed by salespeople searching for price tags and/or display sign-out stickers. Everything should be fixed or changed. There are usually after-inventory sales on almost all the merchandise in the store to make room for the new season's goods. Sales merchandise usually is not put on display (check with your management about policy) because the new merchandise is generally being promoted and advertised. A store obviously earns more profit from a full-price sale than a reduced-price sale, so new displays are most often encouraged.

A successful inventory requires total cooperation from the visual merchandising department. Working hard to help the sales managers and operations staff during this period acts as good public relations for the VM team. The "I'll scratch your back if you'll scratch mine" cliché is a reality in the working world. The operations and financial people will appreciate and remember the VM staff's cooperation and cheerful compliance with the procedures.

January 25 (approx.): Set Up for Valentine's Day

This holiday actually falls on February 14 and is the most popular buying promotion of the winter doldrums. Women tend to buy more than men for this holiday but equal attention should be paid to all related departments. The areas that require attention from visual merchandising are:

Men's accessories: Ties, shirts, belts, underwear (many companies make special packages geared to Valentine's Day with hearts and sayings printed on the underwear), jewelry, and gift items.

Women's accessories: Scarves, hats, belts, handbags, etc.

Women's jewelry: A very important classification in all areas—especially 14 kt. gold.

Women's and junior lingerie: Special attention should be paid to sheer nightgowns, teddies, matching bra and panty sets, garter belts, etc. Flannel nightgowns should not be a big seller at this time.

One easy way to introduce Valentine's Day throughout the store is to bring the red gift merchandise to the front of each department. Red, the traditional color of hearts, psychologically says "Valentine's Day." The customer will recognize the displayed merchandise as an appropriate gift but may buy it in a totally different color or style. The red merchandise serves to identify gift items such as nightgowns or ties, but the customer will usually choose a more conservative color, assured that the merchandise is appropriate as a February 14 gift.

After bringing the red gift items to the attention of the customer, strengthen the presentation with the addition of signs or symbols. There are thousands of different ways to handle even the most cliched symbols. Using the allotted space, merchandise assortment, and theme, a temporary promotional shop can be developed that gives a new and unique feeling to the holiday promotion. Combining a sense of humor along with good design can create an area with more impact than a traditional concept. Humor must be used carefully as not everyone finds the same things amusing. Test your ideas on as many people as possible before implementing a funny theme. If more than one person says that the idea is tasteless or offensive, the chances are good that many more feel that way but don't have the nerve or honesty to express their feelings.

Using current events as a theme for a shop can work equally well for every holiday. The current event is most recognized when it's either regional or personally touches your customers.

The concept of using humor and/or current events is viable for all visual merchandising shops, windows, and smaller item stories.

Valentine's Day is one holiday that the visual merchandiser can enjoy while getting the merchandise and sales concept across to the customer in a visually appealing way. The VM should be able to take a cliché and bend it to fit the store's particular situation using good design sense and a feeling for humor and/or current or historical events (Figure 11–2).

February

February 12—Lincoln's Birthday sales.

February 15—Take down Valentine's Day.

February 22—Washington's Birthday sales.

Figure 11–2

An interesting and humorous way to portray jewelry for Valentine's Day.
Note the hearts at C-3 and 4. The jewelry is in the open drawer of the antique cash register.
Credit: Gene Moore, Display Director, Tiffany & Co., N.Y., N.Y., February, 1965.

February 12 and 22 will both require visual merchandising's help with the sale signs and banners. This is also a large white sale time and the displays that were installed in January may be getting stale by mid-February and need a change or freshening up. The February 12 and 22 are customary days off for schools, banks, post offices, and most industry. They are big shopping days and it may be difficult to get "on-floor" work accomplished. Most holidays are excellent for behind-the-scenes work.

February 15: Take Down Valentine's Day

Nothing looks more absurd than visual merchandising leftovers. Valentine's Day displays on February 15 are old news. Removal of the displays should begin early in the morning of the 15th. The salespeople and department managers should change all the merchandising to deemphasize red and feature the newest items. The VM is responsible for the decor and signing. The departments will need new merchandise on the mannequins and in the caseline presentations. The salespeople can be a tremendous help to display in a take-down procedure when they're properly instructed and treated with respect. Ordering a salesperson to "put the hearts into a bag" will most likely ensure that the bag will then get "lost." Display/visual merchandising personnel often report to different managers but are not in a position to give orders to salespeople. Polite requests will go a long way toward harmony and helpfulness.

March

March 17—St. Patrick's Day

St. Patrick's Day is usually advertised or displayed only in the greeting card department. Specialty shops may highlight the day if their clientele warrants the attention—or if their shops handle a lot of Irish imports.

Most of March is spent installing the spring shops. Some of these shops will highlight sportshirts in the men's and women's departments; sports clothing in both men's and women's areas (all ages and sizes); raincoats in all areas; canvas and straw handbags; lightweight jackets in all areas, the fabric fad of the season (e.g., looped terrycloth, polished cotton, etc.); and the fashion fads of the season in juniors and some misses' contemporary areas (e.g., the sailor, tuxedo, and Victorian looks, the 30's, 40's, 50's, and the hippie look).

April

Mid-End April—Easter

Easter

Although Easter has been deemphasized as a holiday requiring visual merchandising attention, it still is the most important buying holiday of the spring season. Flower shows, fresh floral displays, and flowering trees have all been used to freshen a store for Easter. Traditional Easter displays, such as eggs, bunnies, and the like, are seen today mainly in children's departments. Stuffed animals and dress clothing are important classifications during Easter. Adult coats, dressses, suits, and millinery are also classifications to emphasize. As a result of the current conservative swing in the country, the old-fashioned values of Easter are showing up in retail advertising and merchandise. Visual merchandising may reflect this trend in windows and floor displays by introducing family scenes, i.e., adult male, female, and children dressed in Easter clothing in a family setting. Undecorated eggs are used by Gene Moore of Tiffany's in a different way each Easter. A surreal window for Easter can be seen in Plate 3.

Usually Easter clothing suggestions are displayed on mannequins throughout the store. New spring dresses, hats, suits, and lightweight spring coats should be displayed with like merchandise grouped in front of each department. Sport clothing is usually in the front of each department during the spring but dressier looks are more appropriate for the month of April.

May

First week—WAVM (Western Association of Visual Merchandisers) Market Week in San Francisco.

Second Sunday—Mother's Day.

Mid-May to Mid-June—Graduation.

Last weekend—Memorial Day.

As with the NADI (National Association of Display Industries) show in New York City, this show is a necessary part of the continuing education of all visual merchants as well as other retailers. Many vendors are represented whose merchandise and unique styles of presentation are an inspiration for new displays.

Mother's Day: Second Sunday In May

Setup for Mother's Day should begin May 1. Most people have a mother, a wife, a grandmother, or even a mother-in-law for whom they'll buy a gift or card. Every department that caters to women is important for Mother's Day. Instead of specific displays for each area, most merchants will have Mother's Day signs and toppers printed to remind the customers that Mother's Day is coming and what day to expect it. "Remember Mother on May 14" is basic sign copy. Special Mother's Day outposts can be set up during these two weeks. Favorite outposts are fragrances and 14 kt. gold jewelry shops. Other outposts can be created for watches, small leather goods, and lingerie. Any outpost must be adequately staffed and stocked. Visual interest can be created by the architecture and graphics. Choosing an overall theme for Mother's Day and recreating it around the store is a good way to identify the different outposts and create unity. A different theme for each outpost is equally effective when identified by the theme color. As with Valentine's Day red, Mother's Day needs some type of identifying factor so customers know that the merchandise grouped around that symbol is appropriate for a Mother's Day gift. Remember, as merchandisers, the buyers and visual people are responsible for telling the customers what to buy. VMs identify and sell merchandise specifically bought by the buyers for a promotion.

Graduation Gifts: May to Mid-June

Special graduation advertising and merchandise is promoted from May through mid-June. Usually watches, pen and pencil sets, stationery, books, jewelry, and cameras are important classifications to identify for graduation gifts. Cards, of course, are important for every occasion mentioned throughout the chapter.

Special gift areas can be created within larger departments catering to the graduate. In a specialty store a section can be set aside, or the entire store can advertise special gift ideas through print posters, toppers, and in-store displays.

Memorial Day: May 30

Memorial Day is a large sale day for spring merchandise. Visual merchandising will be involved in any promotions that take place within the store, as well as having responsibility for sale posters and banners.

June

First week—Bridal Week (in some stores), Father's Day setup, NADI Market Week, New York City.

Third Sunday—Father's Day.

Third Monday—Removal of Father's Day displays.

Bridal Week

Bridal week can be held at any point in early June and is usually featured in larger gift shops, department stores, and bridal shops. Sometimes this promotion will be held in May to give more buying time before June weddings. The purpose is to introduce prospective brides to the merchandise available within the store and to encourage brides to register for gifts at that store.

One way to encourage registering is a raffle for bridal gifts. Many stores will raffle off items to prospective brides. The department will thus get a list of many of the women in the area who are planning a wedding in the near future. In a smaller store or in a sales commission situation (where salespeople get a certain percent commission for each sale), the sales staff may invite the prospective brides to the store for a "bridal consultation." This consultation is to ostensibly help the bride to decide what she needs to start out her married life. In reality it also allows the salesperson to introduce and sell many items in the store's domestics, gift, and china/silver/glassware departments. Many consultants also have a good understanding of wedding etiquette and a sincere commitment to provide real service to the bride. This may build her loyalty as a customer throughout her lifetime.

The Bridal Week displays usually have a romantic atmosphere and sell the concept of the full-blown traditional wedding. Depending on the sophistication of the store, the display may include mannequins dressed up in bridal clothing, a table fully set, the illusion of weddings through symbolism, e.g., doves, figures on top of the cake, flowers, etc., and signing designed especially for the event.

One bride registering at a store can bring in many hundreds of dollars in sales. The sales add up and make the promotion viable and important.

Store policy will indicate how much to promote Bridal Week. As with any promotion, the percentage of business gained by a promotion will determine its future budget allocation.

July

July 4—Big swimwear price break.

July 4 is the traditional day for the large advertisements to appear in the newspapers announcing reduced prices on all swimwear. Recently, the ads and prices have been breaking earlier every summer. A special advertisement is still important around July 4 and usually an effort is required by visual merchandising to help the swimwear department get ready for the expected onslaught of eager customers. Special signs and checkout counters are added in some stores during this sale. Floor displays should be simplified so that customers can't ruin them in the (hopeful) crush.

August

Setup of fall trim—all month.

All month—back-to-school, special "young adult" promotions in college towns.

Early fall fashion shows.

Back-to-School

Anyone who is school age belongs in this category. The juniors, young men's, girls', and boys' departments get the major thrust of this promotion. Back-to-school can be worked as a total theme within each department or several separate shop ideas can identify special classifications within an area. Classic props for this promotion are oversized apples, rulers, pencils, crayons, notebooks, and other school accessories. Traffic signs such as "Caution: School Crossing" are also popular. Letting the merchandise act as an inspiration will allow for more creative and practical designs. For several years the classics were in style, e.g., FairIsle sweaters, button-down shirts, blazers, and so on. Themes were created around "a return to classics." Whatever the current theme is, use the merchandise to your advantage and display it to its advantage.

Back-to-school is usually incorporated into the storewide fall trim so there is a tie-in between the two. A successful back-to-school theme trim was employed by Johanna Bohoy of Charrette, a chain of graphic arts supply stores. All the price tags, cases, mailers, posters, and windows used the same graphic drawing of an apple (Figure 11–3).

Sometimes a symbol can be used in the back-to-school area that is originally from the fall trim seen in the rest of the store. The back-to-school shops and decor remain until November when they're almost always replaced by Christmas themes.

Figure 11–3
The graphics of this back-to-school promotion were so strong that the concept was clear to customers as they entered the store. These graphics also coordinated the individual store images so that Charrette presented a unified appearance. All of Charrette's promotions make use of coordinated graphics.
Credit: Johanna Bohoy, Creative Director, Charrette Co., Woburn, MA. Fall, 1981.

September

September 6—Labor Day.

Beginning of month—Back-to-school and continued setup of fall trim.

Fashion shows.

September 6: Labor Day

Another holiday that requires visual merchandising's help with sale signs and banners is Labor Day. The new fall merchandise is often reduced for a few days to bring the customers into the store and introduce them to the pleasures of shopping and to the new merchandise.

Fashion Shows

Another way of introducing fall fashion is through the use of fashion shows. Depending on the needs of a store, visual merchandising plays a varying role in the setup and take-down of a show. If a platform runway (for the models to walk down) already exists in the store, the visual staff's responsibility usually consists of covering the tops and sides of the runway and adding plants, trees, or other decor for atmosphere and softness. Depending on the size of the store and the operations staff, this task can also involve the setup of the runway and folding chairs. Having sheets of Masonite cut and painted to fit over the top of the runway will save time, energy, and expense for the future, although the initial expense is higher than a fabric cover. Also, Masonite nailed or screwed into the top of a runway is much safer for a model to walk on than fabric stapled to the surface, which will pull up, twist, and catch heels. After the runway is set up it is skirted (fabric stapled to the sides to hide the legs of the platform), given some form of display, and the chairs are set in rows. The visual staff may need to help the fashion coordinator with the taped music or in dressing the models.

Shows are constantly becoming more professional and rapidly paced. Fashion shows do not always inspire customers to buy on the same day but create desire for the fashions shown. Eventually the customers will come back and put fashion looks together to recreate the images seen at the show. In the past a lot of time and display money was spent in decorating the runway and the area around it.

Today, fashion shows are less of a display production as more money and energy is put into the models, commentary, and music. A runway model charges from $30 to $60 an hour outside of a large city and often considerably more in a metropolitan area. Models are usually hired through modeling agencies that keep records of their clothing and shoe sizes. With accurate records, a model need not come into the store for a fitting and the store can save on their total fee. Working with a reliable agency in the long run will save money and time. The fashion coordinator can develop the runway lineup from the agencies' records and set up a walking (down the runway) schedule for the models without their being present.

Sometimes fashion shows are held with the salespersons as models and the store manager or visual merchant as the coordinator. This saves a lot of money but for obvious reasons can appear unprofessional.

The store manager will usually request that many folding chairs be set up to accommodate the expected crowds. The crowds can never be anticipated and usually a large portion of the audience stands so they won't feel committed to the entire show. The average show should last 30–40 minutes at the most. A longer show will bore people and too short a show will disappoint the viewers. The shows always end with a grand finale where all the models come out at once, usually in evening clothing or the strongest designs of a group. Coordinating the finale is difficult but the results are well worth a grand finish. Customers will leave the area remembering the last part of the show and the merchandise will be the first to sell.

Removal of the fashion show begins five minutes after the show is over. It should be completely removed within one-half hour because most shows are done on the selling floor and block access to the merchandise.

Fashion shows are usually scheduled for fall for children's back-to-school and fall adult fashion. (Spring is the other fashion show season.) Children's fashion shows are unpredictable and fun. The biggest part of the audience will be the relatives and parents of the child models. Using the children of customers ensures good relations for the store within the community and with the customers.

October

Refurbish Christmas trim.

October 12—Columbus Day.

October 31—Halloween.

Refurbish Christmas Trim

The beginning of October is the perfect time to measure all the areas that need red covering for Christmas. The trim should be looked at during this time and refurbished or totally redone where needed. All the Christmas lights should be tested, bulbs or total sets replaced, and wires checked for any fraying or splitting. Broken or cracked ornaments, statice or baby breath, and faded, dusty ribbon should all be replaced. Old signs and pads for special areas should be redone or cleaned. Breakable items should be checked for condition to avoid last minute replacement panic. In stores that have large walk-through dioramas that feature animated figures, the work for Christmas can take up to six months and a special staff may be assigned to its completion. The larger the store, the more long-term Christmas planning is necessary. Toy departments often get the same amount of special attention as the walk-through areas. The toy section should be one of the most exciting areas in the store.

New props for all the areas should have been ordered in August or September to give the vendors enough time to produce their orders and to ship in time for the

November setup. Last minute items, such as extra light sets and fake snow, can be bought at any time. Larger, more complex props, e.g., animations, electrical items, silkscreened three-dimensional items, or anything unusually large, all must be ordered months in advance to ensure timely delivery.

A separate folder for all the Christmas information can be a very helpful tool for organization. Keep the measurements of all the Christmas areas in this folder as well as a schedule of installation dates and what is needed for each area.

Columbus Day: October 12

The traditional fall and winter coat sales begin on Columbus Day. Visual merchandising is responsible for signs and banners as well as refreshing the department after the sale ends.

Halloween: October 31

Although few in-store displays are set up for this holiday, many windows are assembled to take advantage of the fun that Halloween generates. Halloween doesn't sell any particular merchandise other than costumes, fabric (white sheets for ghosts), and candy, yet it creates a spirit of youth that relates to the merchandise usually advertised at that time. Junior classifications are important during the Halloween season.

November

November 3—Election Day.

Last Thursday—Thanksgiving.

Election Day; November 3

Election Day is important for sales and the visual merchandising department will again be responsible for all signing, sale displays, and banners (if used). This day also signals the beginning of Christmas trim setup.

Christmas is essentially the strongest selling period of the entire year. The six weeks that constitute Christmas sales can make or break a store—large or small. The largest proportion of the fall budget is allocated to this promotion. The Christmas selling period also includes Chanukah, the Jewish holiday in which one gift is given every night for eight nights. In the larger metropolitan areas where the Jewish population is stronger, this holiday accounts for a good percentage of Christmas sales. The Russian Orthodox Christmas comes several weeks after the traditional Christian holiday. Christmas trim and sales stay strong through that day in areas with a large Russian Orthodox population.

Installing the Christmas trim is the hardest and most rewarding work of the year. It requires very long hours, weekend work, and scratched and bleeding hands, but the reward lies in the transformation of the store when it's complete.

Large amounts of red and green effectively communicates the Christmas holiday. Although many alternate colors can be chosen to decorate a store, these seem to get the point across quickly and with the most warmth.

Metallics also are part of the Christmas sparkle, and gold or silver are often used in ribbon or ornaments (Plate 2).

If a store wants to create a total holiday impact, the areas that should be covered in the main color (usually red) are:

Pads in cases

Pads behind cases in core units

Pads on top of core units

Mannequin base pads

T-wall end panels

Wall pads over merchandise

Escalator walls, and

Valances in key Christmas merchandise areas

Many areas can be covered in felt, moire, an inexpensive polyester, or shiny red vinyl to make the store look festive. The easiest for stretching over pads is felt; the toughest is vinyl. These areas can have separate pads already cut and covered in advance or the existing pads can be recovered. Red Plexiglas, red-painted fome-core, and red-painted Masonite are other alternatives to fabric. One important goal is to keep all the reds the same hue. Each area in each branch store should have the same red color. There are hundreds of shades of red and mixing them can look messy and unorganized.

Areas that require trees or Christmas trim are:

Core tops

Escalator wall ledges

Columns

Mannequin platforms

Inside the caseline

Valances

Large blank expanses of wall

Windows, and

Store entryways

The trim traditionally consists of Christmas trees, garland, drops, and wreaths. The trees come in many styles and materials. Individual taste and management will dictate the preferred style. Bloomingdales, New York City, used a basic tree with elegant ornaments in 1982 (Figure 11–4) on their main floor in cosmetics. A general financial rule is that the taller or the more realistic looking the tree, the more expensive it will be. Metallic or colorful trees are not seen as often today because they tend to offend people by their false appearance. The major exception to this is Henri Bendel's in New York City. For many years this elegant store has had a ceiling high white Christmas tree located in front of the elevators on the first floor. The ornaments change yearly but often range between elegant, stylish,

Figure 11–4
This Christmas tree gives a traditional, elegant feeling through the use of ornaments, netting and fabric in an unusual way.
Credit: Colin Birch, V.M.D. Bloomingdales, N.Y., N.Y. 1981.

old-fashioned, and off-beat. Light is shot through the tree with a combination of floor and ceiling spotlights and small white Italian lights strung on the inside near the trunk help to create a glow.

If a trim is done with taste and style it can work beautifully even when it's totally untraditional.

Garlands for Christmas are made up of fake evergreen (like the trees) and joined to create elongated strips (Plate 1). The average garland length is 9'–12' long and is available in many different widths. Like artificial trees, garlands become more expensive with width (fullness) and quality. If the budget does not allow for fullness and quality in the garland or wreaths, opt for fewer or go with other props. Skimpiness is always unattractive. The garland is usually attached to valances or draped from column to column for a swaglike effect. The same ornaments that go on the trees belong on the garland, wreaths, and drops. Drops are large arrangements that attach to columns by hooks. Ideally, they look the same as the trees and garland. As with the trees, the drops are usually lit with strands of lights.

Wreaths belong on walls or hang doubled from the ceiling with garland swagged on either side. The Christmas trim should be consistent on each evergreen piece. The wreaths should have the same lighting and ornaments as the rest of the trim. Wreaths also have hooks on their backs to attach to hooks on the wall.

Special shops for Christmas are a major part of the overall sales plan. Often special merchandise is bought with a shop in mind at the purchase. Some shops are traditionally seen all over the country. One is Trim-a-Tree, which is sometimes set up in late October to get people thinking about Christmas early. Tree-trimming shops consist of artificial trees and all the ornaments and accessories for sale with the trees (Figure 11–5). Such shops require a lot of space and are often set up in the furniture or carpeting sections of large stores. They need overhead signs for customer identification as well as interior lights to highlight the individual trees. In some cases the companies that manufacture the trees and/or ornaments will trim the trees for the stores. Each style of ornament requires a separate sales bin or basket. These temporary fixtures should be kept in good condition so they can be reused yearly.

A good way of displaying light sets is on small wreaths or trees. The lights display should be on the top of the shelving area with the displayed boxed lights below.

Merchandise the ornaments next to the trees on which they're displayed for ease in selling.

Personalized Christmas cards is an area that may be set up in early October to give customers enough time to receive, fill out, and send their cards before Christmas. This area requires a shelving area for all the books and a desk with chairs at which the customers can sit, relax, and go through the selections. An identifying sign is also necessary. This area is an outpost that does especially well if set up in or near a heavily traveled women's shopping area. Women are the primary buyers of personalized Christmas cards and should be catered to by the overall ambience and location of the shop.

Figure 11–5

This shop was carved out of space belonging to the Budget Shop. Temporary walls also form a backdrop for the short-term department. They are 4' × 8' panels covered in red and are attached to the columns. The hanging sign for this shop can be glimpsed in the upper left corner.

Two recent big sellers for Christmas are prepackaged umbrellas and slippers. The vendors most often associated with these products are Totes (umbrellas) (Figure 11–6) and Dearfoam (slippers) (Figure 11–7). Signing, displays, and shelving are needed for the slippers while Totes provides their own fixtures for the umbrellas and only signing and display become necessary.

Fine jewelry and fragrances are two other outpost/shops that are often set up in high-traffic areas to take advantage of last minute impulse shopping. These areas require locked cases, signs, and personnel.

Special gift items, e.g., candles, glassware, silver, and wooden home accessories, are often grouped together in gift outposts. Sometimes they're grouped by price—under $15, under $25, under $35, under $55, or by material—Crystals, Wooden Wonders, Let Us Entertain You (glassware), A Touch of Brass, Old Fashioned Pewter, Candles Glow, etc. Each area requires a special presentation and sign (Figure 11–8).

More temporary shops are installed and more work accomplished in October, November, and December than any other time of the year. The amount of money made during this period justifies the expense, time, and effort.

The religious significance and good feelings of the holiday season can easily be lost by the visual merchandiser and the retail community as hours grow long and

Figure 11–6

This is a temporary Totes outpost on the main floor of a large department store. The floor, fixtures, umbrellas and signing are all painted or covered in the same red.
Credit: Ilene Rosenthal, N.Y., N.Y.

tempers run short. Keeping the Christ in Christmas, the feeling of wonder in Chanukah, and the holiday spirit of good will are goals that are worth working toward while hauling drops and stapling garland.

The trim has to be up by the day before Thanksgiving. The day after Thanksgiving is the biggest shopping day of the year.

Thanksgiving

On this day, eat, be happy, and give thanks that the major part of your work is behind you.

Day After Thanksgiving

The day after Thanksgiving is a good day to devote to behind-the-scenes jobs. Hopefully, the selling floor will be too mobbed with customers to make any headway on floor displays. Many people have this day off and Thanksgiving signals the start of the Christmas shopping season. If your store has a reputation for wonderful Christmas displays, parents with children will be out in full force to check out the store and to marvel at how beautiful everything looks. If Santa comes

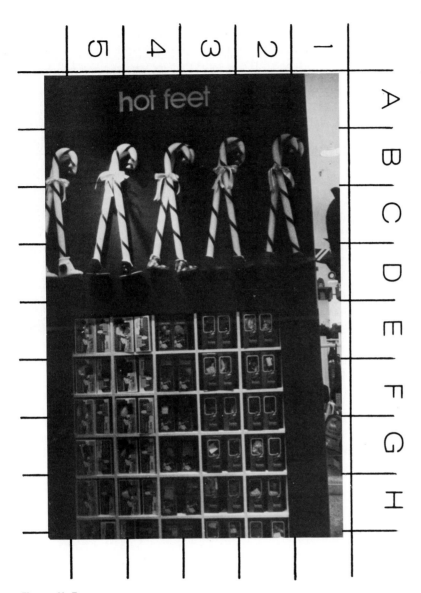

Figure 11–7
This Dearfoam outlet uses temporary space and clever signing to create sales. The wall is covered in red fabric stretched over a board. Note the boots on the feet of the candy canes (D-1-5).
Credit: Ilene Rosenthal, N.Y., N.Y.

to your store, now is the time to set him up in his own highly decorated area complete with oversized chair and goodies for the children.

The setup date will depend on the amount of decor required for Santa's Land or its location within the store. In stores with a special area reserved for Santa, the

Figure 11–8
This successful shop is a temporary outpost in the gift area of a department store. Each item is displayed on top of prewrapped gifts. All the packages and signing are red.
Credit: Ilene Rosenthal, N.Y., N.Y.

decorating can start in September or October because no merchandise will have to be moved elsewhere. If an area for Santa has to be "carved out" of an existing department, the merchandise move will usually wait until the last moment to lose as little business as possible.

December

First week—Set up remainder of shops/NADI Market Week—New York City.

December 25—Christmas.

December 26—Go on vacation if possible, for a needed week or two of rest.

Set Up Remainder of Shops: First Week in December

This finishing up period is a perfect time to fine-tune the existing trim and add an extra touch to hastily installed shops. Additional outposts may be created at this time to take advantage of the merchandising and customer buying trends that are appearing during this period of high sales volume. Some possible trends may include special t-shirts, oversized theme towels, toys that are patterned after television or movie personalities e.g., E.T. or Miss Piggy), a group of decorator pillows, and trendy giftware.

NADI Market Week: First Week in December

The National Association of Display Industries has two shows a year: the Christmas Show in June and the Spring Show in December. Both shows are very well attended and have the largest number of vendors showing their lines to the visual merchandising community. The importance of attending at least one show a year cannot be overemphasized. The show is an excellent barometer of the trends and changes in the field. The personal contacts made at the visual merchandising shows can last a lifetime. It's also very enjoyable to meet in person the people you normally do business with only over the phone.

Christmas: December 25

A day to celebrate either as a religious holiday or as a day off.

A YEAR'S CALENDAR SUMMARIZED

January

1—New Year's Day—national holiday, day off

2—Start taking down Christmas trim

11—Prepare for inventory (if appropriate)

16—Redisplay store after inventory (if needed)

25—Put up Valentine's Day shops

All month—White sales

February

12—Lincoln's Birthday—sales

15—Take down Valentine's Day

22—Washington's Birthday—sales

All month—White sales

End of month—Start installing spring shops

March

17—St. Patrick's Day

All month—Install spring shops

April

Early April—Easter setup

All month—Install spring shops

May

1—WAVM Market Week in San Francisco
   Set up for Mother's Day

Second Sunday—Mother's Day

Second Monday—Take down Mother's Day

Last weekend—Memorial Day

Mid-May to Mid-June—Graduation gifts

June

First week—Set up for Father's Day
            Set up for Bridal Week (if appropriate)
            NADI Market Week—New York City

Third Sunday—Father's Day

Third Monday—Take down Father's Day

July

4—Swimwear price break

Start fall trim

August

Set up fall trim

Back-to-school displays

September

6—Labor Day

Continue fall trim and back-to-school

Fashion shows

October

12—Columbus Day

31—Halloween

Refurbish Christmas trim—all month

Start on walk-through, Santa Land, and toys (if appropriate)

November

3—Election Day

Last Thursday—Thanksgiving

All month—Set up Christmas

December

Set up remainder of shops

NADI Market Week—New York City

25—Christmas

The visual merchandiser tells customers what to buy when he or she highlights or displays certain merchandise. Understanding the promotional themes and planning for them with the buyers and in-store display and sales staff will make installation of theme areas easier and timely.

The seasons may change at different times or not at all but the holidays stay constant. Each store has its own merchandising strategy based on the seasons in its special location and on the calendar year. Although much that was discussed in this chapter relates directly to large department stores, the concepts can be applied to any size and type of retail establishment.

SUMMARY CHECKLIST

Key Concepts

1. The four seasons determine the total look of a store in any three-month period.
2. Understanding the promotional aspects of retailing will help the VMM plan the year's activities.
3. Budgets for theme periods are determined by the amount of money that the particular season is expected to generate.
4. The overall impression of spring should be created on the first floor of a store.
5. Spring displays reflect color, growth, and excitement.

6. Summer signals clearances of spring and summer merchandise.
7. A store has to make 80–85 percent of the yearly income from August through December.
8. Total visual merchandising trims help create, develop, and define a store's image.
9. The overall theme concept works best in smaller stores.
10. Separate themes can work against the total store image if themes compete with one another.
11. Promotions evolve from national holidays, seasons, religious holidays, and special theme concepts.
12. The display department's records of in-store transactions must also be organized during inventory.
13. Valentine's Day is the most popular buying promotion of the winter season.
14. Easter is still the most important buying holiday of the spring season.
15. Planning for the Christmas promotions should begin at the latest, in October.
16. Christmas is the strongest selling period of the entire year.
17. Special shops for Christmas are a major part of the overall sales plan.
18. Each store has its own merchandising strategy based on the seasons, location, and calendar year.

KEY TERMS

1. Trim
2. Low-light plants
3. Case pads
4. Inventory
5. Moire
6. Garland

DISCUSSION QUESTIONS

1. How do the four seasons affect the total look of a store?
2. Summarize the differences between a winter theme in the northern part of the United States and a winter theme in the southern part of the United States.
3. Why does the overall impression of spring have to be created on the first floor of a store?
4. What is the main theme normally found in most stores during the summer season?
5. Fall trim is traditionally based on what theme within the children's, juniors, and young men's/women's areas of a department store?
6. Where is the total visual merchandising trim in a department store usually located?
7. List the three methods for planning display decors.
8. What are the specific points to remember when developing an overall and/or separate theme concept?

9. How do the visual merchandising needs of the Easter holiday differ in the children's department and the men's/women's departments?
10. If a VMM wishes to create a total Christmas impact, what areas should be covered in the main color (red)?

STUDENT EXERCISES

Number 1

Contact three floral shops in your community. Discuss with the owners the possibility of their furnishing greenery (plants) for one of the retail stores located in your community. Attempt to answer the following questions:
1. Would they be willing to furnish the plants to the retail establishments?
2. What would be the cost of their furnishing the plants?
3. What is the cost of maintenance?
4. What types of plants would they provide?

Number 2

Select a major department store in your community or a surrounding community that is utilizing a separate overall theme concept. Analyze their approach and discuss the following questions:
1. Is there any conflict between the separate themes?
2. Are the themes compatible with the merchandise?
3. Are there "resting areas" for the customers' eyes between the theme areas?

CASE PROBLEM 1

The Christmas Trim

Carolyn Brothers is a major full-line department store chain located in the northern United States. At present, the main store is located in Allington, a city of 326,000. They also have 16 branch stores located throughout the state. Carolyn Brothers is a family-owned business that was incorporated in 1930. All stock is family-owned and the corporation is run by a selected board of directors.

During the spring board of directors meetings, the board decided to totally redo the Christmas theme for the main store. The main store is located on two levels with an escalator in the middle to provide access to the second level. The departments located on the first floor include men's furnishings, fashion accessories, stationery/books, women's furnishings, floral shop, and china/dishes/silverware.

The second floor departments are men's clothing, women's clothing, boys' and girls' clothing and accessories, luggage, infant wear, and toys. Lana McKinney, the VMM, has been with the store for 15 years and she has two employees working for her. The Christmas trim has not been changed or upgraded in 10 years due to budget restraints placed on Lana's visual merchandising department. The board of directors has placed the majority of display money into the branch stores over the past few years.

Lana has been directed to prepare a plan for the upcoming Christmas season to be utilized only in the main store. Last year the main store was totally renovated and the Christmas trim should compliment the modern look of the store.

Activities for Completion

Prepare a visual merchandising plan for the Christmas trim for the main store. This plan should be comprehensive and in a format suitable for presentation to the board of directors.

CASE PROBLEM 2

We Need Help

Al's Old-Time Clothing is a men's and women's speciality store located in a small rural town with a population of 35,000. Al's is owned by Bruce and Marian Lebjick. They are both 34 years old and have been involved in two other successful retail businesses. Al's has been opened approximately a year and is already one of the ten highest grossing businesses in the community.

The storefront has been redone to reflect an old-time image. Bruce and Marian have spent considerable time collecting antiques which are used as the main display fixtures in the store. The floor is wooden, display cases and fixtures are from a 1900s general store, and overall the store has a 1920s atmosphere.

The main floor has approximately 2,500 square feet of selling space. There is a spiral staircase in the back of the store that leads to a balcony which overlooks the main floor and has 600 square feet of space. All major clothing items and furnishings are found on the main floor with a jean shop located on the balcony.

One afternoon in January, Marian and Bruce were discussing the past year's business and Marian exclaimed, "We have a problem! We both graduated from college with degrees in marketing, the business is doing fine, and financially we are secure. However, we have no yearly visual merchandising plan for the business." Quickly looking at the financial records, they felt they could increase their sales by 8 percent if they used a visual merchandising plan.

Activities for Completion

1. Do you believe that Bruce and Marian need a visual merchandising plan? (justify your response)
2. Prepare a yearly visual merchandising plan for Al's to include all major holidays and/or special yearly events.

CHAPTER 12

What's New —
What's Not:
A Look Into the Future

LEARNING OBJECTIVES

At the completion of this chapter, you will be able to:

1. Analyze past display trends and their effect on new display concepts.

2. Explain the movement from traditional store windows to the more elaborate and entertaining display windows.

3. Summarize the modernization of display from the 1800s through the 1980s.

4. Cite the importance of mannequins as they relate to the changes in society.

5. Describe the importance of computerized movement in the display function.

6. Discuss the effects of large amount of merchandise in display windows or the use of more space.

7. Trace the women's movement in terms of its importance to the fashion industry.

8. Identify the importance of boutiques as a retail display medium.

9. Outline the effects of modern lighting trends on window display.

Trends in visual merchandising are as ephemeral as trends in fashion. A chapter written in one year can only make an educated guess as to where fashion and display will be headed in the next few years.

The most important aspect of understanding current trends is the realization that nothing is written in stone: nothing is "in" forever, nor is it forever "out." Something that worked as a design element in 1955 may not work well with the graphic sensibilities of 1982 but will again be perfect in a slightly different form for 1985. A necessary skill for the visual merchandiser is the ability to recognize the trends, absorb them, and learn their lessons so that their artistic/design strengths can evolve into something better.

This chapter will discuss past display trends and how they have influenced the newer concepts. Future directions that visual merchandising may take will be anticipated based on emerging trends in the early 1980s.

BACKGROUND

In the 1700s stores used only their names and a hanging sign or symbol to identify their purpose. Most stores operated out of the front rooms of private homes so the windows appeared like most of those in a family neighborhood. Shutters and small panes lent a feeling of privacy to the shops.

As many people were illiterate in the 1700s and 1800s, the shop symbols, e.g., the barber shop pole, cigar store Indian, shoes, keys, eyeglasses, and pawnbrokers balls were hung over each shop until the late 1800s (Figure 12–1). At this time shopkeepers helped to pass laws banning the profusion of symbols in order to lend a more dignified air to the shopping streets.

During the 1800s, the windows in the front of the private home/stores were becoming larger and less obstructed. Gas lights were introduced in the evenings to illuminate the merchandise displayed in the windows. Proprietors painted and polished their stores to make them attractive from the street as well as inside. As the American economic life grew and the population prospered in the 1800s, people turned more to window shopping and browsing as a pleasurable leisure time activity. The stores at that time seemed to display everything they had in stock and more (Figure 12–2). It was considered a sign of wealth to be on the physically heavy side as it showed the financial ability to buy and eat great quantities (and quality) of food. This philosophy of economic indulgence related directly to the overabundance of merchandise shown in stores during that time. The general dry goods store that carried a little (or lot) of everything evolved with the industrial revolution (Figure 12–3) and economic expansion into full-line department stores. Display took on new importance in the late 1800s and early 1900s and by 1907 there were several schools, an organization (National Association of Window Trimmers of America), and a magazine, *The Merchants Record and Show Window.*

The overindulgent jumble of merchandise that was previously found in windows began to turn into narrow assortments displayed as an artistic statement. Two trends that developed during this period were (1) moving displays, such as ferris

Figure 12–1
Clock and eyeglass sign in front of the shop of C. P. Reber, Optician, St. Louis, Missouri. Circa 1900, Library of Congress.

wheels, turntables, and other carnivallike props; and (2) large "sculptures" made of ordinary packaging, such as cracker boxes, salt containers, and special soaps. Print advertising (Figure 12–4) and graphics were the most important window ingredient. Illustrations were added because "a picture is worth one thousand words." Lighting became even more important as after-workday window shopping to compare prices evolved as a form of nighttime entertainment. Shop owners put as much light as possible in each window so their respective stores would be a beacon on the street in the evenings. In the 1920s several display people experimented with showing less merchandise and using spotlights to highlight only specific areas. The store managers were less enthusiastic than the artist/display people. The theory "less is more" began to take shape and it took courageous display people to convince their store managers to try it in the windows. After many trials it became an accepted practice to display the expensive merchandise on its own in elegant settings that imparted a feeling of space. Space around merchandise became a synonym for luxury and exclusivity that is just as relevant today as in the early 1900s.

Figure 12–2
Interior View of L. S. Driggs Lace and Bonnet Store, Boston. 1852 wood engraving by Mallory from Gleason's Pictorial, Vol. 3, p. 244. Library of Congress.

Figure 12–3
Stock poster advertisement showing a crowd of shoppers outside the store. Lithograph copyright 1873 by Gibson. Library of Congress.

A CHANGED MAN.

This Man by his Wife's advice,   Reader his advice to you,
Bought one of our Suits so nice,   Is "Walk in and do so too."

Figure 12–4
"A Changed Man," Drawing by I. Cameron. Lithograph by Currier and Ives, 1880. Library of Congress.

In the mid-1920s Art Deco became an important interior design and architectural influence in both the art and fashion worlds. The Bauhaus mixture of simple artistic design for useful objects and the development of art in industry changed the look of display props and mannequins forever. Architecture became an important aspect of window design and gained more prominence inside the stores as well. Building materials such as brick, cork, asbestos, and various woods were tested for their different textures and functions. Metals were introduced, such as chrome and bronze, and all the props started to take on a cleaner, more manufactured, hard-edge look (Figure 12–5). Paper maché mannequins were starting to give way in the mid-1930s to more lifelike plastic forms. Traditional floral arrangements, once a staple prop, were losing ground to more inventive theatrical situations.

Surrealism, an art form that was developed in the late 1930s in Europe, came to America by way of store windows and amused and provoked the passersby. The surreal windows had a quality of both reality and unreality at the same time (Figure 12–6). Everyday situations were parodied with a sardonic or humorous twist. Surrrealisms start as bizarre lifelike situations, evolving into more beautiful absurdities. Dresses floating in air, invisible mannequins fully dressed (done with thin wires), using the advent of psychoanalysis as wish-fulfilling dreams about beautiful clothing were all themes based on surreal principles.

In the 1940s World War II influenced display art, which attained new heights of realism and a short-term period of feminism. Gasoline was rationed during this

Figure 12–5
An example of revived classic design from the Art Deco period. The rise of the metallic-finished column combined with the metallic bust form shows the use of metals during that period.
Credit: Bonwit Teller, October, 1939. Photo by Worsinger Photo, N.Y.C.

period so the walk-by traffic increased. More complicated windows were installed (Figure 12–7). Budgets were low but that only inspired the creative use of handmade and found-object props. The main thrust was the expanding role of women in society and the new mannequins reflected this individuality and assertiveness. War bonds were advertised in many store windows. Lord and Taylor in New York City opened its corner window by removing the glass and had a spokesperson selling bonds to the Fifth Avenue shoppers all day from the window.

Because many men were in the armed services and not working in the stores, the self-service merchandising concept began to gain favor. Strong in-store display evolved as a necessity to visually sell the merchandise without the accompaniment of a salesperson. "Visual merchandising" became a retailing term during the early 1940s and encompassed store planning and design; interior and exterior identification; fixturing, window, interior, and counter display; and all signing.

In 1950, influenced by the French retailers, boutiques started to show up in stores. Boutiques were small areas, set aside in stores, that merchandised either related items or showed a select group from one designer. These boutiques were decorated and set up in theatrical ways that made use of elaborate, centrally located props.

The 1950s celebrated the end of the war and rationing, and the beginning of a new period of prosperity. Windows always had identifying cards prominently displayed inside with a description or a message about the merchandise on view. These messages became more amusing and tongue-in-cheek and the window designs reflected this lighter mood (Figure 12–8).

As television gained acceptance in the 1950s and more people spent time at home in front of the set, window shopping as a leisure time activity became less popular. Large shopping malls and strip malls (a line of five to ten stores in a straight line along a road) became very popular as the number of shoppers owning automobiles increased. Windows were virtually ignored in drive-up shopping malls because few shoppers were walking or strolling. Consumers would go to the mall for a purpose, take care of their errands, and leave.

Figure 12–6
Surrealism is carried out in this window in a humorous way. The disembodied heads are meant to "float" in the frame of the hanging picture.
Credit: Bonwit Teller, July, 1944.

Figure 12–7
Advertising overseas GI gifts in August prompted early Christmas shopping.
Credit: Bonwit Teller, August, 1944.

The 1960s were times of political unrest as represented by the Viet Nam war, the civil rights movement, and the emergence of the strong liberal in politics. Display had no unifying theme on which to develop ideas. Television was in its teens, the automobile was firmly established as mass transportation—the American way of life—and everyone started to look inward to find their own beliefs and standards. Black female mannequins were first introduced in the finest stores, followed by Orientals, and some customers were outraged while others applauded. Through the 1960s window design became cleaner and more simple using space as a positive design element. Newer, more realistic mannequins were on the market. Adel Rootstein from England developed mannequins whose features and poses seemed real. Attitude began to mean more than a mere fashionable pose. The Rootstein mannequins often looked bored, amused, angry, and sexy. The D. G. Williams mannequins designed by Mary Brosnan were softer and more feminine, but were also becoming more modern with personal attitudes. Other mannequin houses, such as Greneker, Wolf & Vine, Hingsual, and Nissan, started developing more lifelike figures. With the availability of mannequins with personality, display started to take on more realism. With the confusion of ideas, uninspired display windows consisted of a prop, a mannequin, and a foam core printed panel. The panels were new, inexpensive, and solved the problem of what to do in a window.

Figure 12–8
*These mannequins are modeled after Audrey Hepburn. (See the floor card on
the lower right.) The phones are "found-object" props. The use of found-object props
started showing up more in the early 1950s.*
Credit: Bonwit Teller, August, 1953.

Pop art and other art forms were introduced to the public in more avant garde
windows such as Tiffanys' in the late 1960s and early 1970s.

In the early 1970s, the display people partially used the surrealists' concepts
while also adding shocking realism. Sex, drugs, and rock-and-roll became subjects
for windows and these influences lasted until the late 1970s. Many different
situations were alluded to in these windows and many bordered on being tasteless.
Some were actually offensive or violent and were removed as soon as the store
management saw them. These windows reflected the violence seen in the news.
Windows and interiors became more theatrical. Entire blocks of windows were
sometimes used to tell a continuous story. Display became exciting, controversial,
and fun. People started to look forward to the new windows in anticipation not
only of the new merchandise but of the new stage set and the story it would tell.

"Flying" merchandise evolved in the 1960s (and continues today) as a way to show off clothing in an active way without the use of expensive mannequins. The flying was done mainly in junior shops and chainstore, junior-oriented establishments. Wires were used to give the clothing a sense of motion. The clothing was hung from the ceiling with either chains, wires, or the hangers still holding the merchandise in shape. The legs, arms, and skirts were then made to appear to be moving in air by means of wire or fishing tackle. The use of ladders and display people became equally important to the stores that used flying as their main visual statement. The flying technique is still being employed although it damages merchandise, takes a lot of time to do properly, and doesn't show the items off to their best advantage. The future of this technique rests in the flexibility of junior stores to develop their ideas and progress into the 1980s.

Shopping malls gained popularity in the 1970s, enabling people to shop in all kinds of weather. When attractive rooftops were also provided, people spent more time strolling and by the mid 1970s shopping malls had taken on the function of Main Street 100 years ago. People went to shopping malls for entertainment as well as to window shop. Windows, once ignored in mall stores, took on a new importance and vitality. There is a combination now of see-through windows (seeing into the store) and formal window areas. The level of visual merchandising is not yet as creative or trend setting in enclosed shopping malls as it could or should be. Mall merchants are reluctant to give the visual designers a free hand or adequate budget.

In New York City, Colin Birch developed a more graphic approach for Bonwit Teller in the mid 1970s that ignored the theatrical scenes and introduced a sparse, space style (Figure 12–9). Space and graphics became larger and more important, and mannequins were placed off-center to force the viewer to look for them. The bizarre scenes of the early 1970s caused people to wonder about the sensibilities and psychological health of the display designers. The new, clean style gave no sense of individual personality or emotion. The windows were designed as works of art to stand on their own visual presence as opposed to telling the viewer a strange story (Figure 12–10). The impact of the clean style and strong graphics started a new trend in 1978. The 1980s began with the use of this clean style and added a sense of humor and an occasional reference to current events.

Each year different artists/display people/visual merchandisers influence the design of interiors and windows. Rather than one style disappearing completely when another appears, they evolve from each other and selectively take from the past. "What's in" is determined by the popular and commercial acceptance of a new style developed by a creative visual merchandiser. Lessons and trends from the past that will develop and continue past the 1980s will be broken down into what's new and what's not. Each style and development borrows from other influences. Styles change but good design will carry the message over the years.

MANNEQUINS

Chapter 7 gave insight into the images, poses, "attitudes," and practical aspects of mannequins. More than any other visual merchandising prop or fixture, mannequins have reflected the ongoing changes in society. From the bland, boring early

Figure 12–9
This window is important for its sheer simplicity and wonderful use of lighting and negative space.
Credit: Colin Birch, V.M.D., Bonwit Teller, N.Y., N.Y., June, 1976. Photo by: Jerry P. Melmed.

Figure 12–10
A classic window that employs a tongue-in-cheek concept. Ice and tongs are used to highlight a perfect diamond.
Credit: Gene Moore, Display Director, Tiffany & Co., N.Y., N.Y., 1978.

forms to the assertive, forceful figures of today, the mannequin has evolved into a strong contemporary statement about femininity and masculinity.

What's new: Action mannequins are the strongest classification so far being seen in the 1980s. From the diving mannequin by DeStephano Studios to the runners and acrobats of Pucci, these athletic forms reflect society's growing concern for physical fitness (Figure 12–11).

Mannequins' attitudes are changing to parallel the growth in numbers of businesswomen as opposed to housewives, and the acceptance of gentleness and intellectuality in men (Figure 12–12).

What's not: Lacquered, old-styled wigs have given way to newer, more natural styles. Horsehair wigs are only appropriate for fantastic styles that cannot be achieved with the more natural fibers. Outlandish poses that say nothing about attitude and just show movement look foolish when not shown in a context to lend meaning. A trio of moving mannequins without a theme looks old and outdated. Female mannequins without nipples and bikini lines appear outdated and unnatural. Lots of makeup and long fake eyelashes are used only for special effects today and faces are generally left simple and pale. Putting the arms into positions not intended by the manufacturer is an old concept that never worked in the past and should not be continued in the future.

Two trends—active forms and a better balance of masculine and feminine attributes for each sex—seem to be the most important innovations of the 1980s.

Figure 12–11
Active male mannequins from Pucci, New York.

Figure 12–12
This window is a departure from the feminine glamor often seen in 1982 as a result of the Reagan White House influence. These mannequins look as if they belong to an exclusive club for wealthy female executives. They interact through their postures yet they all seem to be very alone.
Credit: Colin Birch, V.M.D., Bloomingdales, N.Y., N.Y. September, 1982.

MOVEMENT

Nothing attracts the eye like movement and its use has been constant since the early 1900s. All sorts of turntables, fans, and moving figures have been and are still being used to catch the customer's attention.

What's new: The age of computerized movement is the most important new trend in theatrical motion control. Mechanical functioning figures will continue to be important throughout the 1980s but the addition of the computer will give visual merchandisers a new way of considering their environment. A single computer can control an entire bank of windows. Individual movements for each figure, light, prop, or piece of merchandise will be programmed into the software and when this is inserted into the board, movement will occur. Hydraulic (water-powered), pneumatic (air-powered), and electrical-mechanical movements are all possible with this computer system. Each system works with pistons or pumps inserted or attached to the object to be moved. An electrical source is needed to power the pistons and the computer. In pneumatics, the pistons are powered by an air compressor (which is powered by electricity) and are regulated by pneumatic valves that control the amount and speed of air into the valves. What makes any of these systems expensive at present is the amount of time necessary to program the movements and to adjust individual pistons, valves, and other machinery to allow for flowing (not jerky) movement. The advantages of these systems are the ability to program intermittent movement that simulates human patterns and the potential to change the movement of human-looking mannequins so that their scenerios are different each week.

Holograms are seen at each visual merchandising show. A hologram is a three-dimensional light form that is created by laser beams when the laser light is split by a high-quality optic filter. These have been used by some of the more adventurous artists in small jewelry windows, e.g., Raymond Mastrobuoni for Cartier. Much excitement and anticipation surrounds the eventual wide-scale use of holograms for visual display and the potential of 3-D television.

Full-color holograms are created by using red, green, and blue lasers. The standard helium red light laser is the least expensive, retailing for about $600. The blue and green lasers cost in the low thousands to buy and make the total cost of full-color holograms prohibitive at present. Holograms show movement and the refinement of this technique has shown great development in the last 20 years. Holograms were first introduced in the early 1960s and there have been few breakthroughs in technology since then. The main experimental thrust has been toward the use of white or natural light rather than expensive blue and green lasers. The coherence or clarity afforded by white light at present is vastly inferior to the manufactured and controlled blue, red, and green lights. Unfortunately, as with fiber optics and video cassettes, it takes American businesses between 15 and 20 years to develop a product so that its manufacturing process is inexpensive enough to generate a substantial profit. Hologram research needs to be funded by future patrons (people with money who want the product) so that the process can be developed to bring the cost down. If the demand increases, we can expect to see holograms in daily use within 15–20 years.

Basic mechanical vignettes are developing more current and/or futuristic themes instead of relying on the past for inspiration. The quality of the figures and the constantly improving technology help to keep these mechanicals a part of the visual merchandising world today and will continue to be important tomorrow.

Strawberry Shortcake is a merchandising concept that gained tremendous popularity during the early 1980s. A cutsy little girl, Strawberry Shortcake showed up on innumerable varieties of merchandise. An oversized display doll was created with a rounded translucent face. On this rounded surface was projected Strawberry's face moving as if she were talking. A recorded voice was run at the same time and the total effect was mesmerizing. From a distance of 7 feet (an average amount of space for a customer to be standing away from a display) the face seemed to be

100 percent real. The projector was positioned on the floor about 3½ feet from the feet of the figure. This projection technique is being applied and developed today and will be a strong feature in the 1980s. Getting movement into the rest of the body through light projection is the next step into the future.

Hidden fans blowing fabric or paper in the window is an old tool but may continue to work if handled with skill and a good design sense.

Mechanicals that are too cute, e.g., dirty cats peeking out of trash cans, are a thing of the past in the more forward-looking stores. Mechanicals that move back and forth in one boring, continuous movement have lost their appeal because the surprise of intermittent movement is missing.

The important changes to look for in the future are extensive use of computers, light projection techniques, improved mechanicals, and slowly increasing use of holograms. These new developments will eventually change the face of visual merchandising and possibly retailing as a whole.

QUANTITY OF MERCHANDISE

The plentiful use of merchandise gained favor in the early 1900s and disappeared from view in the "better" (more expensive) stores in the 1930s. The concepts of "less is more" and space as a measure of elegance began to take shape. There are now newer, more artful ways of displaying large amounts of merchandise in store vignettes or windows.

What's new: Using huge photo blowups of large quantities of related or identical merchandise in a window or in-store display with one or two of the actual objects in front, dramatically lit, gives a more modern feeling than actually stacking all the goods in a window. In the future, more back-lit transparencies will be used to create the desired effect of a wide range or large quantity of merchandise. Large-scale projected slides may be used not only to show merchandise but also to create movement. If the physical merchandise is on a revolving track and the appropriate slides are coordinated to appear with the same items, a "show stopper" will occur!

Other than projection techniques, the simple use of geometric handling of merchandise will stay in favor through the early 1980s. Sweaters overlapped on a table to show every color are appearing in many stores. It's a neat, clean, effective technique and will probably continue in use because it works. Pinning or stretching clothing into geometric forms onto a form of art board to display the merchandise allows for more items to be shown in less space. Stacking (as in grocery store display) is enjoying a rebirth in hard-line departments. Book stores now take huge piles of the same book and create a spiral effect by starting the volumes on angles in a circle on the floor and building up the column from there. This spiraling will extend into the 1980s as an effective merchandise presentation technique.

What's not: Putting one of each item into a window as many hardware, novelty, and drug stores tend to do is about as effective as saying "we sell everything." Neither really gains any major individual item response for the store. Although people may at first come into the store in the hopes of getting a certain item and may use that store in the future as a resource for basics, they will not impulse shop for merchandise displayed in the window. After a while, they won't even see what's in the window because it's too crowded to pay attention to any specific idea or item. Using 1,000 bars of the same soap neatly stacked will make more of an artistic statement than showing all the bathing products together. Even a corny sign saying, "We have a full line of imported soaps and bath accessories . . . and that's no soap" in front of the 1,000 stacked bars is more effective than a large variety.

Flying large amounts of merchandise in a window will also only confuse passersby. Too much movement distracts from the merchandise and nothing sells effectively. Many lower end (lower priced) junior chain stores located in malls have ten to fifteen mannequins on either side of their entrances. Their presentations would be more effective if the mannequins related in either color or type of merchandise, or to each other in story vignettes. Instead, they all seem to stare into space in unrelated stances and clothing and have no discernible interaction or meaning.

The use of photography in terms of slides and blowups and the interesting geometric setup of merchandise are the two major themes that will continue into the mid 1980s.

MATERIALS

The use of natural materials developed as the Art Deco movement became influential. It remains active because of the relative low cost associated with untreated materials. While budgets are low, natural materials will remain in favor. When economic conditions improve, these budgets may be geared to high-technology expenses, such as computers and projection techniques. However, to keep costs down natural materials will continue in use.

What's in: Natural objects, such as tree branches, still work in certain settings. Extremely thin, lacquered bamboo poles are in favor and will probably continue to be so due to their relative low cost. Keep an eye out for square bamboo and bamboo shaped into different geometric forms. It was introduced in the California WAVM show in May 1982 and will most likely gain popularity in the future. Sand, feathers, burlap, mirrors, ceramics, glass, dried flowers, seamless paper, rope, fireproofed leaves, and live plants will all remain popular because of their versatility and low cost.

What's not: Materials that appear to be natural but are clever fakes are usually expensive (although they are often fireproofed) and never look as real as the true natural material. Falling in this category are raffia grass mats, grass paper, fake sod, plastic animals, plastic flowers, and so on. These materials will probably always appear, but their appeal is at the low-end (less expensive) store level and their relatively high cost will only be tolerated in good economic times.

The "natural" look, e.g., raw wood risers, barrels, planking on the walls and floors, etc., comes in and out of style every 15–20 years. It may reappear in the late 1980s because it has been fading out for the last 10 years around the country due to the "high-tech" look (which became popular in 1980 and started to wane in 1983).

The trends in natural materials are difficult to predict. Often the materials can be disguised by paint or an artificial covering to appear to be something else. The visual merchandising trends in this case depend on the merchandise directions and what best reflects the new images.

What begins as a visual merchandising trend on the east or west coast usually reaches the middle of the country six months to two years later. There are some extremely innovative visual merchants throughout the United States to whom this statement doesn't apply. There is some very exciting work being done in Salt Lake City, for example, at ZCMI by Ron Nelson and his staff. Many visual merchandisers throughout the country have their own unique styles and may be very avant garde because they are not influenced on a daily basis by what's happening on the two coasts. But the average freelancer, visual merchandising assistant, or manager in a smaller or branch store learns about new trends from their corporate headquarters (hopefully), through *Visual Merchandising and Store Planning* (a monthly magazine), *Inspiration* (a European publication), or through *Views and Reviews.*

SURREALISM

Surrealism is important both today and tomorrow as one of the best ways to catch the eye of the passerby. The absurd and fascinating twists of reality that embody surrealistic display make it an excellent window or interior concept. It allows the visual merchandiser to make a visual statement that can either amuse, shock, or force the viewer to think (Plate 4 and Plate 7).

What's in: Surrealistic scenes using modern technology in machine/people situations will become popular. As computers become a staple alongside the television set in each home, the vocabulary that surrounds them will be more familiar. There will be more use of computers in surreal situations, either as a part of or for creating the scenerios.

What's not: Shock techniques dealing with sexuality were popular in the late 1970s but have given way to visual artistic surprises as opposed to moral bombardment. The illusion of dead mannequins on the floor or bandaged and bruised faces and limbs may be on hold through the 1980s. Crime has risen steadily since 1975 and is now an extremely frightening reality for most large-city residents. Seeing this portrayed in a window just augments and underlines present day fears. It rarely sells merchandise today—unless mace and guns are being displayed.

While outside tensions grow stronger, as in the days of the depression, the displays react by either becoming more fantasy-oriented or commenting directly on the current situation. Although public commentary is intellectually stimulating, people react in a more positive emotional way to fantasy theater and humor.

The future of surrealism in visual merchandising relates closely to the influence of computers in our daily lives. Bizarre sexual and frightening or violent situations will hopefully not reappear for another 15 or 20 years. The VM must always be sensitive to public taste and sentiment, recognizing the impact such a display might have on individuals.

WOMEN'S EMERGING ROLE IN SOCIETY

Starting with Prohibition and the 18th Amendment (Voting Rights Act), women have been asserting their independence and strength in numbers. During each war women became a major factor in the at-home American work force ("Rosie the Riveter") and contributed heavily to the success of both world wars.

After the wars, many women went home to the family and resumed traditional wifely duties. The recognition of skill and worth outside the home grew slowly at first, but very steadily. With the women's rights movement came a temporary denial of the importance of the fashion world—a world that affords women many job opportunities and potential for success. As the movement became calmer and more secure, fashion returned as an allowable pleasure while windows and interiors reflected a new opulence and awareness of the working life of women (Plate 6).

What's new: The business suit and "dressing-for-success" mentality will continue to be important for several years into the mid 1980s. At that point women will either become fed up with the business uniform and corporate dress restrictions and demand (through buying patterns) a change of emphasis or they will embrace the women's career shops. Only buying trends will predict what will happen in this business. The gains made by women during the last 15 years cannot be overemphasized by visual merchandising. Each window and display will reflect through its mannequins' attitudes the new assertiveness and confidence (Plate 9). Sexual confidence is an important aspect of the 1980s. The women are represented in situations that reflect their professional and emotional control.

What's not: Obviously, the women as a victim is not an acceptable portrayal and will cause anger and loss of sales in the 1980s. Its backlash of publicity may either spur on more sales and/or alienate a segment of the population.

Women as assertive, glamorous, and strong is the image that will grow with the 1980s. Passive, sad, fragile creatures with shy demeanors is a concept for the past.

MEN'S EMERGING ROLE AS A FASHION INFLUENCE IN SOCIETY

The role of men in society hasn't changed as much as society's perception of that role. Men have symbolically been given "the green light" by the women's movement to be human, e.g., express emotion, be vulnerable, be playful.

Clothing is an expressive outlet because its vast selection allows people to purchase their public image in the marketplace.

Men's fashion in the 1980s is developing a lightness and expressiveness through pure colors and freedom of movement through style.

What's in: Mixing and matching colors so that they enhance one another is a trend that seems to be firm for the next several years. The use of varying textures, especially natural fibers, will remain popular because such arrangements work well by creating visual interest. The influx of bright colors combined with pastels (traditionally feminine shades) is a liberating influence to the standard tan, khaki, blue, grey, brown, and green usually seen in men's clothing.

Styles are looser and less constructed to allow ease of movement and more life to the garments.

What's out: Matching clothing so perfect that nothing is exciting or even eye catching is a trend that has lost favor. A dash of color, an unusual texture both say to the public, "I'm an individual, I put this together myself, I didn't buy it right off a mannequin." Mannequins and clothing presentations have begun to look unfashionable without the inspired use of color and texture to give personality to the outfit.

BOUTIQUES

Small boutiques developed originally as outposts for a single designer's work. Such outposts were built in a separate section of a department store, away from the bulk of similarly classified merchandise. Boutiques also became the name in the 1960s for small stores that carried a narrow selection of clothing and accessories appealing exclusively to a certain segment of the market.

What's in: Department stores are building more boutiques yearly to segregate designers and special classifications. The circular flowing approach to floor design has become popular at Saks Fifth Avenue on two newly renovated floors. The circular floor pattern encourages customers to walk around the entire floor area because there is only one entrance/exit. The boutiques are separated by walls and interior decoration treatment while their exteriors that face the aisle flow with a uniform facade. Wood or marble veneer is a popular and expensive choice for facade treatments.

This technique of separating areas by no more than two walls or by differences in floor height plus allowing for a traffic flow to occur seems to be the most important trend in renovations and new construction for the 1980s. Expensive classifications and vendors are allocated these spaces while the less expensive merchandise is housed in larger, less defined areas.

Boutiques are similar to shops but are usually more permanent. More budget money is put into the identifying decor of a designer's boutique as the store's management desires customers to become familiar with its location and salespeople. A boutique is an exclusive, personal, small space, and the service usually reflects this attitude.

What's not: Boutiques that are poorly designed and rely totally on props to define their merchandise content are expensive mistakes that cannot be carried into the future for economic reasons.

The boutique as a merchandising concept is not new but its continued success in giving customers a sense of having had a special shopping experience gives it promise for the future.

ART AND ARCHITECTURE

The worlds of art and architecture have played the largest part in influencing both visual merchandising and fashion. Trends that develop in art are seen almost immediately in windows and interiors. Architectural developments are obvious in facades and special visual treatments of interior shops and windows.

What's new: Neoclassicism is strong in the 1980s due primarily to the influence of several prominent architects. It will probably be strong as a trend for another few years and its influence will be felt in visual merchandising for at least 10 years. The neoclassic look combines traditional Roman and Greek sculptural elements, columns, and colors with a slight Art Deco twist and the sparseness of today's minimalist culture. It's a perfect example of how trends build off one another.

Art is moving back 20 years into a resurgence of German expressionism and neoexpressionism. This is in complete contrast to the past 10 years of photorealism and minimalism. Clothing and visual merchandising have not yet begun to react to this change but will do so by 1983. This will be strong for at least another four years and after that it's anyone's guess as to where the art world will focus its attention.

What's not: Amateurish artwork should not be displayed in a store or window because it can give the appearance that the store can't afford the "real thing." Fabric prints, e.g., Marimekko, were strong for 12 years but have lost their novelty and therefore their importance. Elaborate false facades for departments are in or out depending on the ingenuity used in creating the facade and its design credibility.

The painter Mondrian is a perfect example of how art influences fashion and design. A series of his paintings consists of black lines crossing at 90° angles with selected square or rectangular areas of primary colors carefully placed within the uneven grid pattern (Figure 12–13). In the 1960s these paintings influenced both fashion and advertising. Dresses were constructed with black lines and squares of color placed in a geometric pattern while the advertisements were broken into squares of print using dark lines to connect the areas visually. Mondrian is just one artist whose influence on design and fashion has been felt over an extended period. Many others have made their mark: Roy Lichtenstein, Andy Warhol, Jasper Johns, Robert Rauschenberg, René Magritte, Edward Hopper, and Georgia O'Keefe are some of the important continuing influences in the visual merchandising field.

LIGHTING

If a display is not lit, it is not seen. This basic fact has been a major factor in the many advances in lighting techniques over the years. We progressed from candles and kerosene to gas lamps, then to the first electric bulb, and today to a vast variety of electrical devices.

What's new: The use of lights as a prop is becoming more popular. Special rotating lights with attached patterned filters throw colored light "pictures" on white surfaces (walls). The color and movement are exciting visual messages when used to highlight merchandise displayed on a mannequin or form. Spotlights using color and movement also work well in hard-line areas to direct attention and highlight special merchandise.

Every year new advances are made in color spectrum lighting to show the merchandise off in a realistic and flattering light. The quest for the perfect light

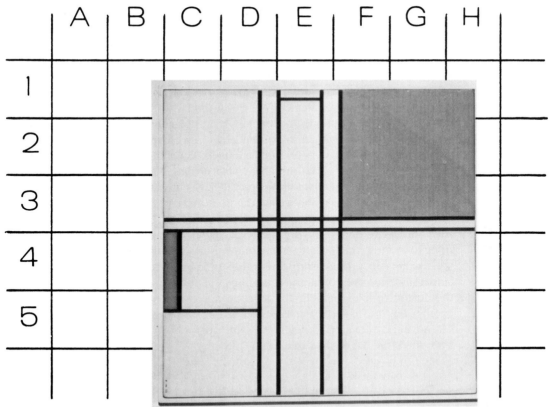

Figure 12–13
Piet Mondrian, Dutch, 1872–1944 "Composition with Blue and Yellow", 1935, oil. Hirshhorn Museum, Smithsonian Institution. The block on the upper right (F-H-1-3) is bright yellow and the small section on the left (C-4 and 5) is bright blue. The composition is part of a series done by Mondrian during those years that influenced clothing, architecture and advertising in the 1960s. His influence is being felt again in the 1980s.

source, i.e., low cost, high energy efficiency, long life span, ease of installation, and pure color accuracy, is a never-ending search.

What's not: There has been a controversy about neon for several years in the New York City area. Most other visual merchants in this country understand the strong impact and excitement that neon generates. However, in their concern for being trendsetters, several large stores in New York City overused neon and then decided when the rest of the retail world picked up the idea that it was "out." Their loss. Neon in art and visual merchandising will be on the scene for many more years. The overuse of neon—or anything for that matter—will eventually make it seem dull and uninspired.

Using floodlights to highlight areas is an inefficient use of both energy and the flood bulb. Spots are for highlighting while floods fill a general area with light.

Mirrored balls come in and out of style depending on the merchandise being displayed. They worked well for disco but fell flat for evening clothes. They are generally considered kitsch today and should be used in a humorous way.

The overuse of flashing lights to create excitement will distract the customer's eye, as will too many lights pointed toward reflective surfaces, e.g., Plexiglas. Combining spots with mirror or plexi is a modern trend that gives excitement and a hard-edged feeling to an area. It has to relate to the concept of the merchandise to work as a visual design element.

Lighting will continue to develop in importance and with the addition of movement will become an important prop as well as a design tool.

The trends that have been listed are just a few of the many influences that have made their mark on visual merchandising design. The most important new development in both merchandising and display is the total theme environment. All the senses participate when a total theme is done well. The merchandise is from one area, country, or people, the music reflects these origins, ethnic foods give off the appropriate odors, and areas are visually created to reflect the theme. Everything works together—sight, smell, touch, hearing, and taste. Each time the senses are touched in a total store promotion memories and sensations are inspired. Hopefully, such memories and sensations, set off by future experiences, will cause the customer to remember the store in a positive way and possibly return for another enjoyable shopping experience.

All trends develop to reach the same goal which is to get a customer to buy from the store more than once.

SUMMARY

Following are some trends to remember:

Mannequins: Their use and evolution.

Movement: From ferris wheels to computers.

Quantity of merchandise: Today less is better.

Graphics and signing: Continued strength.

Materials: The use and abuse of "natural."

Surrealism: From everyday to bizarre and the use of humor.

Women's emerging role: And the future.

Men's emerging role as a fashion influence.

Boutiques: A way of personalizing large areas.

Art used as props: And display as art.

Architecture: Its influence on visual merchandising.

Lighting: Movement and color control.

SUMMARY CHECKLIST

Key Concepts

1. Visual merchandisers must be able to recognize trends and respond to them.
2. Philosophies, techniques, and trends utilized in visual merchandising are affected by annual events such as political unrest, war, and the economic policy of the country.
3. The design of interiors and windows is influenced each year by different artists, display people, and visual merchandisers.
4. Mannequins, more than any other visual merchandising prop or fixture, have reflected the ongoing changes in society.
5. Movement has been used as a constant display technique since the early 1900s.
6. Computerized movement is an important trend in theatrical display.
7. The low cost associated with untreated materials continues to make them the choice for visual merchandising activities.
8. Sexual confidence is an important display aspect of the 1980s.
9. The use of lights as a prop is becoming more popular.
10. The total theme environment is one of the most important new developments in both merchandising and display.

KEY TERMS

1. Surrealism
2. Flying merchandise
3. Holograms
4. Boutiques

DISCUSSION QUESTIONS

1. Describe the display movement during the 1800s.
2. Discuss the impact of architecture on the window display.
3. What effect did the political unrest of the 1960s have on visual merchandising?
4. Discuss the characteristics of display during the pre-1970s, the 1970s, and the 1980s.
5. List the advantages and disadvantages of using "flying merchandise" as a display technique.
6. Compare the relationship of malls to the new interest in window display.
7. Explain how the mannequin has evolved as a strong contemporary statement about femininity and corresponding masculine roles.
8. Discuss the age of computerized movement as it relates to visual merchandising.
9. How can surrealism be utilized in window displays in an exciting way?
10. Summarize the effect of the women's movement on visual merchandising techniques and approaches.

11. Agree or disagree with the following statement and explain your answer: "Art and architecture have played the largest role in influencing both visual merchandising and fashion."

STUDENT EXERCISES

Exercise 1

Visit five community businesses with which you are familiar. Evaluate their visual merchandising/display techniques using the checklist provided. Conduct a discussion with your classmates to determine if any community trends are visible.

Display Trends Checklist

Place an X in the appropriate space next to each question.

_____Yes	_____No	1. Action mannequins are being utilized.
_____Yes	_____No	2. Computerized movement is utilized throughout the displays.
_____Yes	_____No	3. Holograms are used as a basic lighting technique.
_____Yes	_____No	4. Futuristic mechanical themes are being used in display work.
_____Yes	_____No	5. Photo blowups are being used in windows to emphasize specific merchandise.
_____Yes	_____No	6. Geometric handling of merchandise is being emphasized.
_____Yes	_____No	7. Natural materials are being used in display windows.
_____Yes	_____No	8. Surrealistic scenes using modern technology are popular.
_____Yes	_____No	9. The new assertiveness and confidence of women is reflected.
_____Yes	_____No	10. Boutiques are found within the department stores.
_____Yes	_____No	11. The neoclassicism architectural trend is evidenced in display trends.

Comments: _____

_____

_____

Store name_____ Student Name_____

Exercise 2

Assume the role of a VMM. You have been asked to talk to a college visual merchandising class. The topic of your presentation is "The Changing Role of Mannequins in our Current Society."

Develop an outline of your speech and discuss what photos you could use during your presentation.

CASE PROBLEM 1

The Boutique

Looking Good is a small women's clothing store located in the community of Ridge Park which has a population of 60,000. The store was established 15 years ago and has always been a family-owned business. Marge Seton, the owner, has been utilizing an open display arrangement within the store. Similar items are placed together, such as coats, dresses, blouses, etc. Due to the small size of the store, very few accessories are carried.

The total sales volume over the past three years has increased, and the community is continuing to grow at a surprising rate of 5 percent a year. Marge would like to change the image of the store while still utilizing the same selling space. Presently there is no other location in the community as desirable as hers. The present location is very advantageous. The store sits on the corner of the two major streets in the main shopping area and the pedestrian traffic is heavy.

After considerable discussion with employees, family members, customers, and manufacturers' sales representatives, Marge arrived at three possible solutions to her problem.

1. Concentrate on three or four major styles of women's clothing.
2. Continue as is and stay diversified.
3. Develop boutiques within the store that would emphasize certain styles.

Marge finally made the decision to utilize the boutique approach for the upcoming sales season. The first area she will change is women's sport clothes.

Activities for Completion

1. Agree or disagree with Marge's decision and explain your answer.
2. Plan the boutique sales area for the women's sport clothes area of the store.

CASE PROBLEM 2

The New Window

Toys and Such is a toy and hobby store located in a small shopping center approximately three blocks from the main business district of Lineville. The population of Lineville is approximately 35,000. The store is very well situated as the shopping center is on the main thoroughfare into town. Lineville is located 40 miles from a large city of 3 million people and the community continues to grow. A major interstate connecting the two communities was recently completed. The community is composed of middle- to upper middle-income groups.

Toys and Such is owned by Rich Allington, a lifetime resident of Lineville. The store has been in operation approximately five years and until recently Rich felt it was making an adequate profit. During the past year, sales have leveled off and projections indicate that the sales volume for this year is decreasing. Naturally Ralph is concerned about this situation and feels that he should upgrade his displays. The store has two large windows that are used for display purposes. During the past three years, Ralph has won a reputation for having the most decorative and entertaining windows in the community.

After analyzing the window displays, Ralph realized there was very little movement in any of the displays. He decided that by using movement, especially with the help of a newly purchased microcomputer, his displays would draw more customers to the store. This would hopefully increase the sales volume.

Activities for Completion

1. Do you agree that the use of movement would be an asset to the window displays of Toys and Such? (defend your answer)
2. Design a window display for Toys and Such.
   A. Utilize Christmas as your theme.
   B. What type of movement would you include in your display?
   C. Would there be any special type of lighting? (explain)

Appendix

Planning Sequences

The planning sequences listed in this chapter are for reference when starting a job in visual merchandising. They involve basic thought processes that will make any job that is undertaken easier to plan and finish. Some of the sequences have been discussed earlier in the text while others have been added to make this section a complete study guide. Each planning sequence is geared to the most common jobs faced by a beginning visual merchandiser.

COVERING EXISTING PADS

1. Determine the new color and material to be used on the pads.

2. Check this decision with the VMM.

3. Purchase (if necessary) the proper amount of material. Always get one yard extra (at least) to allow for accidents or mistakes. If you come close to finishing the bolt at the fabric store, try to negotiate a lower price for the entire bolt.

4. If the fabric is in stock within the VM shop, premeasure to ensure that there is enough to finish the job.

5. Remove the pads that need recovering from their wall or case.

6. Thoroughly wipe clean a flat area large enough so the fabric won't pick up dirt when it's laid out flat—face down for one or two pads.

7. Lay enough fabric out flat—face down—for one or two pads. Allow the excess to drape over a chair so the ends won't fall on the floor.

8. Place as many pads as possible on the fabric leaving a border of at least 2" around each edge of each pad. If the pad is thicker than 1/2", allow for more border fabric.

9. Using a ruled line, if necessary, cut the fabric out for each pad.

10. Staple and stretch the fabric simultaneously. Start in the middle of one side with two staples and then flip to the opposite side. Pull and staple that side with two staples and then go to another side.

11. Repeat the stapling process so that all the sides are stretched with two staples each and then work the pad in a clock or counterclockwise movement, stapling and pulling.

12. Check the front to make sure there are no wrinkles.

13. Pull and staple each corner.

14. Stack the finished pads in a clean area.

15. Bring all the pads back to the area in which they belong, as well as the appropriate tools needed to reinstall them.

CUTTING PADS

1. Measure the area to be covered.

    A. For a wall pad, take into account the standards and if they are recessed or mounted onto the face of the wall. Stand back from the wall to determine the proper proportionate size for the pad. If there are to be a series of pads all the same size, measure each area if necessary to make sure the pads will fit. Measure the length and the height of the area to be covered by each pad.

    B. In a case pad, measure the depth and length of the case and then measure between the standards. Note where each standard falls and how much space it takes. Use a paper pattern the first few times. The paper pattern is always necessary for an angled case. Cut a piece of paper slightly larger than the case bottom and push it into the case, creasing the paper at the corner angles.

2. For a fomecore pad use a straight edge and a mat knife to cut straight lines. Be careful to cut on a 90° angle, perpendicular to the work bench. An angle cut will appear sloppy.

3. For a hard material, a band saw or table saw is the most accurate tool to use

for cutting clean line pads. The notches for the standards can be cut out with a sabre saw.

SIGNING OR LETTERING

1. Go to the department that requires the new sign and determine the proper size, style, and color of lettering to be used.

2. Pull the needed letters.

3. Paint or clean them if necessary.

4. When dry, take the letters plus the proper adhesive (see the chart in the chapter on signing) and a ruler, T-square, and ladder (if needed) to the area that needs the signage.

5. Check to see where other signs are placed in the area/store and if there is a placement pattern that should be followed.

6. Start heating your glue gun (if that's the attachment method to be used).

7. Place the ladder if needed close enough to the wall so you can work with your body resting forward on the ladder.

8. Measure the area where the letters will be placed and tape your ruler to the wall so that the bottoms of the letters will rest on the ruler. Plan to adjust the lower case g, j, p, q, and y's to fit over the ruler, or allow room for them between the letters and add them after removing the ruler.

9. Use the T-square to determine if the letters are straight.

CHANGING A MANNEQUIN

1. Determine with the sales manager what the mannequin should wear.

   A. What are the predominant colors being featured in the department?

   B. What styles or types of clothing are up front (known as front and forward)?

   C. What type of clothing will work best on the mannequin?

   D. If there is more than one mannequin in the grouping, are there two or more outfits that will work well together in terms of use concept, color, style, price, feeling, and fit? Will they work with what is being presented in the front of the department?

   E. Is the merchandise current and new, or is it on sale and old?

2. After selecting the merchandise, put it in a safe place and sign out matching shoes and accessories.

3. After everything has been gathered to redress the mannequin, begin the undressing procedure.

    A. Take off the arms and the wig. Gently place each item that is removed on the platform.

    B. Remove the torso's clothing.

    C. Twist off the torso.

    D. Take off the skirt or, if wearing slacks, loosen the screw holding the support rod in place and lift the legs off of the stand. Upside down, remove the slacks, stockings/socks, and shoes.

    E. Immediately put on the new socks/stockings and slacks, or shoes (if no slacks will be put on). A seam may have to be split in the seat of the pants (female mannequins) to slide the support rod through.

    F. Place the leg and hip area back on the support rod and tighten both screws top and bottom.

    G. Twist the torso back onto the hips.

    H. Check the makeup and redo if necessary.

    I. Put all the top clothing layers on starting first with the layer closest to the skin.

    J. Pull all the clothing arms through each other so when the mannequin's arms are inserted there are continuous holes to go through.

    K. Attach the arms.

    L. Tuck in all clothing, tags, and pin or tape up hems (only if needed on slacks—never skirts).

    M. Replace the wig and groom.

    N. Make sure the base and platform area are clean.

4. Return all the old clothing and accessories to their parent departments, making sure all signing out and in procedures are followed.

STRIPPING A WINDOW

1. Make sure that everything needed to redo the window is complete and on hand.

2. Turn off the lights in the window.

3. Depending on what props and merchandise are in the window, look at the removal problem logically:

    A. What must be removed before other things can be removed? i.e., a large bed atop a rug.

    B. What can be removed without the help of either another person or a ladder?

C. Where are the removed items going to be stored or placed and how will this affect their removal?

4. Remove everything you can by yourself. Then call for help with the other things that are too heavy, fragile, or bulky for a solo attempt.

5. Remove all the props and ground cover (when appropriate) and vacuum (if needed).

6. Change the walls if needed.

7. Strip and redress the mannequins as quickly as possible.

8. Start setting up the new window.

INSTALLING A WINDOW

A window may take from one hour to a full day depending on the complexity of the design and the amount of people working. The following list is a simplification of a basic window installation.

1. Re-makeup and dress the mannequins in the selected clothing.

2. According to a drawn or visual plan, place the props (if used) where they belong.

3. Wire the mannequins temporarily where they belong.

4. Go outside to see how the window "reads" (looks) from the street.

5. Readjust where necessary.

6. Adjust all the lights.

7. Clean, dust, and vacuum the window area.

8. Add any signing.

9. Check again from the outside.

10. Make any last minute adjustments.

11. Close up the window and check from the street one last time to make sure that nothing was disturbed when the door was shut.

MERCHANDISE PRESENTATION: MEN'S OR WOMEN'S AREA

1. Talk to the department manager about which merchandise to feature.

2. If a display area doesn't exist, discuss with management an appropriate fixture move before moving fixtures to create an area.

3. If the area exists and only a merchandise change is needed, start pulling the new merchandise.

A. Determine the appropriate color of merchandise to display by considering the time of year, the quantities of like merchandise in the same color, and the effect that color will have on the surroundings.

B. Determine the theme of the merchandise presentation and display based on the end use or concept of the merchandise.

C. Have all the merchandise ready before stripping the current display.

D. Change the props as needed.

E. Change the clothing.

F. Return the used merchandise to the department.

G. Clean the area of tools.

An example of this type of merchandise presentation is a long Parsons-style table located in a men's department. On this table sits a male mannequin, a large dried flower arrangement in a terra cotta urn, and twelve sweaters (or shirts) in different colors, overlapped creating a geometric pattern.

4. If the merchandise area has to be created, a table or cube presentation is the most common base choice.

A. After an area has been created within the department for the merchandise presentation, find an appropriate table or cube that will fit into the departmental decor and work with the merchandise.

B. If a prop will enhance both the merchandise and the area, use it.

C. Follow the setup procedure as previously listed for an existing merchandise presentation.

Glossary

Ad breaking—A phrase meaning an advertisement appearing publicly for the first time either in a newspaper, magazine, or on television or radio.

Advertising—The paid use of television, radio, printed materials, or any medium for the purpose of sales.

Aesthetic—Artistic, tasteful, and beautiful. Also used as a noun meaning the standard by which beauty is judged.

Allen wrench—A five-sided metal cylinder with a bend creating a 90° angle. It is used for tightening special screws usually found in fixturing.

Assortment—A noun meaning a mixture of merchandise usually from the same vendor. This assortment is usually put together by price and type.

Balance—Used in display design to mean an equal emphasis on all areas of the design: equality in weight or amount.

Basic stock—Merchandise that is constantly in demand and usually kept in stock all year, e.g., cutlery; basic underwear; or black, blue, and brown socks.

Boutique—A small shop or area of a store characterized by either a deep but limited merchandise assortment or a wide and shallow assortment.

Boutiquing—Creating a small assortment of like merchandise in an artistic manner. Usually in a case or core unit display area.

Braising—A form of soldering used to connect pieces of brass or copper.

Case—A floor unit made to accommodate merchandise. Made of a large variety of rigid materials, cases often have glass shelves and recessed fluorescent lighting to show the merchandise assortment.

Caseline—A series of cases placed next to each other all carrying related classifications of merchandise, e.g., a jewelry caseline with bracelets, necklaces, and earrings in adjoining cases.

Chain store—A group of three or more centrally owned stores, each handling somewhat similar goods which are merchandised and controlled from a central headquarters office (as defined by the Bureau of the Census).

Chase lights—These are a continuous series of flashing lights. They work with an adapter that controls the timing of the lights. Five-watt cosmetic type bulbs are usually used with chase lights.

Classification—An assortment of items or units of merchandise which are related by use, e.g., blouses, t-shirts, and woven shirts are classified as tops.

Color—The reflection off an object when white light (which contains all colors) illuminates it. Color is divided into several properties. Hue corresponds to the name of a color. Intensity is the brightness of a color and tone is the color either lightened or darkened by white or black.

Complementary—Two colors that are opposite each other on the color wheel. Complimentary—Free, gratis, on the house. Also, attractive or lending favor.

Contemporary—Existing at the same time or being of the same general age. Also present day. Contemporary merchandise is that which is geared to the young adult, age range 20s–30s.

Contemporary men's wear—A styling often found in men's department that is geared to the 18- to 30-year-old group. Often referred to as updated, better, or young men's.

Cool—In color usage, those colors that stem from the coolness in nature: water-blue, leaves, grass-green.

Core, core unit—A single fixture unit usually on the main floor of a store. It often houses the sales register, bags, boxes, and has storage space for extra merchandise. It may have shallow built-in windows to display the merchandise that is stocked in the cases. The top of the core unit is often used for large displays, e.g., florals, mannequins, trees.

Decor—The decorative setup of a room, department, store, or theater scene.

Department store—A store that sells general lines of merchandise in each of three categories: home furnishings, household items, and apparel and accessories for all age groups.

Design—In apparel, a version or variation of a style of merchandise known as a number, style, or style number. In art, design is the mental plan, sketch, layout, or pattern for a project.

Diorama—A miniature scene wholly or partially three-dimensional depicting figures or objects in a naturalistic setting.

Discount store—A retail store using self-service techniques to sell its goods. It usually operates on a low profit margin and advertises its pricing policies.

Display—To spread out for view; show, expose to view. Also a merchandise presentation.

Distortion—Used in retailing to indicate an unusual stock enlargement of a piece or classification of merchandise. A buyer will "distort" the stock by buying excess amounts in order to take advantage of a customer buying trend.

Drop—A floral evergreen or leaf arrangement constructed with a flat back and a hook to hang onto a column or wall for decoration/decor. Usually used for Christmas.

End panel—A short wall attached to the end of a free-standing or perpendicular wall. An end panel usually ranges from 8 to 12' high and anywhere from 4 to 8' wide. Often fixturing is attached to an end panel or it may be used for display purposes.

Ennui—Boredom.

Environment—Our surroundings; the conditions for life; the conditions that influence our lives and affect our actions.

Fad—A whim, trend, or passing fashion that affects a small segment of the buying public.

Fashion—An accepted style that is worn or used by many consumers at the same time; style.

Faux—French for fake; used often to describe a surface painted to resemble another material, e.g., faux marble.

Filter—A filter is used in display to color or diffuse a regular white light. Filters come in a large variety of colors and are made to fit over fluorescent tubes and into or on front of the cans for incandescent bulbs.

Fiscal year—The year as determined by business taxes and profits as opposed to the calendar year. The fiscal year varies by company.

Fixture—An object that displays or houses merchandise. It can be floor-standing, counter-top, affixed to a wall, or hanging from a ceiling.

Fluorescent lighting—A system of electrical energy causing phosphers to glow in a tube. Fluorescent lights are used to create overall lighting. They are being developed for energy efficiency.

Flow—Used in display to mean the eye movement from one area to another in a design. Synonymous with rhythm.

Flying merchandise—A display technique that tries to create movement in merchandise by suspending or flying it from a ceiling using thin wire or fishing tackle.

Focal point—The point of convergence, the principal center of attention in a design or work of art.

Font—In typography, an assembly of loose letters in a particular style. A font comprises a complete alphabet with extra necessary characters, such as punctuation and accents marks. Numbers come in separate fonts. Often there is a discounted price for buying a font as opposed to purchasing each letter separately. A sample font: 140 pieces charged as 132 pieces: 10 A's, 4 B's, 6 C's, 4 D's, 12 E's, 3 F's, 4 G's, 3 H's, 6 I's, 2 J's, 2 K's, 6 L's, 4 M's, 8 N's, 8 O's, 4 P's, 2 Q's, 8 R's, 8 S's, 8 T's, 4 U's, 2 V's, 2 W's, 2 X's, 2 Y's, 2 Z's, 2 &'s, 6 .'s, 3 ,'s, and 3 -'s.

Forced blossoms—Flowering branches, flowers, and plants can be made to blossom out of season using the right amount of hot air and the proper water temperature.

Formal balance—Also known as symmetry. This exists when objects of the same visual weight are balanced on both sides of a design.

Frontal projection—Merchandise hung so that its front faces the eye. A blouse frontally projected hangs with its front to the department to show the pattern and detailing. Its back is to the wall.

Garland—A long and usually thin form of display decoration. A garland often is made of fake evergreens for Christmas and runs in length from 6 to 12′ and in width from 4 to 12″ wide. Wire or nylon cord are often used to connect the separate pieces into one long section. Garland is draped over valances, swagged between columns and over long poles, and placed in cases for seasonal decoration. It also comes in flowers, leaves, and the like.

Gild—To put a thin layer of gold on a surface either in leaf or powder or in a mixture with quicksilver.

Goods—Merchandise or items for sale.

Harmony—An agreement or coordination of many parts and aspects to form a complete and acceptable entity.

High tech—A recent trend in interior design and decoration. This trend uses materials normally seen in industry as decorative objects, furniture, and coverings. High tech, i.e., high technology, also makes use of all the technological advances in audio, visuals, lighting, and computers.

Hologram—A recording on a photographic plate of the interference (the variation of light wave amplitude with distance or time caused by the superimposition of two or more waves) patterns produced by coherent light waves. If the subject is a three-dimensional object, a 3-D image can be reproduced by proper illumination of the hologram. If the hologram is made on color film, it can be used to reproduce the subject in its true color. In the display and art worlds holograms are being experimented with to create 3-D moving pictures through the use of laser beams. The technology is very complicated and advanced, and is at this time too expensive to be put into daily use on an artistic level.

Hot—An expression used to describe something terrific or, exciting, in style, an excellent design, e.g., "That display is hot." A "hot item" is a piece of merchandise that sells much more quickly than anticipated.

Hue—That quality expressed by the name of a color, e.g., red, orange, blue, green. The color itself.

Incandescent bulb—A glass globe enclosing a vacuum within which is mounted a filament of conducting material, which is heated to incandescence by an electric current.

Informal balance—That which results when objects on one side of a space are not the same size, color, shape, or proportion as those on the other side. Informal balance works as a positive design feature when the two sides visually balance by weight. This means that although the objects may differ, they are balanced by placement. Possibly the amount of negative/empty space around an object on one side will create the same weighty feeling as the solid objects on the other side. The placement of objects and colors in a manner that is uneven in shape, size, and value yet works together in harmony as a whole design.

Interior decoration—The art or profession of decorating or furnishing the interiors of rooms, houses, and public places.

Interior design—The profession that relates to interior decoration in its final stages but is more concerned with initial space planning, renovation, reconstruction or primary construction, and the design of furniture and objects for home or public use.

Jobber—A person who buys goods in quantity from manufacturers or importers and sells them at a profit to dealers.

Kiosk—A somewhat small structure (usually hexagonal) that is open at one or more sides and used as a newsstand, bandstand, covering for a subway entrance, or public bulletin board (often when all the sides have been enclosed).

Kitsch—Popularization from German used to describe art, writing, a style, and objects of a pretentious but shallow kind that are calculated to have popular appeal.

Leased department—A department that seems to be part of the main store but is actually operated by a separate organization that pays a percentage of the sales to the store as a rental agreement. Departments that are often leased are millinery, shoes, fine jewelry, watches, and sometimes designer dresses.

Ledge line—The visual edge line created by a ledge attached to a wall. A ledge is an architectural horizontal attachment to a wall.

Line—An assortment of new designs offered by manufacturers to their customers. Lines are usually developed on a seasonal basis, e.g., the spring line, the fall/winter line, the cruise line, etc.

Lingerie—A category of women's merchandise that includes slips, petticoats (half-slips), camisoles, underpants, brassieres, night gowns, robes, and pajamas. Night wear consists of the robes, pajamas, and gowns. Day wear comprises undergarments.

Mannequin—A model of the human body used for displaying clothing. A human model, female, who exhibits clothing at fashion shows, stores, and in the showroom.

Manpower—The collective strength, ability, and availability of a group of people to work in a store, plant, state, or nation.

Massing out—The placing of large quantities of merchandise on the selling floor either on fixtures or stacked on the floor.

Merchandise—The objects of commerce, of whatever is bought and sold in the consumer, private, and industrial markets.

Merchandising—The planning and implementation required to have the right merchandise at the right time in the right place in the right quantities and at the right price for specific targeted groups of customers.

Merchandise assortment—A group of items of merchandise with the same general use that are often housed together in a specific area of a store, e.g., table linens, napkin holders, placemats, and napkins.

Broad assortment—many styles

Deep assortment—large range of colors and sizes in each style

Narrow assortment—relatively few styles

Shallow assortment—only a few sizes and colors in each style

Merchandising policies—Those policies or guidelines developed by the store management to attract and sell to the customer who has been targeted by the store's marketing department.

Moonlighting—The practice of holding a second job in addition to a main job, e.g., a person works as a display assistant during the day and an usher at a movie theater at night.

Negative space—In a composition, the area that has nothing on or in it. This area surrounds physical things, e.g., the area surrounding a solid triangle on a piece of paper is the negative space. The triangle is the positive space.

New wave—More an attitude than a style. New wave refers to a clothing, art, music, and life attitude. It is a combination of eclecticism and irony. The attitude presented by new wave is a variant of camp (exaggerated, artificial, ostentatious behavior). Images are taken from the past and used in the present in an expressionless, cynical manner. Rather than copying exactly a style, manner, or image from the past, it is mocked, twisted, and aped at the same time by the new wave subculture. The cultural majority is considered middle class and boring. Twisting culture with a cynical, dark humor gives the new wave its attitude. Traditional art forms have been replaced by American cultural symbols used in collage treatments. A revival of late forties and fifties cheer and purity is often portrayed in strange ways. From an article in *New York* magazine, July 26, 1982, Vol. 15, No. 29, by Craig Unger.

Optics—Relating to vision or sight. Pertaining to the eye. Also relating to the science of optics which deals with the nature and properties of light and vision.

Outpost—An area devoted to a merchandise assortment that is located outside of the parent department.

Pad—A piece of painted or covered board placed into a case or on a wall to give a feeling of color, texture, and softness to the area.

Panel—A piece of wood or board, either stained, painted, or covered, that is attached to a wall. Its purpose is to cover an area with color or texture.

Physical plant—This word is used to describe the material qualities of a building such as square footage, electrical work, ceiling, structure. Physical plant describes the physical totality of a building.

Pin spots—Very small, incandescent spotlights used to highlight small areas of a display. The beam that is thrown is very intense and circular. The beam actually looks (in comparison with the large circle of light thrown by a regular spotlight) like a pin-sized spot. These are most effective in smaller windows or when used in combination with larger spots.

Pop—An expression that means to stand out or to look more exciting than the surroundings. Used in the context, "Make this T-stand pop so that we can sell the merchandise."

Positive space—In a two- or three-dimensional design, the positive space is that which is occupied by the main design elements. If a window has three mannequins and two trees, these are the elements that constitute the positive space.

Price line—The price that is on the merchandise assortment for sale.

Price range—The spread between the top and bottom price at which merchandise is sold.

Promotional—Pertaining to a promotion. An item that is ready or ideal for an interest-stirring event. Offering T-shirts with a picture of people running right before a running marathon would be promotional.

Proportion—The comparative relationship between parts or things with respect to size, amount, and quantity. Also, it can mean a harmonious relationship between parts or things; balance or symmetry.

Purchase order—A contract between a store and a manufacturer/vendor to purchase and pay for certain specified goods with specific conditions applied to the sale.

Ready to wear (RTW)—Apparel made by manufacturers in a factory that is of standard sizes, e.g.:

Misses'—4, 6, 8, 10, 12, 14, 16, 18

Junior—3, 5, 7, 9, 11, 13, 15

Men's—(suit sample) 38 Short (S), Regular (R), Long (L)

(shirt sample) 15–1/2—33 (neck)—(sleeves)

(pants sample) 34—33 (waist)—(leg length)

Receiving apron or Ke-rec—A form, sequentially numbered, that is filled out in the receiving department that records complete information about a shipment of merchandise. This is necessary to prove receipt of merchandise in order to pay an invoice.

Renovate—To make new, freshen up, revive, clean up, or restore an item or area.

Repetition—The reiteration of an act, word, or idea. Used in display as a repeated visual image, e.g., Mugs . . . Mugs . . . Mugs.

Retailing—The business of buying goods from many resources and selling them at a profit from another location(s) to customers. To sell directly to a consumer.

Rhythm—The pattern of an arrangement, or the aesthetic relation of parts of a design to the whole. The regular recurrence of strong and weak elements, such as black and light grey circles on a white background. *See also* Flow.

Rudimentary—The first principle, element, or fundamental of a subject to be learned; elementary, or incompletely or imperfectly developed.

Runway lineup—A chart or schedule listing the models and what they are wearing in sequential order for a fashion show.

Scale—The proportion that an object, model, or map bears to the thing that it represents. The scale or size of an apple can be represented by putting that apple next to a human hand. If the apple is then placed next to an elephant, the scale/proportion/size is viewed differently.

Scapes—A term popularly used to describe a scene—such as a "landscape"—composed of things found in nature. A "city scape" is a scene of a city.

Scatter—A prop used on floors to cover areas either for color, texture, or camouflage, i.e., to hide Styrofoam or mannequin bases. Scatter is usually composed of many small (1/8"–1/2") pieces of material (cork, paper, plastic, wood) that can be thrown on or in an area for coverage.

Sell retail—Sell to a consumer at the full listed price.

Sell wholesale—Sell to a jobber or to someone who will buy in large quantities. Means selling at a lower cost per item.

Serif—In printing or signing, a fine line usually found at the top or bottom of a letter, e.g., I.

Shadow box—A small area in the core unit wired for light and used for display.

Shape—The external outline of a thing; form.

Shop—A small store or an area within a larger store that is stocked with special merchandise for targeted customers. A special interest catered to by merchandise selected for that purpose.

Showcase—A floor fixture with shelves and sliding back doors covered on top and in front either partially or totally with glass. It is used to display and/or stock merchandise.

Signing—The use of letters to make signs. "Signing" can be applied to three-dimensional signs as well as to two-dimensional posters and signs. Also known as lettering. Lettering can also imply hand lettering or calligraphy.

Solder—To fuse or unite two or more metallic surfaces using high heat and solder (a metal or metallic composition used for joining or patching metal parts of surfaces. A metallic cement).

Hard solder—A solder that requires a red heat to melt it; used for joining brass and iron.

Soft solder—A solder that melts at a relatively low temperature; used for fusing lead and tin.

Spots—An abbreviation of the word spotlight. A spotlight is an incandescent light fixture that is trained on a small area for highlighting.

Sprinklers—The smoke and heat-sensitive watering heads that are installed in the ceilings of public buildings. They are attached to a water system that is kept in reserve in case of fire. Sprinkler heads are sensitive to touch and can be set off by careless handling.

Specialty store—a store that carries limited lines of apparel, accessories, or home furnishings (as defined by the Bureau of Census). In retailing, the specialty store is a store that is current with fashion trends and carries merchandise for men, women, and/or children.

Spectrum—The series of colored bands that are diffracted and arranged in the order of their respective wavelengths by the passage of white light through a prism. They shade continuously from red to violet: red, orange, yellow, green, blue, violet. A spectrum is referred to in display as a way of showing colorful merchandise above the fixturing in a natural way by using the natural order of the light/color spectrum.

Standards—In this book standards refers to fixturing. Standards are slightly rounded metal bars that are screwed vertically onto walls. They have slots that run vertically that are made to accept the hooks on brackets. The brackets hold up metal rods to create a hanging area or shelves for folded goods.

Stock—To keep in supply, to have for sale, to carry. Stock also means to put out for sale, as in "Stock the shelves." "We have lots of stock" makes stock a synonym of merchandise.

Store image—The identity or distinctive attitude that a store presents to the public.

Style—In retailing, a style is the combination of characteristics that make one item different from another. The line, shape, color, size, design, and texture are all involved in differentiating one style from another. Style is also a manner or mode of expression in language, a way of dressing, a characteristic manner of self-expression through body language, and the distinction and elegance of hearing and speech.

Story—The retailing use of story is concerned with the term as it refers to a merchandise presentation. Merchandise that works together either with color, end use, style, size, image, or place of origin "tells a story." It is an overused term. An example of "telling a story": In a lingerie department at Valentine's Day, all the red and black merchandise is placed in the front of the department as well as on all the mannequins. This merchandise is telling a story by reminding the customers that it's Valentine's Day and that's a time for love—and sexy lingerie.

Surrealism—This is characterized by an irrational and/or out-of-context arrangement of material used either in art or literature. It was a modern movement in the art and literary worlds in which an attempt was made to portray the workings of the subconscious mind and to use the dream state as a reality.

Swag—A long piece of garland attached at both ends to columns or walls that is used for decoration. It is often pulled up in the center to create a very large and spread out W. It is most often used for Christmas trim and Bridal Week.

Symmetry—A similarity of form or arrangement on either side of a dividing line. Both sides correspond in size, shape, and position.

T-wall—A wall that is built in the shape of a T. A T-wall is created when a half wall (8–9′ high) is built out into the selling floor from a main wall. A wall of the same height but of shorter width is then attached to the end of the half-wall creating the cross on the T. The T-walls are often used for individual merchandise statements and small shops.

Terms—The conditions of a contract, agreement, sale, etc., that limit or define its scope or the action involved, e.g., terms of a contract, terms of an agreement, terms of a sale.

Texture—The character of a surface.

Thematic—Consisting of a theme or themes. Thematic refers to the total, overall concept of a promotion, work of art, piece of music.

Topper—A piece of promotional cardboard literature that slides into a sign holder and is taller than the holder. The part that stands above the holder holds the promotional message on both sides.

Transitional—A passing from one condition to another. Transitional means that something is in the process of transition, or in the act of changing or passing.

Transparency—A piece of transparent (see-through) or translucent (diffused light) material having a picture or design that is visible when light shows through it. Used in conjunction with slide projectors or, on its own, blown up, mounted with a built-in light source in the light box.

Trendy—In vogue, in current style. Trendy also indicates that it is not of a lasting style, that it will go out of fashion quickly.

Trim—An ornamental decoration. Trim also encompasses a total decorative package for a store.

Trompe l'oeil—A still-life deception done with paint; an illusion or camouflage.

Trunk show—A garment manufacturer sends a representative to a store with samples of the current line and shows the samples to customers at scheduled, advertised showings, usually within the department the merchandise is carried in.

Typesetting—The act, art, or process by which type is set. Type is a raised letter either set in a block to be grouped with others to make a word, or printed on a wax paper so it can be rubbed off onto a clean surface. Typesetting is the effort used to group the letters into a formal presentation.

U-bin—A countertop fixture usually formed of Plexiglas or wood. It is used as a buildup for merchandise presentations. Its height acts to raise the merchandise above the counter or cube surface and the empty part between the legs of the upside-down U is an extra space for merchandise.

Unity—Oneness, harmony, agreement, singleness. An arrangement of parts or material that will produce a single, harmonious design or effect in a display.

Unrenovated—An older store that hasn't repainted, carpeted, put in new flooring, updated its fixturing, still has 6" wood strip valances, and looks generally out-of-date.

Urn—A vase in any form usually having a definite base or pedestal.

Valance—An architectural facing on a wall of wood or metal used to define an area. It is hung at least 1' over the merchandise and lights are often attached to the rear of the valance structure.

Velcro—A material that comes in two parts that attach to each other through a textural alignment of the two different surfaces. When one piece of Velcro is attached to an object and the other, corresponding piece is attached to another object, the two objects will stick together when the Velcro strips are joined.

Viable—Possible, capable of occurring or being done.

Vignettes—A picture, illustration, or display with no defined border. An ornamental design.

Visual merchandising—The combined art of display and merchandise presentation designed to create and sell an image and merchandise to a designated customer.

Warm—Suggesting warmth. Having a yellow, red, orange hue. A term for colors. The opposite of cool.

Waterfalled—A term used for merchandise placed on a slanted wall or floor fixture that will accept up to six pieces of merchandise without overlapping.

Weld—To unite two pieces of metal by heating until molten and fused or until soft enough to hammer or press together.

Wholesale—To sell in large quantities at reduced prices to someone for resale.

Work—Used in the expression, "Does it work?" Work means does it do the job it intends to do. It also indicates the manner, style, and quality of workmanship.

Index